easy
Writer

easy **Writer**

third edition

Andrea A. Lunsford
STANFORD UNIVERSITY

with a section for
multilingual writers by

Franklin E. Horowitz
TEACHERS COLLEGE
COLUMBIA UNIVERSITY

A POCKET REFERENCE

BEDFORD/ST. MARTIN'S
Boston ◆ New York

For Bedford/St. Martin's

Senior Developmental Editors: Kristin Bowen/Carolyn Lengel
Production Editor: Bernard Onken
Marketing Manager: John Swanson
Art Director: Lucy Krikorian
Text Design: Delgado and Company
Copy Editor: Denise P. Quirk
Indexer: Riofrancos & Co. Indexes
Cover Design: Donna Dennison
Composition: Monotype, LLC
Printing and Binding: Quebecor World Eusey Press

President: Joan E. Feinberg
Editorial Director: Denise B. Wydra
Editor in Chief: Nancy Perry
Director of Marketing: Karen Melton Soeltz
Director of Editing, Design, and Production: Marcia Cohen
Managing Editor: Erica T. Appel

Library of Congress Control Number: 2009924674

Manufactured in the United States of America.
4   3   2   1   0   9
f   e   d   c   b

For information, write: Bedford/St. Martin's, 75 Arlington
Street, Boston, MA 02116 (617-399-4000)

ISBN-10: 0-312-59459-3
ISBN-13: 978-0-312-59459-6

Acknowledgments
Acknowledgments and copyrights appear at the back
of the book on page 304, which constitutes an extension
of the copyright page.

How to Use This Book

Whether you're a writing student, an engineer, or a psychologist, chances are that you're called on to write and do research often, maybe even every day. Chances are also good that you often have questions about writing and research. *EasyWriter* aims to provide answers to such questions.

Ways into the book

BRIEF CONTENTS. Inside the front cover you will find a flap listing the book's contents. Once you locate a general topic in the Brief Contents, it will point you to the chapter of the book that contains specific information on the topic.

USER-FRIENDLY INDEX. The index lists everything covered in the book. You can find information by looking up a topic ("articles," for example) or, if you're not sure what your topic is called, by looking up the word you need help with (such as *a* or *the*).

CONTENTS. If you're looking for specific information within a general topic, inside the back cover a brief but detailed table of contents lists chapter titles and major headings.

FIND IT. FIX IT. Following "How to Use This Book," advice on the twenty most common errors provides hand-edited examples and brief explanations to guide you toward recognizing, understanding, and editing the most common errors. This "Find It. Fix It." section includes cross-references to other places in the book where you'll find more detail.

PRACTICAL ADVICE ON RESEARCH AND DOCUMENTATION. Source maps walk you step by step through the processes of selecting, evaluating, and citing sources. Documentation models are easy to find in four color-coded sections — one each for MLA, APA, *Chicago,* and CSE styles.

REVISION SYMBOLS. If your instructor uses revision symbols to mark your drafts, consult the list of symbols on the inside back cover and its cross-references to places in the book where you'll find more help.

GLOSSARIES. The Glossary of Terms, on blue-green pages (pp. 281–92) at the back of the book, provides definitions of grammatical terms. The Glossary of Usage, on yellow pages (pp. 293–303), gives help with troublesome words (*accept* and *except,* for example). Note that all terms highlighted in the book are included in the Glossary of Terms.

Ways to navigate the pages

The descriptions below correspond to the numbered elements on the sample page opposite.

① GUIDES AT THE TOP OF EVERY PAGE. Headers tell you what chapter or subsection you're in, the chapter number and section letter, and the page number. Icons that link to the name of the section (sunglasses for *Sentence Style,* for example) also appear at the top of the page.

② HAND-EDITED EXAMPLES. Most examples are hand-edited in blue, allowing you to see the error and its revision at a glance. Blue pointers and boldface type make examples easy to spot on the page.

③ FOR MULTILINGUAL WRITERS BOXES. Advice for multilingual writers appears in a separate section (Chapters 33–37) and in boxed tips throughout the book. You can find a list of topics covered, including language-specific tips, on p. 325.

④ CROSS-REFERENCES TO THE WEB SITE. The *EasyWriter* Web site expands the book's coverage. The cross-references to the Web site point you to practical online resources — from a tutorial on avoiding plagiarism to grammar exercises, model essays, a writer's almanac, and links to other Web resources. Inside the front cover, you can find a directory for the model student essays and the Writer's Almanac's coverage on the Web site.

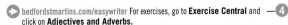

72 **9a** Adjectives and Adverbs ——————— ➊

▶ You can feel the song's meter if you listen ~~careful.~~ —— ➋
  carefully.

▶ The audience was ~~real~~ disappointed by the show.
  really
  ^

Good, well, bad, and *badly.* The modifiers *good, well, bad,* and *badly* cause problems for many writers because the distinctions between *good* and *well* and between *bad* and *badly* are often not observed in conversation. Problems also arise because *well* can function as either an adjective or an adverb.

▶ I look ~~well~~ in blue.
  good
  ^

▶ Now that the fever has broken, I feel ~~good~~ again.
  well
  ^

▶ He plays the trumpet ~~good.~~
  well.
  ^

▶ I feel ~~badly~~ for the Toronto fans.
  bad
  ^

▶ Their team played ~~bad.~~
  badly.
  ^

FOR MULTILINGUAL WRITERS

Using Adjectives with Plural Nouns —— ➌

In Spanish, Russian, and many other languages, adjectives agree in number with the nouns they modify. In English, adjectives do not change number in this way: *her dogs are small* (not *smalls*).

9b Comparatives and superlatives

Most adjectives and adverbs have three forms: **positive**, **comparative**, and **superlative**. You usually form the comparative and superlative of one- or two-syllable adjectives by adding *-er* and *-est: short, shorter, shortest.* With some two-syllable adjectives, longer adjectives, and most adverbs, use *more* and *most* (or *less* and *least*): *scientific, more*

---

 bedfordstmartins.com/easywriter For exercises, go to **Exercise Central** and —— ➍
click on **Adjectives and Adverbs.**

easy
Writer

Find It. Fix It.

Although many people think of correctness as absolute — based on hard-and-fast, unchanging rules — instructors and students know better. We know that there are rules but that the rules change all the time. "Is it okay to use *I* in essays for this class?" asks one student. "My high school teacher wouldn't let us." Such questions show that rules clearly exist but that they are always shifting and thus need our ongoing attention.

Shifting standards do not mean that there is no such thing as correctness in writing — only that *correctness always depends on some context*. Correctness is not so much a question of absolute right or wrong as a question of the way a writer's choices are perceived by readers. As writers, we all want to be considered competent and careful. We know that our readers judge us by our control of the conventions we have agreed to use. As Robert Frost once said of poetry, trying to write without honoring the conventions and agreed-upon rules is like playing tennis without a net.

A major goal of this book is to help you understand and control the surface conventions of academic and professional writing. Since you already know most of these rules, the most efficient way to proceed is to focus on those that are still unfamiliar or puzzling.

To aid you in this process, we have identified the twenty error patterns (other than misspelling) most common among U.S. college students and listed them here in order of frequency. This section provides brief examples and explanations to help you recognize, understand, revise — and learn from — the twenty most common errors. Each of the items ends with cross-references to other places in this book where you can find more detailed information and additional examples.

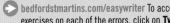 bedfordstmartins.com/easywriter To access this advice online and for exercises on each of the errors, click on **Twenty Most Common Errors.**

1 Missing comma after an introductory element

▶ Determined to get the job done, we worked all
  weekend.
  <small>∧</small>

▶ In German, nouns are always capitalized.
  <small>∧</small>

Readers usually need a small pause between an introductory word, **phrase**, or **clause** and the main part of the sentence, a pause most often signaled by a comma. Try to get into the habit of using a comma after every introductory element. When the introductory element is very short, you don't always need a comma after it. But you're never wrong if you do use a comma. (See 19a.)

2 Vague pronoun reference

POSSIBLE REFERENCE TO MORE THAN ONE WORD

▶ Transmitting radio signals by satellite is a way of

  overcoming the problem of scarce airwaves and
                          the airwaves
  limiting how ~~they~~ are used.
           <small>∧</small>

  Does *they* refer to the signals or the airwaves? The editing clarifies what is being limited.

REFERENCE IMPLIED BUT NOT STATED

▶ The company prohibited smoking, ~~which~~ many
                                   a policy
  employees resented.
            <small>∧</small>

  What does *which* refer to? The editing clarifies what employees resented.

A **pronoun** — a word such as *she, yourself, her, it, this, who,* or *which* — should clearly refer to the word or words it replaces (called the **antecedent**) elsewhere in the sentence or in a previous sentence. If more than one word could be the antecedent or if no specific antecedent is present in the sentence, edit to make the meaning clear. (See 11c.)

Missing comma in a compound sentence

▶ The words "I do" may sound simple, but they mean a
   life commitment.

A **compound sentence** consists of two or more parts that could
each stand alone as a sentence. When the parts are joined by a
coordinating conjunction — *and, but, so, yet, or, nor,* or *for* —
use a comma before the conjunction to indicate a pause
between the two thoughts. In very short sentences, the comma
is optional if the sentence can be easily understood without it.
But you'll never be wrong to use a comma. (See 19b.)

 Wrong word

▶ *Paradise Lost* contains many ~~illusions~~ *allusions* to classical
   mythology.

   Illusions means "false ideas or appearances," and *allusions*
   means "references."

▶ Working at a computer all day often means being
   ~~sedate~~ *sedentary* for long periods of time.

   Sedate means "composed, dignified," and *sedentary* means
   "requiring much sitting."

Wrong-word errors can involve mixing up words that sound
alike, using a word with the wrong shade of meaning, or using
a word with a completely wrong meaning. Many wrong-
word errors are due to the improper use of homonyms —
words that are pronounced alike but spelled differently, such
as *their* and *there*. (See Chapter 32 and the Glossary of Usage.)

 Missing comma(s) with a nonrestrictive
   element

▶ Marina, who was the president of the club, was first to speak.

   The reader does not need the clause *who was the president of
   the club* to know the basic meaning of the sentence: Marina
   was first to speak.

A **nonrestrictive element** — one that is not essential to the basic meaning of the sentence — could be removed and the sentence would still make sense. Use commas to set off any nonrestrictive parts of a sentence. (See 19c.)

6   Wrong or missing verb ending

▶ The United States ~~drop~~ *dropped* an atomic bomb on Hiroshima on August 6, 1945.

It's easy to forget the **verb** endings -*s* (or -*es*) and -*ed* (or -*d*) because they are not always pronounced clearly when spoken. In addition, some varieties of English use these endings in ways that are different from uses in academic and professional English. (See Chapters 7 and 8.)

7   Wrong or missing preposition

▶ We met ~~in~~ *on* Union Street *in* San Francisco.

In and *on* both show place, but use *on* with a street and *in* with a city.

▶ President Richard Nixon compared the United States ~~with~~ *to* a "pitiful, helpless giant."

Compare to means "regard as similar"; *compare with* means "to examine to find similarities or differences."

Many words in English are regularly used with a particular **preposition** to express a particular meaning. Throwing a ball *to* someone is different from throwing a ball *at* someone. Because many prepositions are short and not stressed or pronounced clearly in speech, they are often accidentally left out or mixed up in writing. (See Chapter 36.)

8   Comma splice

▶ Westward migration had passed Wyoming by*;* even the discovery of gold in nearby Montana failed to attract settlers.

▶ I was strongly attracted to her,^*for*^ she had special qualities.

▶ We hated the meat loaf,^*that*^ the cafeteria served ~~it~~ every

Friday.

A **comma splice** occurs when only a comma separates **clauses** that could each stand alone as a sentence. To correct a comma splice, you can insert a semicolon or period, connect the clauses clearly with a word such as *and* or *because*, or restructure the sentence. (See Chapter 12.)

9 Missing or misplaced possessive apostrophe

▶ Overambitious parents can be very harmful to a ~~childs~~^*child's*^

well-being.

▶ Pedro Martinez is one of the ~~Met's~~^*Mets'*^ most electrifying

pitchers.

To make a noun **possessive**, add either an apostrophe and an -s (*Ed's book*) or an apostrophe alone (*the boys' gym*). (See 22a.)

10 Unnecessary shift in tense

▶ A few countries produce almost all of the world's
illegal drugs, but addiction ~~affected~~^*affects*^ many
countries.

▶ Priya was watching the great blue heron take off. Then
she ~~slips~~^*slipped*^ and ~~falls~~^*fell*^ into the swamp.

Verb tenses tell readers when actions take place: saying *Ron <u>went</u> to school* indicates a past action whereas saying *he <u>will</u> go* indicates a future action. Verbs that shift from one tense to another with no clear reason can confuse readers. (See 18a.)

11 Unnecessary shift in pronoun

▶ When one first sees a painting by Georgia
  O'Keeffe, ~~you are~~ impressed by a sense of
         ⌃ *one is*
  power and stillness.

An unnecessary pronoun shift occurs when a writer who
has been using one **pronoun** to refer to someone or something shifts to another pronoun for no apparent reason.
(See 18c.)

12 Sentence fragment

NO SUBJECT

▶ Marie Antoinette spent huge sums of money on
  herself and her favorites. ~~And~~ helped bring on the
                      Her extravagance
                            ⌃
  French Revolution.

NO COMPLETE VERB

▶ The old aluminum boat sitting on its trailer.
                    was
                     ⌃

  Sitting cannot function alone as the verb of the sentence. The
  auxiliary verb *was* makes it a complete verb.

BEGINNING WITH SUBORDINATING WORD

▶ We returned to the drugstore. ~~Where~~ we waited for our
                        where
                         ⌃
  buddies.

A **sentence fragment** is part of a sentence that is written as
if it were a whole sentence, with a capital letter at the
beginning and a period, a question mark, or an exclamation point at the end. A fragment may lack a **subject**, a
complete **verb**, or both. Other fragments may begin with a
subordinating conjunction, such as *because*, and so
depend for their meaning on another sentence. Reading
your draft out loud, backwards, sentence by sentence, will
help you spot sentence fragments. (See Chapter 13.)

13 Wrong tense or verb form

▶ By the time Ian arrived, Jill *~~died~~* died.
   had

The verb *died* does not clearly state that the death occurred *before* Ian arrived.

▶ Iris has *~~went~~* to the store.
   gone

The verb *go* has irregular past-tense forms.

Errors of wrong **tense** include using a **verb** that does not clearly indicate when an action or a condition is, was, or will be completed — for example, using *walked* instead of *had walked*, or *will go* instead of *will have gone*. Errors of wrong form include confusing the forms of **irregular verbs** (such as *go, went,* or *gone*) or treating these verbs as if they followed the regular pattern — for example, using *beginned* instead of *began*. (See 18a and Chapters 7 and 35.)

14 Lack of subject-verb agreement

▶ A strategist behind the scenes *~~create~~* the candidate's
   creates
   public image.

The subject is the singular noun *strategist*, not *scenes*.

▶ Each of these designs *~~coordinate~~* with the others.
   coordinates

The subject is the singular pronoun *each*, not *designs*.

▶ There *~~is~~* two main reasons that I want to become a
   are
   lawyer.

The subject, *reasons*, is plural, so the verb is plural.

▶ My brothers or my sister *~~come~~* every day to see Dad.
   comes

Here, the noun closest to the verb is singular (*sister*). The verb must agree with that singular noun.

▶ Johnson was one of the athletes who *~~was~~* disqualified.
   were

Here, *who* refers to *athletes*, so the verb is plural.

A **verb** must agree with its **subject** in **number** and in **person**. In many cases, the verb must take a form depending on whether the subject is **singular** or **plural**: The *old man is angry and stamps into the house,* but *The old men are angry and stamp into the house.* Lack of subject-verb agreement is often just a matter of carelessly leaving the *-s* ending off the verb or of not identifying the subject correctly. (See Chapter 8.)

15 Missing comma in a series

▸ Sharks eat mostly squid, shrimp, crabs, and other fish.
                                         ^

When three or more items appear in a series, many disciplines require them to be separated from one another with commas. Although newspapers and magazines do not use a comma between the last two items, the best advice in writing other than journalism is to use a comma because a sentence can be ambiguous without one. (See 17a and 19d.)

16 Lack of agreement between pronoun and antecedent

▸ Each of the puppies thrived in ~~their~~ *its* new home.
                                  ^

Many **indefinite pronouns**, such as *everyone* and *each*, are always **singular**.

▸ Either Nirupa or Selena will be asked to give ~~their~~ *her*
  speech to the graduates.
                                                  ^

When **antecedents** are joined by *or* or *nor*, the **pronoun** must agree with the closer antecedent.

▸ The team frequently changed ~~its~~ *their* positions to get varied
  experience.
                               ^

A **collective noun** can be either singular or **plural**, depending on whether the people are seen as a single unit or as multiple individuals.

▸ **Every student must provide his *or her* own uniform.**

With an antecedent that can refer to either a man or a woman, use *his or her*, *he or she*, and so on. When the singular antecedent refers to either a male or a female, you can also rewrite the sentence to make the antecedent and pronoun plural or to eliminate the pronoun altogether.

Pronouns must agree with their antecedents in **gender** (for example, using *he* or *him* to replace *Abraham Lincoln* and *she* or *her* to replace *Queen Elizabeth*) and in **number**. (See 11b and 11c.)

17 Unnecessary comma(s) with a restrictive element

▸ **People, who wanted to preserve wilderness areas, opposed the plan to privatize national parks.**

The reader needs the clause *who wanted to preserve wilderness areas* because it announces which people opposed the plan. The clause should not be set off with commas.

A **restrictive element** is essential to the basic meaning of the sentence. It is not set off from the rest of the sentence with commas. (See 19c and 19i.)

18 Fused sentence

▸ **The current was swift. *He* he could not swim to shore.**

▸ **Klee's paintings seem simple, *but* they are very sophisticated.**

▸ **Although she She doubted the value of meditation, she decided to try it once.**

A **fused sentence** (also called a **run-on sentence**) is created when **clauses** that could each stand alone as a sentence are joined with no punctuation or words to link them. Fused sentences must be either divided into separate sentences or joined by adding words or punctuation. (See Chapter 12.)

19   Misplaced or dangling modifier

MISPLACED MODIFIER

With binoculars, the
▶ ~~The~~ hikers could see the eagles swooping and diving.
   ^
~~with binoculars.~~   ^

Who was wearing the binoculars — the eagles?

Every **modifier** (whether a word, **phrase**, or **clause**) should
be as close as possible to the word it describes or relates to.
Misplaced modifiers may confuse your readers by seem-
ing to modify some other element in the sentence. (See 10a.)

DANGLING MODIFIER

                             we see that
▶ Looking down the sandy beach, people are tanning
                                ^

themselves.

A **dangling modifier** hangs precariously from the beginning or end of a sentence, attached to no other part of the
sentence. The element that the phrase modifies may exist
in your mind but not in your draft. Each modifier must
refer to some other element in the sentence. (See 10c.)

20   Its/It's confusion

                       its   *It's*
▶ The car is lying on ~~it's~~ side in the ditch. ~~Its~~ a white 2006
                             ^   ^

Passat.

Use *its* to mean *belonging to it*; use *it's* only when you mean
it is or *it has*. (See 22b.)

FOR MULTILINGUAL WRITERS

Language-Specific Tips

Is your first language Arabic? Chinese? Spanish? something else? See
the directory for multilingual writers at the back of the book to find
tips about predictable error patterns in twenty different languages.

Writing

Writing

Sentence
Grammar

Sentence Style

Punctuation/
Mechanics

Language

Multilingual
Writers

Research

Documentation

1   A Writer's Choices

You sit down to dash off a quick email message to your best friend about a weekend reunion in Chicago. Later on, you put together an analysis of several cost-cutting possibilities for the manager of the wholesale produce company you're working for. And later still, just before calling it a day, you pull out the notes you took on your biology experiment and write up the lab report that is due tomorrow. In between, you probably do a lot of other writing as well — notes, lists, blog entries, and so on.

These are the kinds of writing most of us do every day, more or less easily, yet each demands that we make various important choices. In your email message, you may choose to use a kind of shorthand, not even bothering to write complete sentences, since it's just a quick note to a friend. For your boss, however, you will probably choose to be more formal and "correct." And for your lab report, you will probably choose to follow the format demonstrated in your textbook. In each case, the choices you make are based on what is most appropriate for your purposes and audience.

1a   Assignments and purposes

- If you have a specific writing assignment, what does it ask you to do? Look for words such as *define, explain, prove,* and *survey*. Keep in mind that these words may differ in meaning from discipline to discipline or from job to job.

- What information do you need to complete the assignment? Will you need to do research? What graphics or visual information will you need?

- What are the assignment's specific requirements? Consider length, format, organization, and deadline.

- What is the primary purpose for writing — to explain, summarize, or persuade? to respond to a question, learn about a topic, or make recommendations? to express certain feelings? If you are unclear about the primary purpose, talk with the person who gave you the assignment.

1b   Topic

To choose a topic, try answering the following questions:

- Is the topic interesting and important to you?

- Is the topic focused enough for you to write about it in the time and space allowed?
- Do you have some ideas about how to pursue the topic?

To identify and begin exploring a viable topic, try these techniques:

- Brainstorm with a friend, classmate, or co-worker about ideas and subjects you'd like to explore further or that puzzle you.
- Write for ten to fifteen minutes, without stopping, about one of these ideas or subjects.
- Read over what you've written, looking for the most interesting or provocative phrase or sentence. Then begin another ten-minute writing session, using that phrase or sentence as a starting point.
- If after these activities you have not come up with useful material, consider trying another subject.

1c Working thesis

Once you have chosen a topic, craft a working thesis that includes two parts: a topic, which states what you are writing about, and a comment, which makes an important point about the topic.

            TOPIC   COMMENT

▶ Recent studies of depression suggest that it is much

more closely related to physiology than scientists had

previously thought.

            TOPIC   COMMENT

▶ The current health-care crisis arises from three major

causes.

A successful working thesis has three characteristics:

1. It is potentially interesting to the intended audience.
2. It is as specific as possible.
3. It limits the topic enough to make it manageable.

---

bedfordstmartins.com/easywriter To see student drafts, click on **Student Writing.** For more help with writing, go to **Links** and click on **The Art and Craft of Writing.** For more about online writing, go to **Links** and click on **Working Online.**

FOR MULTILINGUAL WRITERS

Stating a Thesis

In some cultures, it is considered rude to state an opinion outright. In the United States, however, academic and business practices require writers to make key positions explicitly clear.

1d Audience

- Whom do you most want to reach — people already sympathetic to your views? people who disagree with your views? members of a group you belong to? members of a group you don't belong to?

- In what ways are the members of your audience different from you? from one another? Consider such factors as education, region, age, gender, occupation, social class, ethnic and cultural heritage, politics, religion, marital status, and sexual orientation.

- What assumptions can you legitimately make about your audience? What might they value? Think about brevity, originality, conformity, honesty, adventure, wit, seriousness, thrift, and so on.

- What sorts of information and evidence will your audience find most compelling — quotations from experts? personal experiences? photographs? diagrams or charts?

- What response(s) do you want as a result of what you write? How can you make clear what you want to happen?

(For more on audience, see 29d.)

1e Stance and tone

Knowing your own stance — where you are coming from — can help you think about ways to get your readers to understand and perhaps share your views.

- What is your overall attitude toward the topic — approval? disapproval? curiosity? indifference? What social, political, religious, or other factors account for your attitude?

- What do you know about the topic? What preconceptions do you have about it?

- What seems important — or unimportant — about the topic?

- What do you expect to conclude about the topic?
- Think about your audience. Will they have similar attitudes and interests?
- What tone do your purpose, audience, and stance call for? Should your tone be humorous? serious? impassioned? helpful?

1f Genres and formats

- What genre, or form, of writing does your task call for — a report? a review? a poem? a letter? a blurb? Have you considered the design conventions appropriate to the kind of document you are creating? Find out which formats are most often used in similar situations. If you are unsure what format to use, ask your instructor or supervisor for guidance.
- What organizational patterns are most appropriate for your subject, purpose, and audience? Will you use chronological order or some other order, such as problem-solution or cause-effect? Should you use headings and subheadings to help readers follow your organization? (For more on headings, see 5c.)

1g Visuals

Pay special attention to how well your text and visuals work together and fit the purpose of the writing and the intended audience. In addition, think carefully about when to put more emphasis on words and when to put more emphasis on visuals.

- What kinds of visuals does your topic call for? Visuals should add meaning or clarity, not just decoration.
- Consider using visuals when you want to capture your reader's attention and interest in a vivid way, emphasize a point you have already made in your text, present information that is difficult to convey in words, or communicate with audiences with different language skills and abilities.
- Place each visual as near as possible to the text it illustrates.
- Remember to introduce each visual clearly: *As the map to the right depicts . . .*
- Comment on the significance or effect of the visual: *Figure 1 corroborates the claim made by geneticists: while the human genome may be mapped, it is far from understood.*
- Does the particular visual you are considering convey the tone you want to achieve? Is that tone appropriate for your audience, purpose, and topic?

1h Evidence

What kinds of evidence will be most persuasive to your audience and most effective in the field you are working in — historical precedents? expert testimony? statistical data? experimental results? personal anecdotes? Knowing what kinds of evidence count most in a particular field or with particular audiences will help you make appropriate choices.

1i Language and style

- What level of formality is most appropriate — extremely informal, as in an email to a friend? moderately formal, as in a letter to someone you know only slightly? very formal, as in legal or institutional documents?

- What forms of address are most appropriate for your audience? Do you know them well enough to use nicknames or slang? Are words from another language or varieties of English appropriate? Should you use *he* or *she* or some gender-neutral way to refer to your readers?

- What kind of sentence style will be most appropriate — simple, straightforward sentences that convey information clearly and concisely? longer descriptive sentences that create a picture in readers' minds or evoke emotional responses? lists of phrases to give directions? brief **sentence fragments** to get a point across quickly online?

FOR MULTILINGUAL WRITERS

Bringing in Other Languages

Even when you write in English, you may want or need to include words, phrases, or whole passages in another language. If so, consider whether your readers will understand that language and whether you need to provide a translation, as in this example from John (Fire) Lame Deer's "Talking to the Owls and Butterflies":

> Listen to the air. You can hear it, feel it, smell it, taste it. *Woniya waken* — the holy air — which renews all by its breath. *Woniya, woniya waken* — spirit, life, breath, renewal — it means all that.

In this instance, more than one translation is necessary because the phrase Lame Deer is discussing has multiple meanings in English.

1j Research

Writing will often call for research. First, determine what research you need to do:

- Make a list of what you already know about your topic (and where you learned it, since these sources may be useful later on).
- Decide what other information — including visuals — you are most likely to need.
- Jot down ways to get this additional information. Will you need to visit libraries? search the Web? interview someone?

(For more on research, see Chapters 38–41.)

1k Planning and drafting

Sketch out a rough plan for organizing your writing, as in the following example:

WORKING THESIS

Increased motorcycle use demands reorganization of parking lots.

INTRODUCTION

— Give background and overview of the current situation (motorcycle use is up).
— State my purpose (to offer solutions to the problem identified in the thesis).

BODY

— Describe the current situation (tell about my research in area parking lots).
— Describe the problem in detail (report on statistics; cars vs. cycles).
— Present two possible solutions (enlarge lots or reallocate space).

CONCLUSION

— Recommend against first solution because of cost and space limitations.
— Recommend second solution and summarize its benefits.

Once you have come up with a plan, these guidelines can help you complete a draft:

- Keep all information close at hand and arranged in the order of your plan.

- Draft at a computer if possible. Before beginning, create a folder for your project and, within it, create two subfolders — one labeled "sources" and the other labeled "drafts." As you write, remember to save often into the "drafts" folder. Choose a file name that you will recognize instantly, and include the draft number in the file name: *human genome draft 1*. As you revise, use the SAVE AS command to make a copy of each new draft (*human genome draft 2*). Also back up your work on a disk.

- Try to write in stretches of at least thirty minutes; writing will get easier as you go along.

- Don't get bogged down with details such as word choice or mechanics.

- Remember that a draft is never perfect. Concentrate on getting all your ideas down.

- Stop writing at a logical place, one where you know what will come next. Doing so will make it easier to resume writing later.

1l Revising

Revising means taking a fresh look at your draft to make sure it is complete, clear, and effective. These questions can help you revise:

- Does the draft accomplish its purpose?
- Does the title tell what the draft is about?
- Is the thesis clearly stated, and does it contain a topic and a comment?
- Does the introduction catch readers' attention?
- Will the draft interest and appeal to its audience?
- How does the draft indicate your stance on the topic?
- What are the main points that illustrate or support the thesis? Are they clear? Do you need to add material to the points or add new points?
- Are the ideas presented in an order that will make sense to readers?
- Are the points clearly linked by logical transitions?
- How are visuals and other sources (if any) integrated into your draft? Are they clearly labeled and referred to in the draft? Have you commented on their significance?

- How does the draft conclude? Is the conclusion memorable?
- Have you read your draft aloud to make sure it flows smoothly and to find typos or other mistakes?
- Are all sentences complete and correct?
- Have you used the spell checker?
- Have you proofread one last time, going word for word?

(For more on drafting and revising, see Chapter 41.)

1m Writing and collaborating online

The contexts for online communication are changing and multiplying daily, offering many new ways to get information and join conversations. Since much of your writing may take place online, consider these questions:

- What is your purpose for writing online? If it is to gather information, what is the best way to phrase questions for a discussion-list posting or in an email to an expert?
- Have you considered your online audience carefully? How well does your audience know you? Are your tone and level of formality appropriate?
- Have you observed the rules of online etiquette? If you are writing to a listserv or a chat room, are you following expected conventions?
- Have you considered what design elements you should use? a template? color to signal responses to email? graphics that can be quickly downloaded?
- If you are relying on information you found online, are you sure of its accuracy and validity?

More and more online writing is social and collaborative. You can learn to work more effectively with others online by planning ahead and observing some simple rules of online etiquette:

- Plan collaborative projects carefully so that each person knows the exact responsibilities of every member. Also plan to keep in touch by email, on a discussion list, or on the phone.
- Create a group name in your email program so that you can send messages to the entire group.
- When doing collaborative work via a discussion list, save copies of messages in a folder unless your email program automatically saves them to a Sent folder.

- When sharing emailed writing with co-authors, save your work as rich text format (RTF) or HTML so that it can be read and edited across platforms (PC, Macintosh, Linux) and word processors. When all else fails, copy and paste your document directly into an email message.

- Give credit where credit is due. In an online discussion, remember the name of the writer whose ideas you are referring to, and credit him or her. In team projects, acknowledge all members' contributions as well as any help you receive from outsiders.

2 Analyzing and Constructing Arguments

In one sense, all language use has an argumentative edge: even when you greet friends, you want to convince them that you are genuinely glad to see them. In much academic and professional writing, however, **argument** is more narrowly defined as a text — whether verbal or visual — that makes a claim and supports it fully.

2a Identifying basic appeals in an argument

Identify emotional appeals.   Emotional appeals stir our emotions and remind us of deeply held values. In analyzing any argument, look for what the writer or creator is doing to tug on the audience's emotions, and you'll be on your way to identifying the emotional appeals.

Identify ethical appeals.   Ethical appeals support the credibility, moral character, and goodwill of the writer. To find these appeals, ask yourself what the writer or creator is doing to show that he or she is knowledgeable and has really done homework on the subject. Ask what kind of character the writer or creator builds and how he or she does so. Most important, ask if the writer or creator seems

---

▶ bedfordstmartins.com/easywriter For additional help with argumentation, go to **Links** and click on **Argument**. To read a complete sample argument essay, click on **Student Writing**.

CHECKLIST

Analyzing Verbal and Visual Arguments

- What cultural contexts — the time and place the argument was written; the economic, social, and political events surrounding the argument; and so on — inform the argument? What do they tell you about where the writer or creator is coming from?
- What is the main issue of the argument?
- What emotional, ethical, or logical appeals is the argument making?
- How has the writer or creator established credibility?
- What sources does the argument rely on? How current and reliable are they? Are some perspectives left out, and if so, how does this exclusion affect the argument?
- What claim does the argument make, and what evidence supports it?
- How has the writer or creator used visuals to support the argument? How well do words and images work together to make a point?
- What effect do highlighted or foregrounded visual details, words, or images have on your response to the argument?
- How effectively does the argument use color, sound, or video to convey a message?
- What overall impression does the argument create? Are you convinced?

trustworthy and has the best interests of the audience in mind.

Identify logical appeals.   Logical appeals are often most persuasive to Western audiences — as some say, "the facts don't lie." In addition to checking the facts of any argument, look for firsthand evidence drawn from observations, interviews, surveys or questionnaires, experiments, and personal experience as well as secondhand evidence drawn from the testimony of others, statistics, and other print and online sources. As you evaluate these sources, ask yourself how trustworthy they are and whether terms are clearly defined.

2b Analyzing the elements of an argument

According to philosopher Stephen Toulmin, most arguments contain a **claim** or claims; reasons for the claim(s); **warrants** (often in the form of assumptions, whether stated or not); **evidence** (facts, authoritative opinions, examples, and so on); and **qualifiers**, which limit the claim in some way. Nailing down the major claim(s) and these other elements will put you well on your way to a good, strong analysis.

Suppose you have read a brief argument about providing sex education for children. The following diagram shows how you can use the elements of argument for analysis:

Toulmin's System Applied to Sex-Education Argument

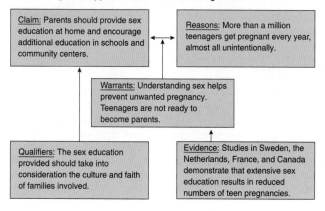

Claim: Parents should provide sex education at home and encourage additional education in schools and community centers.

Reasons: More than a million teenagers get pregnant every year, almost all unintentionally.

Warrants: Understanding sex helps prevent unwanted pregnancy. Teenagers are not ready to become parents.

Qualifiers: The sex education provided should take into consideration the culture and faith of families involved.

Evidence: Studies in Sweden, the Netherlands, France, and Canada demonstrate that extensive sex education results in reduced numbers of teen pregnancies.

2c Making an argument

Chances are you've been making convincing arguments since early childhood, and your family slowly learned to respond to these arguments. But if family members and friends are not always easy to convince, then the job of making effective arguments to those unfamiliar with you presents even more challenges. It is especially difficult to argue constructively with people who are thousands of miles away and are encountering your argument in cyberspace.

Arguable statements.   An arguable statement should meet three criteria:

1. It should seek to convince readers of something, to change their minds, or to urge them to do something.
2. It should address a problem that has no obvious or absolute solution or answer.
3. It should present a position that readers can have varying perspectives on.

ARGUABLE STATEMENT	Video games lead to violent behavior.
UNARGUABLE STATEMENT	Video games earn millions of dollars every year.

Argumentative thesis or claim. To move from an arguable statement to an argumentative thesis, begin with an arguable statement:

ARGUABLE STATEMENT	Pesticides should be banned.

Attach at least one good reason.

REASON	because they endanger the lives of workers

You now have a working argumentative thesis.

ARGUMENTATIVE THESIS	Because they endanger the lives of workers, pesticides should be banned.

Develop the underlying assumption that supports your argument.

UNDERLYING ASSUMPTION (WARRANT)	Workers have a right to a safe working environment.

Identifying this assumption will help you gather evidence in support of your argument. Finally, consider whether you need to qualify your claim in any way.

Ethical appeals. To make any argument effective, you need to establish your credibility. Here are some good ways to do so:

- Demonstrate that you are knowledgeable about the issues and topic.
- Show that you respect the views of your audience and have their best interests at heart.
- Demonstrate that you are fair and evenhanded.

Logical appeals. Audiences almost always ask, "So where's your proof," and by this question they are pointing toward those logical reasons that back up your argument. You can create good logical appeals in the following ways:

- Provide strong examples that are representative and that clearly support your point.
- Introduce precedents — particular examples from the past — that support your point.
- Use narratives or stories in support of your point.
- Cite authorities and their testimony, as long as the authority is timely and is genuinely qualified to speak on the topic.
- Establish that one event is the cause — or the effect — of another.

Emotional appeals.   You can make strong emotional appeals to your audience in several ways:

- Introduce a powerful image (either verbal or visual) that supports your point.
- Use detailed description and concrete language to make your points more vivid to the audience.
- Use figurative language — metaphors, similes, analogies, and so on — to make your point both lively and memorable.

Visual appeals.   Remember that visuals make strong appeals to audiences; in some instances, a picture really is worth a thousand words. Following are visuals that make ethical, logical, and emotional appeals.

The first visual is one that makes an ethical appeal. The National Endowment for the Humanities home page begins to establish its credentials through its title and motto, "great ideas brought to life." These elements help to create an ethical appeal; they say, in essence, "you can trust us; we're THE national endowment that supports the humanities, and we are associated with bringing great ideas to life."

The second visual appeal, which appeared in *Business Week*, makes a logical appeal. It uses a simple bar graph to deliver a logical message about equality of pay for men and women. A quick glance will reveal how long it would take to explain in words alone all the information this chart contains.

Visual That Makes an Ethical Appeal

Visual That Makes a Logical Appeal

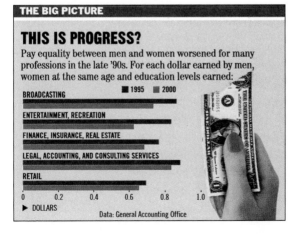

The following visual, from a "My Turn" essay in *Newsweek,* depicts the author, Joseph C. Phillips, standing tall and proud in front of an American flag, an image intended to capture his identification with flag and country. This visual supports Phillips's argument that black Americans should claim the American freedom they have fought so long to gain rather than rejecting America.

Visual That Makes an Emotional Appeal

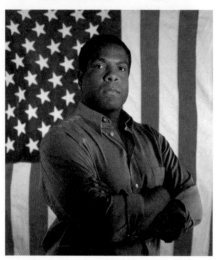

2d Organizing an argument

Although there is no universal "ideal" organizational framework for an argument, the following pattern (often referred to as the classical system) has been used throughout the history of the Western world:

INTRODUCTION

- Gets readers' attention and interest
- Establishes your qualifications to write about your topic
- Establishes common ground with readers
- Demonstrates fairness
- States or implies your argumentative thesis

BACKGROUND

- Presents any necessary background data or information, including pertinent personal narratives or stories

LINES OF ARGUMENT

- Present good reasons and evidence (including logical and emotional appeals) in support of your thesis, usually in order of importance
- Demonstrate ways your argument is in readers' best interest

CONSIDERATION OF ALTERNATIVE ARGUMENTS

- Examines alternative or opposing points of view
- Notes advantages and disadvantages of alternative views
- Explains why one view is better than other(s)

CONCLUSION

- May summarize the argument briefly
- Elaborates on the implication of your thesis
- Makes clear what you want readers to think and/or do
- Makes a strong ethical or emotional appeal in a memorable way

2e Designing an argument

Like all writing, most arguments no longer appear only in print form. Rather, they are designed carefully to make the best use of space, font style and type size, color, visuals, and digital technology.

- Check out the conventions of the kind of argument you are writing. What is expected in a Web-based report? in a brochure presentation?
- Choose fonts that will help create the overall impression you are trying to achieve, and use a readable type size appropriate to your medium and genre.
- Think visually, considering the use of white space, titles, headings, and the "look" of each segment of the project. Choose titles, headings, and subheadings that will guide readers from point to point, and set each one off consistently.
- Plan where each visual will go, keeping each one as close to the text that refers to it as possible, giving each a title, labeling each as a figure or table if appropriate, and providing the source for the visual.
- Remember that you may need to request permission to use something taken from another source, especially if your work will be posted to a public space on the Web.
- Choose colors carefully, keeping your audience in mind; in some cultures, for example, red suggests war, and blue purity. You may want to stick to black and white for much

of your text because it is easy to read, and reserve color for headings, illustrations, and so on. If you are posting your argument to the Web, remember that you need to have a strong contrast between the background color and print and illustrations.

2f A student argument essay

In this essay, Teal Pfeifer argues that images in the media affect how women see themselves, and she offers a solution to a problem. Her essay has been excerpted to show some key parts of her argument as well as her good use of reasons, evidence, and appeals to logic and emotion.

Teal Pfeifer

Professor Rashad

English 102

13 April 2007

Devastating Beauty

Collarbones, hipbones, cheekbones — so many bones. She looks at the camera with sunken eyes, smiling, acting beautiful. Her dress is Versace, or Gucci, or Dior, and it is revealing, revealing every bone and joint in her thin, thin body. She looks fragile and beautiful, as if I could snap her in two. I look at her and feel the soft cushion of flesh that surrounds my own joints; then I look away and wonder what kind of self-discipline it takes to become beautiful like this.

By age seventeen a young woman has seen an average of 250,000 ads featuring a severely underweight woman whose body type is, for most people, unattainable by any means, including extreme ones such as anorexia, bulimia, and drug use, ("The Skinny"). The media promote clothing, cigarettes, fragrances, and even food with images like these, and the women in these images are a smaller size than ever before. In 1950, the White Rock Mineral Water girl was 5'4" tall and weighed 140 pounds; now she is 5'10" tall and weighs only 110 pounds, signifying the growing deviation between the weight of models and that of the normal female population (Pipher 184).

This media phenomenon has had a major effect on the female population as a whole, both young and old. Five to ten million women in America today suffer from an eating disorder related to poor self-image, and yet advertisements continue to prey on insecurities fueled by a woman's desire to be thin. Current estimates reveal that 80 percent of women are dissatisfied with their appearance and 45 percent of those are on a diet on any given day ("Statistics"). Yet even the most stringent dieting will generally fail to create the paper-thin body so valued in the media, and continuing efforts to do so can lead to serious psychological problems such as depression.

While many women express dissatisfaction with their bodies, they are not the only victims of the emaciated images so frequently presented to them. Young girls are equally affected by these images, if not more so. Eighty percent of girls under age ten have already been on a diet and expressed the desire to be thinner and more beautiful (*Slim Hopes*). Thus from a young age, beauty is equated with a specific size. The message girls get is an insidious one: in order to be your best self, you should wear size 0 or 1. The pressure only grows more intense as girls grow up. According to results from the Kaiser Family Foundation Survey "Reflections of Girls in the Media," 16 percent of ten- to seventeen-year-old girls reported that they had dieted or exercised to look like a TV character. Yet two-thirds of teenage girls acknowledged that these thin characters were not an accurate reflection of "real life" (qtd. in Dittrich, "Children").

It is tragic to see so much of the American population obsessed with weight and reaching an ideal that is, for the most part, ultimately unattainable. Equally troubling is the role magazines play in feeding this obsession. When a researcher asked female students from Stanford University to flip through several magazines containing images of glamorized, super-thin models, 68 percent of the women felt significantly worse about themselves after viewing the magazine models (qtd. in Dittrich, "Media"). Another study showed that looking at models on a long-term basis leads to stress, depression, guilt, and lowered self-worth (qtd. in Dittrich, "Media").

How can we reject images that are so harmful, especially to young women? Perhaps the most effective way to rid the print medium of emaciated models and eliminate the harmful effects they cause is to mount a boycott. If women stopped buying magazines that target them with such harmful advertising, magazines would be forced to change the kinds of ads they print. Such a boycott would send a clear message: women and girls reject the victimization that takes place every time they look at a skeletally thin model and then feel worse about themselves. Consumers can ultimately control what is put on the market: If we don't buy, funding for such ads will dry up fast.

In the past, boycotts have been effective tools for social change. Rosa Parks, often identified as the mother of the modern-day civil rights movement, played a pivotal role in the Montgomery bus boycott in December 1955. When Parks refused to give up her seat to a white rider, she was arrested, and this incident inspired the boycott. For more than a year, African Americans in Montgomery chose to walk instead of ride the buses. The boycott was eventually successful: segregation on buses was declared illegal by the U.S. Supreme Court.

As a society, we have much to learn from boycotts of the past, and their lessons can help us confront contemporary social ills. As I have shown, body-image dissatisfaction and eating disorders are rising at an alarming rate among young girls and women in American society. The anorexia and bulimia that women suffer from are not only diseases that can be cured; they are also ones that can be prevented — if women will take a solid stand against such advertisements and the magazines that publish them. This is where power lies — in the hands of those who hand over the dollars that support the glorification of unhealthy and unrealistic bodies. It is our choice to exert this power and to reject magazines that promote such images.

Works Cited

Dittrich, Liz. "About-Face Facts on Children and the Media."
    About-Face. About-Face, 1996-2008. Web. 10 Mar. 2007.

---. "About-Face Facts on the Media." *About-Face*. About-Face,
    1996-2008. Web. Mar. 2007.

Pipher, Mary. *Reviving Ophelia: Saving the Selves of Adolescent Girls*.
    New York: Ballantine, 1994. Print.

"The Skinny on Media and Weight." *Common Sense Media*. Common
    Sense Media Inc., 27 Sept. 2006. Web. 15 Mar. 2007.

Slim Hopes. Dir. Sut Jhally. Prod. Jean Kilbourne. Media Education
Foundation, 1995. Videocassette.

"Statistics." *National Eating Disorders Association*. National Eating
Disorders Association, 2005. Web. 14 Mar. 2007.

3 Writing in Any Discipline

Writing is important in almost every profession, but it
works in different ways in different disciplines. You may
begin to get a sense of such differences as you prepare
essays or other assignments for courses in the humanities,
the social sciences, and the natural sciences.

3a Analyzing academic assignments and expectations

When you receive an assignment in any discipline, your
first job is to make sure you understand what that assignment is asking you to do. Whatever your assignment, use
the questions in the checklist on p. 32 to analyze it.

3b Understanding disciplinary vocabularies

A good way to enter into the conversation of a field or discipline is to study its vocabulary. Highlight key terms in
your reading or notes to help you distinguish any specialized terms. If you find only a little specialized vocabulary,
try to master the new terms quickly by reading your textbook carefully, asking questions of the instructor, and looking up key words or phrases.

---

bedfordstmartins.com/easywriter For information on multidisciplinary inven-
tion techniques, go to **Links** and click on **The Art and Craft of Writing.** For
sample student writing, go to **Student Writing** and click on **Writing in the
Disciplines.**

> ✔ CHECKLIST
>
> **Analyzing an Assignment in Any Discipline**
>
> 1. What is the purpose of the assignment? Does it serve as a basis for class discussion or brainstorming about a topic, or is the purpose to demonstrate your mastery of certain material and your competence as a writer?
>
> 2. What is the assignment asking you to do? Are you to summarize, explain, evaluate, interpret, illustrate, or define? If you are to do more than one of these tasks, does the assignment specify an order?
>
> 3. Do you need to ask for clarification of any terms?
>
> 4. What do you need to know or find out to complete the assignment?
>
> 5. Do you understand the expectations regarding background reading and preparation, use of sources (both written and visual), method of organization and development, format, and length?
>
> 6. Can you find an example of an effective response to a similar assignment? If so, you can analyze it and perhaps use it as a model for developing your own approach to the current assignment.
>
> 7. Does your understanding of the assignment fit with that of other students? Talking over an assignment with classmates is one good way to test your understanding.

If you find a great deal of specialized vocabulary, any of the following procedures may prove helpful:

- Keep a log of unfamiliar or confusing words used in context. Check the terms in your textbook's glossary or in a specialized dictionary. Students entering the discipline of sociology, for instance, may refer to the *Dictionary of the Social Sciences*.

- Check to see if your textbook has a glossary of terms or sets off definitions in italics or boldface type.

- Try to start using or working with key concepts. Even if they are not yet entirely clear to you, working with them will help you come to understand them. For example, try to plot the narrative progression in a story even if you are still not entirely sure of the definition of *narrative progression*.

- If you belong to listservs or online discussion groups — or even if you are browsing Web sites related to a particular field — take special note of the ways technical language or disciplinary vocabulary is used there. Look for definitions of terms on a Web site's FAQ page.

3c Identifying the style of a discipline

Another important way to learn about a particular discipline is to identify its stylistic features. Study pieces of writing in the field with the following questions in mind:

- How would you describe the overall tone of the writing?
- To what extent do writers in the field strive for an objective stance? (See 39a.)
- In general, how long are the sentences and paragraphs?
- Are verbs generally active or passive — and why? (See 7e.)
- Do the writers use first person (*I*) or prefer terms such as *one* or *the investigator*? What is the effect of this choice?
- How does the writing use and integrate visual elements such as graphs, tables, charts, photographs, or maps?
- What role, if any, do headings and other formatting elements play in the writing?
- What bibliographic style (such as MLA, APA, CSE, or *Chicago*) is used?

Of course, writings within a single discipline may have different purposes and different styles. For example, a chemist may write a grant proposal, lab notebook, literature review, research report, and lab report, each with a different purpose and style.

3d Understanding the use of evidence

As you grow familiar with any area of study, you will develop a sense of just what it takes to prove a point in that field. As you read assigned materials, ask yourself the following questions about evidence:

- How do writers in the field use precedent and authority? (See 2c.)
- What use is made of quantitative data (items that can be counted and measured) and qualitative data (items that can be systematically observed)?
- How is logical reasoning used? How are definition, cause and effect, analogy, and example used in this discipline?
- What are the primary materials — the firsthand sources of information — in this field? What are the secondary materials — the sources of information derived from others? (See 38b.)
- How are quotations used and integrated into the text?

3e Using conventional disciplinary patterns and formats

You can gather all the evidence in the world and still fail to produce effective writing in your discipline if you do not know the field's generally accepted formats for organizing and presenting evidence. Again, these formats vary widely from discipline to discipline and sometimes from instructor to instructor, but patterns do emerge. The typical laboratory report, for instance, follows a fairly standard organizational framework whether it is in botany, chemistry, or parasitology. A case study in sociology or education or anthropology likewise follows a typical organizational plan.

4 Writing with Computers: The Basics

How often do you find yourself at a computer? Many writers today use a word-processing program to draft and revise documents from start to finish; read and write email, instant messages, and Web logs; and visit chat rooms to keep in touch with colleagues, family, and friends. In fact, many writers feel that their computers are an extension of themselves, so closely connected are they to these machines and the acts of communication they make possible.

4a Using word-processing tools

The metaphor of word *processing* deserves attention: we use computers to literally process our words — to discover ideas, to format them in various ways, and to experiment with organization and style. Here are some ways to use word-processing software efficiently and effectively.

---

bedfordstmartins.com/easywriter For resources and more information, click on **Working Online**. For additional help, click on the **Designing for the Web Tutorial**.

Saving and sharing files. Save each file with a clear name (*Rhetorical Analysis draft 1*, for example, instead of *Paper 1*) that you will recognize later. Save related files in the same folder. Here are some additional tips for saving and sharing files:

- If you are sending a file to an instructor or someone else, include your name in the file name along with other pertinent information so that the recipient can easily identify it.

- Before sending a draft electronically, check with your recipients on the file types they can receive. Some email accounts limit the size of files, and larger files take longer to download.

- Use your word processor's AUTO SAVE function. Or if not available, save your files every five minutes or right after you've made an important change.

- Take the extra precaution of saving a backup copy of every file — with a slightly different name (*Rhetorical Analysis draft 1 dup*) — on a disc or in another location.

Formatting. The following list of format recommendations includes some keywords (in *italics*) that you can search for in your word processor's HELP menu to learn how to use each specific feature:

- Most word processors set the default *margins* at 1 inch for top and bottom and 1.25 inches for left and right sides. You may need to adjust margins for some documents.

- For text you want to *indent*, don't use the *enter* key for hard returns. Instead, highlight the text, and then use the FORMAT menu or ruler bar to align the text.

- Use the word processor to insert *page numbers* automatically. Include additional information with the page number by using *headers* and *footers*. You can also automatically add and number *footnotes* and *endnotes*.

- Format your lists by using *bullets* and *numbering*. For some documents, you may want to create *columns*.

- Many word processors include graphics tools for creating charts, graphs, tables, and other illustrations. Choosing *insert* may also help you easily add a *picture*, *symbol*, or *hyperlink* to your document.

- Use PRINT PREVIEW before printing to check that your format looks correct.

Cutting and pasting.   Here are some tips to help you CUT, COPY, and PASTE text efficiently as you revise:

- Select text for copying by highlighting a passage and then clicking on COPY in the EDIT menu. Copied text will stay where it was in your document while you experiment with moving it to a more appropriate place. If the passage fits better somewhere else, you can PASTE it there and then go back and delete it from its original location.

- Work from a copy of the file if you plan to revise the organization of a document extensively.

- Remember that too much cutting and pasting can result in an incoherent text. After cutting and pasting, reread your entire text to make sure it still moves logically from point to point.

Other basic tools.   Several other word-processing tools may help you improve the quality of your writing.

- Use the OUTLINE function to check the logical connections in a document you create.

- Spell checkers can go a long way toward identifying typos and other misspellings. But a spell checker will fail, for instance, to flag misspelled proper names, confused homonyms (*there, their, they're*), and wrong words that are nevertheless spelled correctly (*form* when it should be *from*). In short, you still need to proofread.

- Use grammar and style checkers carefully. Grammar and style checkers can miss errors and are more problematic than spell checkers because they are looking at your text out of context, without knowing your purpose or audi-

Incorrect Suggestion from a Grammar Checker

ence. Furthermore, grammar and style checkers sometimes give the wrong advice, as shown on p. 37.

- If you're using Microsoft Word, experiment with the TRACK
  CHANGES and COMMENT tools. The TRACK CHANGES function
  records additions, deletions, and so on, and allows you to
  later accept or reject those changes. Both of these tools are
  useful for revising and working collaboratively.

- Use the FIND and REPLACE functions to search for certain
  kinds of errors. For example, if you sometimes mistype *it's*
  for *its,* you can search for all uses of *it's* and correct them if
  necessary.

4b Following conventions for email, discussion lists, and Web logs (blogs)

Though much of your online communication may be very
informal, you must know when to adjust your style and
voice for specific audiences and occasions.

Email. As with any kind of writing, email calls on you to
consider your purpose and audience when you write messages. The following advice will help ensure that your email
is effective:

- Use a subject line that states your topic accurately and
  clearly — whether you are writing an email message or
  responding to one.

- Be pertinent; include only the information your readers
  need.

- Break your long paragraphs into shorter paragraphs, and
  when a message has several points, create sections with
  headings.

- Avoid flaming — using intentionally rude or insulting
  language — and remember that tone is very hard to convey in online postings; what you intend as a joke may
  come across as an insult.

- Many readers find messages in ALL CAPS irritating, as if
  someone were shouting at them.

- Use a more formal tone along with a formal greeting and
  closing when writing to someone you don't know or to an
  authority, such as a supervisor or instructor (*Dear Ms.
  Aulie* rather than *Hello*).

- Except in very informal situations, use the conventions
  of academic and professional English. If you want your

message to be taken seriously, be sure it is clearly written and error free. Proofread email just as you would other writing.

- Avoid using color fonts or other special formatting unless you know the formatting will appear as you intend on your reader's screen.

- Remember that the Internet is public and that online readers can easily print or forward your messages. When privacy is important, think twice before communicating by email.

- Before attaching files of text or visuals, check with your recipients to make sure they will be able to download them.

- Conclude your message with your name and email address. Your email program likely includes a command that lets you place this information in a signature file.

The sample message that follows is succinct and direct, with a specific subject line and the writer's contact information since it is an email to someone the writer doesn't know.

Email

```
To: techsoup@indirect.com
From: Andrea Lunsford <lunsford@stanford.edu>
Subject: help finding a correct address

Dear Techsoup:

I am trying to send a message to Irene Whitney
at Pacific Synergies, which is headquartered
in Whistler, B.C. The email address she gave
me is pacsyn@direct.net -- which is obviously
not right since you returned it as undeliver-
able. If you have an address for Pacific
Synergies, I would be very grateful to receive
it.

Andrea Lunsford, Department of English
<lunsford@stanford.edu>
Stanford University
450 Serra Mall
Stanford, CA 94305-2087
(650) 723-0682 phone
(650) 723-0631 fax
```

FOR MULTILINGUAL WRITERS

Following Email Conventions

Email conventions are still evolving, and they differ from one cultural context to another. Especially if you do not know the recipients of your email, stick to a more formal tone (*Dear Ms. Ditembe* and *Sincerely yours,* for example), and follow the conventions of print letter writing — complete sentences, regular capitalization, and so on.

Email lists and discussion forums. When taking part in an online discussion (in forums or on lists, sometimes called listservs), keep the following tips in mind:

- Avoid unnecessary criticism of spelling or other obvious language errors. If you disagree with an assertion of fact, offer what you believe to be the correct information, but don't insult the writer for making a mistake.
- If you think you've been flamed, give the writer the benefit of the doubt. Replying with patience will make you appear credible and mature.
- Follow the conventions of a particular discussion forum regarding the use of acronyms (such as *IOW* for *in other words*). If readers might not understand a particular acronym, write it out.
- Note that many email discussion lists are archived, so more people than you think may be reading your messages. Remember that your postings create an impression of you.

Web logs (blogs). Blogs are Web texts written by one or more persons focusing on a single topic and updated regularly, often daily. For those writing and reading them, blogs provide an ongoing record of thinking, one that is easily recoverable: think of an interactive electronic journal you write in as often as possible. Here are some basic tips for using blogs effectively:

- Remember that blogs, like email, are public — what you wish to remain private should not go on a blog.
- To comment on a blog, follow the same conventions you would for a discussion-list posting. Become familiar with

the conversation before you add a comment of your own, and avoid commenting on blog entries that are several days old.

- A blog makes it easy to post writing to the Web, but how you use a blog — as a journal, research log, and so on — is determined by your purpose, audience, and imagination.

The sample discussion-list posting that follows responds to an earlier query in a tone that is engaged and polite. It is signed with only a first name and initial, since this is a closed discussion for a class.

Posting to a Discussion List

```
To: alenglh167@lists.acs.ohio-state.edu
From: Kristen Convery <convery.8@osu.edu>
Subject: Re: class discussion of "self"

At 03:48 PM 04/17/04 -0500, Kate wrote:

>Has anyone had any interesting or pertinent
>discussions of the "self" in other classes
>this term?

I'm taking psychology this quarter and have
found some information that pertains to our
discussion on the self.

Carl Rogers studied the self and self-concept,
theorizing that people do things in line with
their concept of themselves in order to avoid
having to rework that self-concept. For
instance, if I think of myself as an artist and
not as a musician and I want to go to a concert,
I will go to the art museum just so that I do
not have to rethink and maybe change the way I
view myself.

It strikes me as interesting that we seem to
feel as if we must fit one mold, and that that
mold nullifies all other concepts of the self.
Why can't we be both artists and musicians?
Comments from other class members?

Kristen C.
```

Responses to email and postings. When responding to a particular message, keep these guidelines in mind:

- Change the subject line if you are writing about something different from the original subject.

- Check to make sure you are responding to the appropriate person or persons. If you receive a message that is copied to several others, decide whether you want to reply to the author (REPLY) or to the whole group (REPLY TO ALL). Accidentally sending personal messages to an entire group can be embarrassing.

- Include only those parts of the original message that you are writing about, and delete the rest.

4c Creating Web texts

As you take advantage of the opportunities Web texts offer, think carefully about the design of effective Web pages.

Planning Web texts. As in preparing any important document, you need to plan your Web text with a keen eye on your deadlines and rhetorical situation, including purpose, audience, topic, and stance. (See Chapter 1.)

- Make sure you have access to space on a server so that you can both preview your pages as you design them and post them "live" to the Web.

- Consider the overall impression you want to create. Do you want your site to be bold? soothing? serious? This overall impression should guide your decisions about text, navigational aids, visuals, color, video, sound clips, and so on.

- Visit several Web sites you admire. Look for effective design ideas and ways of organizing navigation and information.

- Map (or storyboard) your Web document, and be ready to move elements around to improve organization. Think about creating a template for consistent layout of pages or sections.

- Plan your use of visuals very carefully, making sure that each one helps get your message across. Make sure your visuals are saved in browser-supported formats such as GIF or JPEG. Check the file size and resolution of photos and other visuals to make sure they can be downloaded quickly.

- Give considerable thought to the colors you will use, remembering that colors carry strong emotional associations. (See 5b.)

- Consider the technical limitations readers may face, and test your Web text from a dial-up modem and in different browsers to see how it loads and looks.

- Web texts are dynamic, so plan to reassess, revise, and maintain your Web text on an ongoing basis and to note when the site was last updated.

Mapping Web texts.   Just as you might outline a print document, you should develop a clear structure for a Web text. These tips can help you map your Web text:

1. Inventory the content material you have, and make a list of what you still need to find or create.

2. Using a word-processing program or old-fashioned pencil and paper, sketch the basic text and visuals for each page of your text, beginning with the homepage.

3. Indicate the links among the pages — and make sure all sections of your Web text link to the homepage.

Following design principles.   For any Web document, you should follow some basic principles of good design.

- At the top of the homepage, put a title (and subtitle, if necessary) along with an eye-catching and easy-to-process visual or statement that makes clear what the Web site is about.

- Think of each page beyond the homepage as having two main parts: navigation areas (such as menus or links) and content areas. Make these two areas distinct from one another, and make the navigation clear to your readers.

- Use a design template to make the elements on each page consistent. You can find such templates in some Web writing tools and on Web design sites, or you may take cues from existing Web designs (but be sure to give proper credit).

- Create a navigation area for every main page, listing links to the key sections of the site along with a link back to the homepage.

- Use visuals that can be downloaded quickly and easily by your readers.

- Remember that the top left of a page is always visible and thus the most important spot.

- Include your name and contact information on every page.

- Get responses to a rough draft of your pages, especially the homepage. How understandable and readable are these pages? How easy are they to navigate? How effective is your use of color, visuals, fonts, sound, and so on?

Coding Web texts. Essentially, codes tell a Web browser how to interpret the various elements on a page. One set of codes (usually called document tags) governs the larger aspects of the text (such as the title, body elements, background color, and so on), while another set (usually called appearance tags) governs smaller aspects (italics, boldface, underlining, and so on). You can write your own code from scratch, or draft on a word processor and save the material as HTML. But you will most likely use a text editor (such as Microsoft FrontPage or Dreamweaver) that does the hard work for you and lets you see each page as it is created.

Once you have coded your document, asking for responses from readers is crucial before you make your document available on the Web. To preview your text:

- Proofread every page, looking for any typos, errors, or confusing passages.
- Check the navigation of the site, verifying that all links work and that readers can find their way around with ease.
- Check the site using several different browsers and computers, if possible, to see that each page displays properly.

Using visuals and multimedia. The following tips will help you think carefully about how best to use visuals and multimedia in your Web texts:

- Visuals may add to but are not a substitute for text, so integrate the two very carefully. Don't use visuals for mere decoration.
- Readers may not see the connection between a visual and text; make that relationship clear in the text or in labels or captions. (See 5d.)
- Most work on the Web is protected by copyright, so unless there is an explicit statement that the information is available for free use, you must request permission to use a visual or sound clip that you have not created yourself. Free icons, clip art, and other visuals are widely available on the Web; check archives of free visuals and most search engines. Government documents are in the public domain and thus free for use, but always include source information.

- To download and save a visual image from the Web using Windows on a PC, place your cursor over the visual, right click with your mouse, and select SAVE IMAGE AS. To download a visual image on a Mac, hold down the mouse until a menu appears and select SAVE THIS IMAGE AS.

- The file space a JPEG or GIF visual takes up may make downloading the image difficult, so limit individual visuals to 30 to 40 kilobytes — or use a smaller thumbnail version as a link to the original, larger file.

- Experiment with scanning objects and taking pictures with a digital camera — and using photo-editing software to clarify and improve them. (See 5d.)

- Remember that visuals and audio will often not be accessible to those with disabilities and those with browsers that can't display them. Test your Web site to see how accessible it is.

5 Designing Documents

Computers have made it easier for us to use headings, lists, graphics, and other visuals when we write. Because these visual elements can help us get and keep a reader's attention, they bring a whole new dimension to writing — what some refer to as *visual rhetoric*.

5a Understanding design principles

Most design experts begin with several very simple principles that guide the design of print and Web-based texts.

Contrast. The contrast in a design is what attracts your eye to the page and guides you around it. You may achieve contrast through the use of color, icons, boldface or large type, headings, and so on. To capture your readers' attention, begin with a focal point — the dominant point, visual, or words on the page — and structure the flow of your visual information from this point.

---

bedfordstmartins.com/easywriter For more on effective design, click on **Roger Munger's Designing Documents Tutorial.** For sample documents, click on **Student Writing.**

The National Geographic Web site above uses high-contrast yellow and blue effectively.

Proximity. Parts of a page that are closely related should be together (*proximate* to one another). Your goal is to position related points, texts, and visuals as close to one another as possible and to use clear headings to identify them.

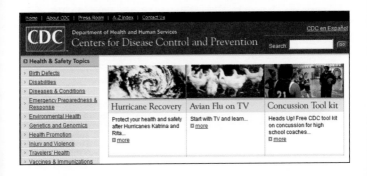

This CDC site demonstrates proximity by placing each image above its label and supporting text.

Repetition. Readers are guided in large part by the repetition of key words or elements. You can take advantage of this design principle by using a consistent design throughout your document for elements such as color, typestyle, and visuals.

Bartleby.com's navigation tabs are repeated at the top of every page on the site. The main ways to navigate the site are repeated in the sidebar.

Alignment.   This principle refers to how visuals and text on a page are lined up, both horizontally and vertically. The headline, title, or banner on a document, for example, should be carefully aligned horizontally so that the reader's eye is drawn easily along one line from left to right. Vertical alignment is equally important. In general, you can choose to align things with the left side, the right side, or the center. If you begin with left alignment, for example, stick with it. The result will be a cleaner and more organized look.

The U.S. Postal Service site effectively aligns content under three major headings. The box rules and the vertical lines in between them help make the alignment clear. Text under each heading is aligned at left.

Overall impression. Aim for a design that creates the appropriate overall impression, or mood, for your document. For an academic essay, you will probably make conservative choices that strike a serious scholarly note. In a newsletter for a campus group, you might choose bright colors and arresting images.

5b Using format effectively

Because writers have so many design possibilities to choose from, it's important to spend some time thinking about the most appropriate format for a document.

Margins and white space. For most print documents, frame your page with margins of between 1 inch and 1.5 inches (Web pages require wider margins). Since the eye takes in only so much data in one movement, very long lines can be hard to read. Wider margins help, particularly if the information is difficult or dense. To make Web pages easier to read, set margins so that the average text line includes about 10 words (or 75 characters).

Use white space, or negative space, to emphasize and direct readers to parts of the page. For example, you can use white space around graphics, headings, or lists to make them stand out.

Color. Your use of color should depend on the purpose(s) of your document and its intended audience.

- Use color to draw attention to elements you want to emphasize: headings, bullets, or parts of charts or graphs, for example.

- Be consistent in your use of color; use the same color for all main headings, for example.

- For most documents, keep the number of colors fairly small; too many colors can create a jumbled or confused look. In addition, avoid colors that clash or that are hard on the eyes (certain shades of yellow, for example). Check to make sure that all color visuals and text are legible.

- Some colors (red, for example) can evoke powerful responses, so take care that the colors you use match the message you are sending and the mood you want to create.

- Remember that when colors are printed or projected, they may not look the same as they do on your computer screen.
- Look for examples of effective use of color. Find color combinations that you think look especially good — and then try them out.

Certain color combinations clash and are hard to read.	Other combinations are easier on the eyes.

Paper.   The quality of the paper and the readability of the type affect the overall look and feel of print documents. Although inexpensive paper is fine for your earlier drafts, use 8 1/2″ × 11″ good-quality white bond paper for your final drafts. For résumés, you may wish to use parchment or cream-colored bond. For brochures and posters, colored paper may be most appropriate. Try to use the best-quality printer available to you for your final product.

Pagination.   Except for a separate title page, which is usually left unnumbered, number every page of your print document. Your instructor may ask that you follow a particular format (see Chapters 42–45); if not, beginning with the first page of text, place your last name and an Arabic numeral in the upper right-hand corner of the page, about one-half inch from the top and aligned with the right margin.

Type.   Most personal computers allow writers to choose among a great variety of type sizes and typefaces, or fonts. For most college writing, 10- to 12-point type sizes are best. For print documents, a serif font (as used in the main text of this book) is generally easier to read than a sans serif font, though sans serif is often easier to read online. And although unusual fonts might seem attractive at first glance, readers may find such fonts distracting and hard to read over long stretches of material. Most important, be consistent in the size and style of type you choose.

Spacing.   Final drafts for most of your college writing should be double-spaced, with the first line of paragraphs indented one-half inch or five spaces. Other documents, such as letters, memorandums, lab reports, and Web texts, are usually single-spaced, with no paragraph indentation. Single-spaced text usually adds a blank line between paragraphs instead of indenting paragraphs to make the text easier to read. Other kinds of documents, such as flyers and newsletters, may call for multiple columns of text.

5c Using headings effectively

Headings call attention to the organization of a text and thus aid comprehension. Some kinds of reports have standard headings (like *Abstract* or *Summary*), which readers expect (and writers should therefore provide). If you use headings, you need to decide on type size and style, wording, and placement.

Type size and style. In college papers, you will usually distinguish levels of headings using indents along with type — for example, centered capitals and lowercase boldface for the first-level headings, capitals and lowercase boldface aligned at the left for the second level, capitals and lowercase italics aligned left for the third level, and so on.

First-Level Heading

Second-Level Heading

Third-Level Heading

Consistent headings. Look for the most succinct and informative way to word your headings. Most often, state the topic in a single word, usually a noun (*Toxicity*); in a phrase, usually a noun phrase (*Levels of Toxicity*) or a gerund phrase (*Measuring Toxicity*); in a question that will be answered in the text (*How Can Toxicity Be Measured?*); or in an imperative that tells readers what steps to take (*Measure the Toxicity*). Whichever structure you choose, make sure you use it consistently for all headings of the same level, and remember to position each level of heading consistently throughout your paper.

5d Using visuals effectively

Visuals can often make a point more vividly and succinctly than words alone could. In this way, visuals help draw your audience into your document. Try to choose visuals that will help you make your points most emphatically and help your audience understand your document. (See the table on p. 51 for advice on using a variety of visuals.)

Number your visuals (number tables separately from other visuals) and give them informative captions. In some instances, you may need to give readers additional data, such as source information (see checklist on p. 52).

Table 1. Word Choice by Race: *Seesaw* and *Teeter-totter,*
Chicago 1986

Using scanners and image editors. Tools such as scanners and image editors allow you to do the following:

- make visuals larger or smaller
- adjust or rotate a visual to a particular angle
- adjust colors to make them brighter or to heighten contrast
- crop visuals to create close-ups or emphasis
- sharpen a visual or create particular effects
- save a file in the right format for printing or posting to a Web page

Remember that resolution affects the quality of the visual you are scanning. Choose a higher resolution for a sharper picture — but remember, too, that the higher the resolution the bigger the file size.

Analyzing and altering visuals. As you would with any source material, carefully assess any visuals you find online for effectiveness, appropriateness, and validity.

- Check the context in which the visual appears. Is it part of an official government, company, or library site?
- If the visual is a photograph, are the date, time, place, and setting shown or explained? If the visual is a chart, graph, or diagram, are the numbers and labels explained? Are the sources of the data given?
- Is biographical and contact information for the designer, artist, or photographer given?

If you do alter a visual, do so ethically:

- Make sure the visual does not attempt to mislead readers. Show things as accurately as possible.
- Tell your audience what changes you have made.
- Include all relevant data and information about the visual, including the source.

Type of Visual		When to Use It
Pie Chart	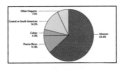	Use *pie charts* to compare a part to the whole.
Bar Graph	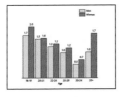	Use *bar graphs* and *line graphs* to compare one element with another, to compare elements over time, to demonstrate correlations, and to illustrate frequency.
Table		Use *tables* to draw attention to particular numerical information.
Diagram		Use *drawings* or *diagrams* to draw attention to dimensions and to details.
Map		Use *maps* to draw attention to location and to spatial relationships.
Cartoon		Use *cartoons* to illustrate or emphasize a point dramatically or comically.
Photo		Use *photographs* to draw attention to a graphic scene (such as devastation following an earthquake) or to depict people or objects.

> ✔ **CHECKLIST**
>
> **Using Visuals Effectively**
>
> - Use visuals as a part of your text, never as decoration.
> - In print texts, refer to the visual before it actually appears. For example: *As Table 1 demonstrates, the cost of a college education has risen dramatically in the last decade.*
> - Tell the audience explicitly what the visual demonstrates, especially if it presents complex information. Do not assume readers will "read" the visual the way you do; your commentary on it is important.
> - Number and title all visuals. Number tables and figures separately.
> - Follow established conventions for documenting visual sources, and ask permission for use if necessary. (See 40c.)
> - Use clip art sparingly, if at all. Clip art is so easy to cut and paste that you may be tempted to slip it in everywhere, but resist this urge.
> - Get responses to your visuals in an early draft. If readers can't follow them or are distracted by them, revise accordingly.
> - Do a test-run printout of all visuals just to make sure your printer is adequate for the job.
> - Use scanners and image editors to prepare drawings, photographs, or other illustrations for insertion into your document. But remember to do so ethically.

6 Making Oral and Multimedia Presentations

When the Gallup Poll reports on what U.S. citizens say they fear most, the findings are always the same: public speaking is apparently more frightening to us than almost anything else, even scarier than an attack from outer space.

6a Making effective oral presentations

More and more students report that formal presentations are becoming part of their work both in and out of class. As you begin to plan for such a presentation, you should consider a number of issues.

Considering the task, purpose, and audience. Think about how much time you have to prepare; where the presentation will take place; how long the presentation is to be; whether you will use written-out text or note cards; whether visual aids, handouts, or other accompanying materials are called for; and what equipment you will need. If you are making a group presentation, you will need time to divide duties and to practice with your classmates.

Consider the purpose of your presentation. Are you to lead a discussion? teach a lesson? give a report? engage a group in an activity?

Consider your audience. What do they know about your topic, what opinions do they already hold about it, and what do they need to know to follow your presentation and perhaps accept your point of view?

Emphasizing the introduction and conclusion. Listeners tend to remember beginnings and endings most readily. Consider making yours memorable by using a startling statement, opinion, or question; a vivid anecdote; or a powerful quotation.

Using explicit structure and signpost language. Organize your presentation clearly and carefully, and give an overview of your main points at the outset. (You may wish to recall these points toward the end of the talk.) Then pause between major points, and use signpost language as you move from one idea to the next. Such signposts should be clear and concrete: *The second crisis point in the breakup of the Soviet Union occurred hard on the heels of the first* instead of *Another thing about the Soviet Union's problems . . .* You can also offer signposts by repeating key words and ideas; avoiding long, complicated sentences; and using as many concrete verbs and nouns as possible. If you are talking about abstract ideas, try to provide concrete examples for each.

bedfordstmartins.com/easywriter For other examples of effective presentations, click on **Student Writing.** For additional help, click on **Jon Battalio's Preparing Presentation Slides Tutorial.**

Preparing the text for ease of presentation. If you decide to speak from a full text of your presentation, use fairly large double- or triple-spaced print that will be easy to read. End each page with the end of a sentence so that you won't have to pause while you turn a page. Whether you speak from a full text, a detailed outline, note cards, or points on flip charts or slides, mark the places where you want to pause, and highlight the words you want to emphasize. (If you are using transparencies or presentation software, print out a paper version and mark it up.)

Using visuals. Visuals are often crucial to conveying a message. Because of their importance, visuals must be large enough to be easily seen and read by your audience. Be sure that the information on any visual is simple, clear, and easy to read and understand. And remember not to simply read from visuals (such as PowerPoint slides) or to turn your back on your audience when referring to any visuals. Most important, make sure that all visuals engage and help your listeners rather than distract them from your message.

You may also want to prepare handouts for your audience: pertinent bibliographies, for example, or text too extensive to be presented otherwise. Unless the handouts include material you want your audience to consult while you speak, distribute them at the end of the presentation.

Practicing the presentation. Leave enough time to practice your presentation — including the use of all visuals — at least twice. You might also audiotape or videotape your rehearsals, or practice in front of a mirror or with friends who can give comments on content and style.

Note how long your presentation takes, and make sure you will stay within the allotted time. Allow roughly two and a half minutes per double-spaced 8 1/2" × 11" page of text (or one and a half minutes per 5" × 7" card).

Making the presentation. The best strategy for calming your nerves and getting off to a good start seems to be to know your material really well. You may also be able to use the following strategies to good advantage:

- Consider how you will dress and how you will move around, making sure that both are appropriate to the situation.

- Visualize your presentation with the aim of feeling comfortable during it; go over the scene of your presentation in your mind.
- Consider doing some deep-breathing exercises to relax before the presentation; avoid too much caffeine.
- Remember that most speakers make a stronger impression standing rather than sitting.
- Pause before you begin, concentrating on your opening lines.
- Face your audience at all times and make eye contact as much as possible.
- Allow time for the audience to respond and ask questions.
- Thank your audience at the end of your presentation.

6b Using presentation slides effectively

Many speakers use presentation software, such as PowerPoint, to help them create a memorable multimedia presentation. (See the examples on p. 56.) Before you begin designing such a presentation, make sure that the computer equipment and projector you need will be available. Then keep some simple principles in mind:

- Use 44- to 50-point type for headings, 30- to 34-point type for subheads, and smaller but still readable type for other text.
- Use bulleted or numbered lists instead of paragraphs, with three to five bullet points per slide, or no more than fifty words. Keep these items concise and logically related, and use clear language.
- Create a clear contrast between any text or visuals and the background. Light backgrounds work better in a darkened room, dark backgrounds in a lighted one.
- Be careful of becoming overly dependent on presentation-software templates. The choices of layout, color, font, and so on offered by such "wizards" may not always match your goals or fit your topic.
- Use the slides to illustrate or summarize points. Never simply read the text of slides to your audience.
- Use only visuals that are sharp and large enough to be clearly visible to your audience.
- Make sure any sound or video clips are audible and that they relate directly to your topic.
- Use animation and other special effects sparingly.

Sample Slides from an Effective PowerPoint Presentation

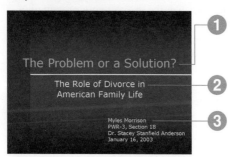

① Heading in large, easy-to-read type

② Clear contrast between light-colored type and dark background

③ Presenter, course, instructor, and date identified

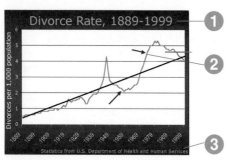

① Heading clearly identifies the topic of the graph

② Arrows point out specific years for the purpose of this presentation

③ Source of statistics included at bottom of graph

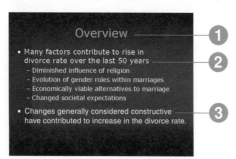

① Light type against dark background is easy to read onscreen in a well-lit room

② Bulleted points announce presentation's topics and subtopics

③ Bulleted points kept brief

Sentence
Grammar

Writing

Sentence
Grammar

Sentence Style

Punctuation/
Mechanics

Language

Multilingual
Writers

Research

Documentation

7 Verbs

One famous restaurant in Boston offers to bake, broil, pan-fry, deep-fry, poach, sauté, fricassee, blacken, or scallop any of the fish entrees on its menu. To someone ordering — or cooking — at this restaurant, the important distinctions lie entirely in the **verbs**.

7a Regular and irregular verb forms

The **past tense** and **past participle** of a **regular verb** are formed by adding *-ed* or *-d* to the **base form**.

BASE FORM	PAST TENSE	PAST PARTICIPLE
love	loved	loved
honor	honored	honored
obey	obeyed	obeyed

An **irregular verb** does not follow the *-ed* or *-d* pattern. If you are unsure about whether a verb is regular or irregular, or what the correct form is, consult the following list or a dictionary. Dictionaries list any irregular forms under the entry for the base form.

Some common irregular verbs

BASE FORM	PAST TENSE	PAST PARTICIPLE
arise	arose	arisen
be	was/were	been
beat	beat	beaten
become	became	become
begin	began	begun
bite	bit	bitten, bit
blow	blew	blown
break	broke	broken
bring	brought	brought
build	built	built
burn	burned, burnt	burned, burnt
burst	burst	burst
buy	bought	bought
catch	caught	caught
choose	chose	chosen
come	came	come
cost	cost	cost
cut	cut	cut

58

BASE FORM	PAST TENSE	PAST PARTICIPLE
dig	dug	dug
dive	dived, dove	dived
do	did	done
draw	drew	drawn
dream	dreamed, dreamt	dreamed, dreamt
drink	drank	drunk
drive	drove	driven
eat	ate	eaten
fall	fell	fallen
feel	felt	felt
fight	fought	fought
find	found	found
fly	flew	flown
forget	forgot	forgotten, forgot
freeze	froze	frozen
get	got	gotten, got
give	gave	given
go	went	gone
grow	grew	grown
hang (suspend)[1]	hung	hung
have	had	had
hear	heard	heard
hide	hid	hidden
hit	hit	hit
keep	kept	kept
know	knew	known
lay	laid	laid
lead	led	led
leave	left	left
lend	lent	lent
let	let	let
lie (recline)[2]	lay	lain
lose	lost	lost
make	made	made
mean	meant	meant
meet	met	met
pay	paid	paid
prove	proved	proved, proven
put	put	put
read	read	read

[1]*Hang* meaning "execute by hanging" is regular: *hang, hanged, hanged.*
[2]*Lie* meaning "tell a falsehood" is regular: *lie, lied, lied.*

 bedfordstmartins.com/easywriter For exercises, go to **Exercise Central** and click on **Verbs.**

BASE FORM	PAST TENSE	PAST PARTICIPLE
ride	rode	ridden
ring	rang	rung
rise	rose	risen
run	ran	run
say	said	said
see	saw	seen
send	sent	sent
set	set	set
shake	shook	shaken
shoot	shot	shot
show	showed	showed, shown
shrink	shrank	shrunk
sing	sang	sung
sink	sank	sunk
sit	sat	sat
sleep	slept	slept
speak	spoke	spoken
spend	spent	spent
spread	spread	spread
spring	sprang, sprung	sprung
stand	stood	stood
steal	stole	stolen
strike	struck	struck, stricken
swim	swam	swum
swing	swung	swung
take	took	taken
teach	taught	taught
tear	tore	torn
tell	told	told
think	thought	thought
throw	threw	thrown
wake	woke, waked	waked, woken
wear	wore	worn
win	won	won
write	wrote	written

7b *Lie* and *lay, sit* and *set, rise* and *raise*

These pairs of verbs cause confusion because both verbs in each pair have similar-sounding forms and somewhat related meanings. In each pair, one verb is **transitive**, meaning that it is followed by a **direct object** (*I lay the package on the counter*). The other is **intransitive**, meaning that it does not have an object (*He lies on the floor unable to move*). The best way to avoid confusing these verbs is to memorize their forms and meanings.

BASE FORM	PAST TENSE	PAST PARTICIPLE	PRESENT PARTICIPLE	-S FORM
lie (recline)	lay	lain	lying	lies
lay (put)	laid	laid	laying	lays
sit (be seated)	sat	sat	sitting	sits
set (put)	set	set	setting	sets
rise (get up)	rose	risen	rising	rises
raise (lift)	raised	raised	raising	raises

▶ The doctor asked the patient to ~~lay~~ *lie* on his side.

▶ She ~~sat~~ *set* the vase on the table.

▶ He ~~rose~~ *raised* himself to a sitting position.

7c Verb tenses

Tenses show when the verb's action takes place. The three **simple tenses** are the **present tense**, the **past tense**, and the **future tense**.

PRESENT TENSE	I *ask, write*
PAST TENSE	I *asked, wrote*
FUTURE TENSE	I *will ask, will write*

More complex aspects of time are expressed through **progressive**, **perfect**, and **perfect progressive** forms of the simple tenses.

PRESENT PROGRESSIVE	she *is asking, is writing*
PAST PROGRESSIVE	she *was asking, was writing*
FUTURE PROGRESSIVE	she *will be asking, will be writing*
PRESENT PERFECT	she *has asked, has written*
PAST PERFECT	she *had asked, had written*
FUTURE PERFECT	she *will have asked, will have written*
PRESENT PERFECT PROGRESSIVE	she *has been asking, has been writing*

| PAST PERFECT PROGRESSIVE | she *had been asking, had been writing* |

| FUTURE PERFECT PROGRESSIVE | she *will have been asking, will have been writing* |

The simple tenses locate an action only within the three basic time frames of present, past, and future. Progressive forms express continuing actions; perfect forms express completed actions; perfect progressive forms express actions that continue up to some point in the present, past, or future.

Using the present tense for special purposes. When writing about action in literary works, use the present tense.

▸ Ishmael slowly ~~realized~~ *realizes* all that ~~was~~ *is* at stake in the search for the white whale.

General truths or scientific facts should be in the present tense, even when the **predicate** in the **main clause** is in the past tense.

▸ Pasteur demonstrated that his boiling process ~~made~~ *makes* milk safe.

In general, when you are quoting, summarizing, or paraphrasing a work, use the present tense.

▸ Keith Walters ~~wrote~~ *writes* that the "reputed consequences and promised blessings of literacy are legion."

But when using APA (American Psychological Association) style, report the results of your experiments or another researcher's work in the past tense (*wrote, noted*) or the present perfect (*has discovered*). (For more on APA style, see Chapter 43.)

▸ Comer (1995) ~~notes~~ *noted* that protesters who deprive themselves of food are seen not as dysfunctional but rather as "caring, sacrificing, even heroic" (p. 5).

7d Sequencing verb tenses accurately

Careful and accurate use of tenses is important for clear writing. When you use the appropriate tense for each action, readers can follow time changes easily.

▶ By the time he lent her the money, she ^*had* declared

bankruptcy.

The revised sentence makes clear that the bankruptcy occurred before the loan.

7e Using active and passive voice appropriately

Voice tells whether a **subject** is acting (*He questions us*) or being acted upon (*He is questioned*). When the subject is acting, the verb is in the **active voice**; when the subject is being acted upon, the verb is in the **passive voice**. Most contemporary writers use the active voice as much as possible because it makes their prose stronger and livelier. To shift a sentence from passive to active voice, make the performer of the action the subject of the sentence.

▶ ^*My sister took the* The prizewinning photograph ~~was taken by my sister.~~

Use the passive voice when you want to emphasize the recipient of an action rather than the performer of the action.

▶ DALLAS, NOV. 22 — President John Fitzgerald Kennedy was shot and killed by an assassin today.

—TOM WICKER, *New York Times*

In scientific and technical writing, use the passive voice to focus attention on what is being studied.

▶ The volunteers' food intake was closely monitored.

7f Selecting the appropriate mood

The **mood** of a verb indicates the writer's attitude toward what he or she is saying. The **indicative mood** states facts or opinions and asks questions: *I <u>did</u> the right thing.* The

imperative mood gives commands and instructions: *Do the right thing.* The **subjunctive mood** (used primarily in **dependent clauses** beginning with *that* or *if*) expresses wishes and conditions that are contrary to fact: *If I <u>were</u> doing the right thing, I'd know it.*

The present subjunctive uses the base form of the verb with all subjects.

▷ It is important that children *be* psychologically ready for a new sibling.

The past subjunctive is the same as the simple past except for the verb *be,* which uses *were* for all subjects.

▷ He spent money as if he *had* infinite credit.
▷ If the store *were* better located, it would attract more customers.

Because the subjunctive creates a rather formal tone, many people today tend to substitute the indicative mood in informal conversation.

▷ If the store *was* better located, it would attract more customers.

For academic or professional writing, use the subjunctive in the following contexts:

CLAUSES EXPRESSING A WISH

▷ He wished that his mother w̶a̶s̶ *were* still living nearby.

***THAT* CLAUSES EXPRESSING A REQUEST OR DEMAND**

▷ The plant inspector insists that a supervisor i̶s̶ *be* on site at all times.

***IF* CLAUSES EXPRESSING A CONDITION THAT DOES NOT EXIST**

▷ If the federal government w̶a̶s̶ *were* to ban the sale of tobacco, tobacco companies and distributors would suffer a great loss.

One common error is to use *would* in both clauses. Use the subjunctive in the *if* clause and *would* in the other clause.

▶ If I ~~would have~~ ^{had} played harder, I would have won.

8 Subject-Verb Agreement

In everyday terms, the word *agreement* refers to an accord of some sort: you reach an agreement with your boss about salary; friends agree to go to a movie; the members of a family agree to share household chores. This meaning covers grammatical **agreement** as well. **Verbs** must agree with their **subjects** in **number** (singular or plural) and in **person** (first, second, or third).

To make a verb in the **present tense** agree with a third-person singular subject, add *-s* or *-es* to the **base form**.

▶ **A vegetarian diet** *lowers* **the risk of heart disease.**

To make a verb in the present tense agree with any other subject, use the base form of the verb.

▶ **I** *miss* **my family.**

▶ **They** *live* **in another state.**

Have and *be* do not follow the *-s* or *-es* pattern with third-person singular subjects. *Have* changes to *has; be* has irregular forms in both the present tense and the **past tense**.

▶ **War** *is* **hell.**

▶ **The soldier** *was* **brave beyond the call of duty.**

8a Subjects and verbs separated by other words

The subject is sometimes separated from the verb by other words. Make sure the verb agrees with the **simple subject** and not with another **noun** that falls in between.

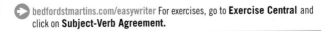

bedfordstmartins.com/easywriter For exercises, go to **Exercise Central** and click on **Subject-Verb Agreement.**

▶ **Many books on the best-seller list $\overset{have}{\underset{\wedge}{\text{has}}}$ little literary value.**

The simple subject is *books,* not *list.*

Be careful when you use *as well as, along with, in addition to, together with,* and similar phrases. They do not make a singular subject plural.

▶ **A passenger, as well as the driver, $\overset{was}{\underset{\wedge}{\text{were}}}$ injured in the accident.**

Though this sentence has a grammatically singular subject, it suggests a plural subject and would be clearer with a compound subject: *The driver and a passenger were injured in the accident.*

8b Compound subjects

Compound subjects joined by *and* are generally plural.

▶ **A backpack, a canteen, and a rifle $\overset{were}{\underset{\wedge}{\text{was}}}$ issued to each recruit.**

When subjects joined by *and* are considered a single unit or refer to the same person or thing, they take a singular verb form.

▶ **George W. Bush's older brother and political ally *is* the governor of Florida.**

▶ **Drinking and driving $\overset{remains}{\underset{\wedge}{\text{remain}}}$ a major cause of highway accidents and fatalities.**

In this sentence, *drinking and driving* is considered a single activity, and a singular verb is used.

With subjects joined by *or* or *nor,* the verb agrees with the part closer to the verb.

▶ **Neither my roommate nor my neighbors *like* my loud music.**

▶ **Either the witnesses or the defendant *is* lying.**

If you find this sentence awkward, put the plural noun closer to the verb: *Either the defendant or the witnesses <u>are</u> lying.*

8c Collective nouns as subjects

Collective nouns — such as *family, team, audience, group, jury, crowd, band, class,* and *committee* — and fractions can take either singular or plural verbs, depending on whether they refer to the group as a single unit or to the multiple members of the group. The meaning of a sentence as a whole is your guide.

▶ **After deliberating, the jury *reports* its verdict.**

The jury acts as a single unit.

▶ **The jury still *disagree* on a number of counts.**

The members of the jury act as multiple individuals.

▶ **Two-thirds of the park *~~have~~* burned.**
   has

Two-thirds refers to the single portion of the park that burned.

▶ **One-third of the students *~~was~~* commuters.**
   were

One-third here refers to the students who commuted as individuals.

Treat phrases starting with *the number of* as singular and with *a number of* as plural.

SINGULAR   The number of applicants for the internship *was* unbelievable.

PLURAL   A number of applicants *were* put on the waiting list.

8d Indefinite-pronoun subjects

Indefinite pronouns do not refer to specific persons or things. Most take singular verb forms.

SOME COMMON INDEFINITE PRONOUNS

another	each	much	one
any	either	neither	other
anybody	everybody	nobody	somebody
anyone	everyone	no one	someone
anything	everything	nothing	something

▶ **Of the two jobs, neither *holds* much appeal.**

▶ **Each of the plays ~~depict~~ a hero undone by a tragic flaw.**
       depicts ∧

Both, few, many, others, and *several* are plural.

▶ **Though many *apply*, few *are* chosen.**

All, any, enough, more, most, none, and *some* can be singular or plural, depending on the noun they refer to.

▶ **All of the cake *was* eaten.**

▶ **All of the candidates *promise* to improve the schools.**

8e   *Who, which,* and *that* as subjects

When the **relative pronouns** *who, which,* and *that* are used as subjects, the verb agrees with the **antecedent** of the pronoun (11b).

▶ **Fear is an ingredient that *goes* into creating stereotypes.**

▶ **Guilt and fear are ingredients that *go* into creating stereotypes.**

Problems often occur with the words *one of the.* In general, *one of the* takes a plural verb, while *the only one of the* takes a singular verb.

▶ **Carla is one of the employees who always ~~works~~ overtime.**
       work ∧

    Some employees always work overtime. Carla is among them. Thus *who* refers to *employees,* and the verb is plural.

▸ Ming is the only one of the employees who always ~~work~~ *works* overtime.

Only one employee always works overtime, and that employee is Ming. Thus *one,* and not *employees,* is the antecedent of *who,* and the verb form must be singular.

8f Linking verbs and complements

A **linking verb** should agree with its subject, which usually precedes the verb, not with the **subject complement**, which follows it.

▸ These three key treaties ~~is~~ *are* the topic of my talk.

The subject is *treaties,* not *topic.*

▸ Nero Wolfe's passion ~~were~~ *was* orchids.

The subject is *passion,* not *orchids.*

8g Subjects with plural forms but singular meanings

Some words that end in *-s* seem to be plural but are singular in meaning and thus take singular verb forms.

▸ Measles still ~~strike~~ *strikes* many Americans.

Some nouns of this kind (such as *statistics* and *politics*) may be either singular or plural, depending on context.

SINGULAR   Statistics *is* a course I really dread.

PLURAL   The statistics in that study *are* questionable.

8h Subjects that follow the verb

In English, verbs usually follow subjects. When this order is reversed, make the verb agree with the subject, not with a noun that happens to precede it.

▶ Beside the barn ~~stands~~ *stand* silos filled with grain.

The subject, *silos*, is plural, so the verb must be *stand*.

In sentences beginning with *there is* or *there are* (or *there was* or *there were*), *there* serves only as an introductory word; the subject follows the verb.

▶ There *are* five basic positions in classical ballet.

The subject, *positions*, is plural, so the verb must also be plural.

8i Titles and words referred to as words

Titles and words referred to as words always take singular verb forms, even if their own forms are plural.

▶ *One Writer's Beginnings* ~~describe~~ *describes* Eudora Welty's child-hood.

▶ *Steroids* ~~are~~ *is* a little word that packs a big punch in the world of sports.

8j Habitual actions in African American vernacular

In African American varieties of spoken English, third-person singular verbs that do not end with *-s* or *-es* indicate that the action described is habitual — that it occurs regularly.

▶ She go to work seven days a week.

▶ He need to follow through.

You may see verb forms such as these in writing that reports or imitates spoken language. In most academic and professional writing, however, it's usually advisable to add *-s* or *-es*.

9   Adjectives and Adverbs

Adjectives and **adverbs** often add indispensable differences in meaning to the words they modify (describe). In basketball, for example, there is an important difference between a *flagrant* foul and a *technical* foul, a layup and a *reverse* layup, and an *angry* coach and an *abusively angry* coach. In each instance, the **modifiers** are crucial to accurate communication.

Adjectives modify **nouns** and **pronouns**; they answer the questions *which? how many?* and *what kind?* Adverbs modify **verbs**, adjectives, and other adverbs; they answer the questions *how? when? where?* and *to what extent?* Many adverbs are formed by adding *-ly* to adjectives (*slight, slightly*), but some are formed in other ways (*outdoors*) or have forms of their own (*very*).

9a   Adjectives versus adverbs

When adjectives come after **linking verbs** (such as *is*), they usually describe the **subject**: *I am patient.* Note that in specific sentences, some verbs may or may not be linking verbs — *appear, become, feel, grow, look, make, prove, seem, smell, sound,* and *taste,* for instance. When a word following one of these verbs modifies the subject, use an adjective; when it modifies the verb, use an adverb.

ADJECTIVE   Otis Thorpe looked *angry.*

ADVERB   He looked *angrily* at the referee.

Linking verbs suggest a state of being, not an action. In the preceding examples, *looked angry* suggests the state of being angry; *looked angrily* suggests an angry action.

In everyday conversation, you will often hear (and perhaps use) adjectives in place of adverbs. For example, people often say *go quick* instead of *go quickly.* When you write in academic and professional English, however, use adverbs to modify verbs, adjectives, and other adverbs.

bedfordstmartins.com/easywriter For exercises, go to **Exercise Central** and click on **Adjectives and Adverbs.**

> ### FOR MULTILINGUAL WRITERS
>
> **Using Adjectives with Plural Nouns**
>
> In Spanish, Russian, and many other languages, adjectives agree in number with the nouns they modify. In English, adjectives do not change number in this way: *her dogs are small* (not *smalls*).

▸ You can feel the song's meter if you listen ~~careful.~~ *carefully.*

▸ The audience was ~~real~~ *really* disappointed by the show.

Good, well, bad, and *badly*.   The modifiers *good, well, bad,* and *badly* cause problems for many writers because the distinctions between *good* and *well* and between *bad* and *badly* are often not observed in conversation. Problems also arise because *well* can function as either an adjective or an adverb.

▸ I look ~~well~~ *good* in blue.

▸ Now that the fever has broken, I feel ~~good~~ *well* again.

▸ He plays the trumpet ~~good.~~ *well.*

▸ I feel ~~badly~~ *bad* for the Toronto fans.

▸ Their team played ~~bad.~~ *badly.*

9b Comparatives and superlatives

Most adjectives and adverbs have three forms: **positive**, **comparative**, and **superlative**. You usually form the comparative and superlative of one- or two-syllable adjectives by adding *-er* and *-est*: *short, shorter, shortest*. With some two-syllable adjectives, longer adjectives, and most adverbs, use *more* and *most* (or *less* and *least*): *scientific, more scientific, most scientific; elegantly, more elegantly, most elegantly*. Some short adjectives and adverbs have irregular comparative and superlative forms: *good, better, best; badly, worse, worst*.

Comparatives versus superlatives.   In academic writing, use the comparative to compare two things; use the superlative to compare three or more things.

▶ Rome is a much *older* city than New York.

▶ Damascus is one of the ~~older~~ cities in the world.
            ^oldest^

Double comparatives and superlatives.   Double comparatives and superlatives are those that unnecessarily use both the *-er* or *-est* ending and *more* or *most*. Occasionally, these forms can add a special emphasis, as in the title of Spike Lee's movie *Mo' Better Blues.* In academic and professional writing, however, do not use *more* or *most* before adjectives or adverbs ending in *-er* or *-est.*

▶ Paris is the ~~most~~ loveliest city in the world.

Absolute concepts.   Some adjectives and adverbs — such as *perfect, final,* and *unique* — are absolute concepts, so it is illogical to form comparatives or superlatives of these words.

▶ Anne has ~~the most~~ unique sense of humor.
           ^a^

---

10   Modifier Placement

To be effective, **modifiers** should clearly refer to the words they modify and be positioned close to those words. Consider this command:

> DO NOT USE THE ELEVATORS IN CASE OF FIRE.

Should we really avoid the elevators altogether in case there is ever a fire? Repositioning the modifier *in case of fire* eliminates such confusion — and makes clear that we are to avoid the elevators only if there is a fire: IN CASE OF FIRE, DO NOT USE THE ELEVATORS.

---

 bedfordstmartins.com/easywriter For exercises, go to **Exercise Central** and click on **Modifier Placement.**

10a Misplaced modifiers

Modifiers can cause confusion or ambiguity if they are not close enough to the words they modify or if they seem to modify more than one word in the sentence.

▶ She teaches a seminar this term ~~on voodoo~~ at Skyline
   ^ *on voodoo*

College.

The voodoo is not at the college; the seminar is.

▶ ~~Billowing from the window,~~ He saw clouds of smoke. *billowing from the window.*
   ^ ^

People cannot billow from windows.

▶ *After he lost the 1962 race,*
   Nixon told reporters that he planned to get out of
   ^
   politics ~~after he lost the 1962 race.~~
   ^

The unedited sentence implies that Nixon planned to lose the race.

Limiting modifiers. Be especially careful with the placement of limiting modifiers such as *almost, even, just, merely,* and *only.* In general, these modifiers should be placed right before or after the words they modify. Putting them in other positions may produce not just ambiguity but a completely different meaning.

AMBIGUOUS   The court *only* hears civil cases on Tuesdays.

CLEAR   The court hears *only* civil cases on Tuesdays.

CLEAR   The court hears civil cases on Tuesdays *only.*

Squinting modifiers. If a modifier can refer either to the word before it or to the word after it, it is a **squinting modifier**. Put the modifier where it clearly relates to only a single word.

SQUINTING   Students who practice writing *often* will benefit.

REVISED   Students who *often* practice writing will benefit.

REVISED   Students who practice writing will *often* benefit.

10b Disruptive modifiers

Disruptive modifiers interrupt the connections between parts of a sentence, making it hard for readers to follow the progress of the thought.

▸ Vegetables will, *If they are cooked too long, vegetables will* ~~if they are cooked too long,~~ lose most
∧
of their nutritional value.

Split infinitives. In general, do not place a modifier between the *to* and the **verb** of an **infinitive** (*to often complain*). Doing so makes it hard for readers to recognize that the two go together.

▸ Hitler expected the British to fairly quickly *surrender*. ~~surrender.~~
∧ ∧

In some sentences, however, a modifier sounds awkward if it does not split the infinitive. Try rewording the sentence to eliminate the infinitive altogether.

SPLIT   I hope *to* almost *equal* my last year's income.

REVISED   I hope that I will earn almost as much as I did last year.

10c Dangling modifiers

Dangling modifiers are words or **phrases** that modify nothing in the rest of a sentence. They often *seem* to modify something that is implied but not actually present in the sentence. Dangling modifiers frequently appear at the beginnings or ends of sentences.

DANGLING   Driving nonstop, Salishan Lodge is two hours from Portland.

REVISED   Driving nonstop from Portland, you can reach Salishan Lodge in two hours.

To revise a dangling modifier, often you need to add a **subject** that the modifier clearly refers to; sometimes you have to turn the modifier into a phrase or a **clause**.

▶ Reluctantly, the hound ~~was given~~ to a neighbor.
  our family gave ^

In the original sentence, was the dog reluctant, or was someone else who is not mentioned reluctant?

▶ ~~As~~ a young boy, his grandmother told stories of her
  When he was ^
  years as a country schoolteacher.

His grandmother was never a young boy.

▶ ~~Thumbing through the magazine, my~~ eyes automati-
  _My_ ^　　　　　　　　_as I was thumbing through the magazine._
  cally noticed the perfume ads.
  　　　　　　　　　　　^

Eyes cannot thumb through a magazine.

11　Pronouns

As words that stand in for **nouns**, **pronouns** carry a lot of weight in everyday discourse. These directions show why it's important for a pronoun to refer clearly to a specific noun or pronoun **antecedent**:

> When you see a dirt road on the left side of Winston Lane, follow it for two more miles.

The word _it_ could mean either the dirt road or Winston Lane.

11a　Pronoun case

Most speakers of English know intuitively when to use _I,_ _me,_ and _my._ Our choices reflect differences in **case**, the form a pronoun takes to indicate its function in a sentence. Pronouns functioning as **subjects** or **subject complements** are in the **subjective case** (_I_); those functioning as **objects** are in the **objective case** (_me_); those functioning as possessives are in the **possessive case** (_my_).

⬀ bedfordstmartins.com/easywriter For exercises, go to **Exercise Central** and click on **Pronouns.**

SUBJECTIVE	OBJECTIVE	POSSESSIVE
I	me	my/mine
we	us	our/ours
you	you	your/yours
he/she/it	him/her/it	his/her/hers/its
they	them	their/theirs
who/whoever	whom/whomever	whose

Case problems tend to occur in the following situations.

In subject complements. Many Americans routinely use the objective case for subject complements, especially in conversation: *Who's there? It's me.* If the subjective case for a subject complement sounds stilted or awkward (*It's I*), try rewriting the sentence using the pronoun as the subject (*I'm here*).

▶ She was the
 ~~The~~ first person to see Kishore after the awards ~~was~~
  ^   ^
 ~~she.~~

Before gerunds. Pronouns before a **gerund** should be in the possessive case.

▶ The doctor argued for ~~him~~ writing a living will.
                        his
                         ^

With *who, whoever, whom,* and *whomever*. A common problem with pronoun case is deciding whether to use *who* or *whom*. Two particular situations lead to confusion with *who* and *whom*: when they begin a question and when they introduce a **dependent clause** (13c). You can determine whether to use *who* or *whom* at the beginning of a question by answering the question using a **personal pronoun**. If the answer is in the subjective case, use *who*; if it is in the objective case, use *whom*.

▶ Whom
 ~~Who~~ did you visit?
  ^
 I visited *them*. *Them* is objective, so *whom* is correct.

▶ Who
 ~~Whom~~ do you think wrote the story?
  ^
 I think *she* wrote the story. *She* is subjective, so *who* is correct.

The case of a pronoun in a dependent clause is determined by its function in the clause, no matter how that clause functions in the sentence. If the pronoun acts as a subject or subject complement in the clause, use *who* or *whoever.* If the pronoun acts as an object in the clause, use *whom* or *whomever.*

▶ Anyone can hypnotize a person ~~whom~~ *who* wants to be hypnotized.

The verb of the clause is *wants,* and its subject is *who.*

▶ ~~Whoever~~ *Whomever* the party suspected of disloyalty was executed.

Whomever is the object of *suspected* in the clause *whomever the party suspected of disloyalty.*

In compound structures. When a pronoun is part of a compound subject, complement, or object, put it in the same case you would use if the pronoun were alone.

▶ When ~~him~~ *he* and Zelda were first married, they lived in New York.

▶ The boss invited ~~she~~ *her* and her family to dinner.

▶ This morning saw yet another conflict between my sister and ~~I.~~ *me.*

In elliptical constructions. Elliptical constructions are those in which some words are understood but left out. When an elliptical construction ends in a pronoun, put the pronoun in the case it would be in if the construction were complete.

▶ His sister has always been more athletic than *he* [is].

In some elliptical constructions, the case of the pronoun depends on the meaning intended.

▶ Willie likes Lily more than *she* [likes Lily].

She is the subject of the omitted verb *likes.*

▶ Willie likes Lily more than [he likes] *her.*

Her is the object of the omitted verb *likes.*

With *we* and *us* before a noun.   If you are unsure about whether to use *we* or *us* before a noun, use whichever pronoun would be correct if the noun were omitted.

▶ ~~Us~~ fans never give up hope.
   We

Without *fans, we* would be the subject.

▶ The Rangers depend on ~~we~~ fans.
   us

Without *fans, us* would be the object of a preposition.

11b Pronoun-antecedent agreement

The **antecedent** of a pronoun is the word the pronoun refers to. Pronouns and antecedents are said to agree when they match up in **person**, **number**, and **gender**.

SINGULAR   The *choirmaster* raised *his* baton.

PLURAL   The *boys* picked up *their* music.

Compound antecedents.   When a compound antecedent is joined by *or* or *nor*, the pronoun agrees with the nearer or nearest antecedent. If the parts of the antecedent are of different genders or persons, however, this kind of sentence can be awkward and may need to be revised.

AWKWARD   Neither Annie nor Henry got *his* work done.

REVISED   Annie didn't get *her* work done, and neither did Henry.

When a compound antecedent contains both singular and plural parts, the sentence may sound awkward unless the plural part comes last.

▶ Neither the newspaper nor the radio stations would reveal *their* sources.

Collective-noun antecedents.   A **collective noun** such as *herd, team,* or *audience* may refer to a group as a single unit. If so, use a singular pronoun.

▶ The *committee* presented *its* findings to the board.

When a collective noun refers to the members of the group as individuals, however, you should use a plural pronoun.

▶ The *herd* stamped *their* hooves and snorted nervously.

Indefinite-pronoun antecedents. Indefinite pronouns do not refer to specific persons or things. Most indefinite pronouns are always singular; a few are always plural. Some can be singular or plural depending on the context.

▶ *One* of the ballerinas lost *her* balance.

▶ *Many* in the audience jumped to *their* feet.

SINGULAR   *Some* of the furniture was showing *its* age.

PLURAL   *Some* of the farmers abandoned *their* land.

Sexist pronouns. Pronouns often refer to antecedents that may be either male or female. Writers used to use a masculine pronoun, known as the "generic *he*," to refer to such antecedents: *Everyone should know <u>his</u> legal rights.* In recent decades, however, many people have pointed out that such wording ignores or even excludes females — and thus should be revised: *Everyone should know <u>his</u> or <u>her</u> legal rights*, for example, or *People should know <u>their</u> legal rights*.

11c Clear pronoun reference

If a pronoun does not refer clearly to a specific antecedent, readers will have trouble making the connection between the two.

Ambiguous antecedents. When a pronoun can refer to more than one antecedent, revise the sentence to make the meaning clear.

▶ The car went over the bridge just before ~~it~~ *the bridge* fell into the water.

What fell into the water — the car or the bridge? The revision makes it clear that the pronoun *it* refers to the antecedent *the bridge*.

▶ Kerry told Ellen, ~~that she~~ should be ready soon."
_{"I}

Reporting Kerry's words directly, in quotation marks, eliminates the ambiguity.

Vague use of *it*, *this*, *that*, and *which*. The words *it*, *this*, *that*, and *which* often function as a shortcut for referring to something mentioned earlier. Like other pronouns, each must refer to a specific antecedent.

▶ When the senators realized the bill would be

defeated, they tried to postpone the vote but failed.
The entire effort
~~It~~ was a fiasco.

▶ Nancy just found out that she won the lottery, ~~which~~
and her sudden wealth

explains her resignation.

Indefinite use of *you*, *it*, and *they*. In conversation, we frequently use *you*, *it*, and *they* in an indefinite sense in such expressions as *you never know* and *on television, they said*. In academic and professional writing, however, use *you* only to mean "you, the reader," and *they* or *it* only to refer to a clear antecedent.

▶ Commercials try to make ~~you~~ buy without
people

thinking.

▶ ~~On the~~ Weather Channel, ~~it~~ reported that Hurricane
The

Fran will hit Virginia Beach tomorrow morning.

▶ ~~In France, they~~ allow dogs ~~in many restaurants.~~
Many restaurants in France

Implied antecedents. A pronoun may suggest a noun antecedent that is implied but not present in the sentence.

▶ Detention centers routinely blocked efforts by
detainees.
~~detainees'~~ families and lawyers to locate ~~them.~~

12   Comma Splices and Fused Sentences

A **comma splice** results from placing only a comma between **independent clauses** — groups of words that can stand alone as a sentence. We often see comma splices in advertising, where they can give slogans a catchy rhythm.

> It's not just a job, it's an adventure.
>
> — U.S. ARMY RECRUITING SLOGAN

Another common error is a **fused**, or **run-on**, **sentence**, which results from joining two independent clauses with no punctuation or connecting word between them. The army slogan as a fused sentence would be "It's not just a job it's an adventure."

In academic and professional English, using comma splices or fused sentences will almost always be identified as an error.

12a Separating the clauses into two sentences

The simplest way to revise comma splices or fused sentences is to separate them into two sentences.

COMMA SPLICE   My mother spends long hours every spring tilling the soil and moving manure. this part of gardening is nauseating.

If the two clauses are very short, making them two sentences may sound abrupt and terse, so some other method of revision is probably preferable.

12b Linking the clauses with a comma and a coordinating conjunction

If the two clauses are closely related and equally important, join them with a comma and a **coordinating conjunction** (*and, but, or, nor, for, so,* or *yet*).

FUSED SENTENCE   Interest rates fell, so people began borrowing more money.

12c Linking the clauses with a semicolon

If the ideas in the two clauses are closely related and you want to give them equal emphasis, link them with a semi-colon.

COMMA SPLICE   This photograph is not at all realistic⁄it uses
                                              ∧
               dreamlike images to convey its message.

Be careful when you link clauses with a **conjunctive adverb** like *however* or *therefore* or with a **transition** like *in fact*. In such sentences, the two clauses must be separated by a semicolon or by a comma and a coordinating conjunction.

COMMA SPLICE   Many Third World countries have high
               birthrates⁄therefore,most of their citizens
                        ∧   ∧
               are young.

FOR MULTILINGUAL WRITERS

Judging Sentence Length

If you speak a language that tends to use long sentences — Arabic, Farsi, or Chinese, for instance — be careful not to join English sentences in a way that results in comma-splice errors. Note that in standard academic and professional English, a sentence should contain only one independent clause *unless* the clauses are joined by a comma and a coordinating conjunction or by a semicolon.

12d Recasting the two clauses as one independent clause

Sometimes you can reduce two spliced or fused independent clauses to a single independent clause.

FUSED   ~~A large part~~ of my mail is advertisements
SENTENCE   *Most*
             ∧ *and*
             ~~most of the rest is~~ bills.
             ∧

▶ bedfordstmartins.com/easywriter For exercises, go to **Exercise Central** and click on **Comma Splices and Fused Sentences.**

12e Recasting one independent clause as a dependent clause

When one independent clause is more important than the other, try converting the less important one to a **dependent clause** by adding an appropriate **subordinating conjunction**.

COMMA
SPLICE

Although
^ Zora Neale Hurston is regarded as one of America's major novelists, she died in obscurity.

In the revision, the writer emphasizes the second clause and makes the first one into a dependent clause by adding the subordinating conjunction *although*.

FUSED
SENTENCE

The arts and crafts movement, *which reacted against mass production,* called for hand-made objects.~~it reacted against mass production.~~
^

In the revision, the writer chooses to emphasize the first clause (the one describing what the movement advocated) and make the second clause into a dependent clause.

12f Linking the two clauses with a dash

In informal writing, you can use a dash to join the two clauses, especially when the second clause elaborates on the first clause.

COMMA
SPLICE

Exercise trends come and go, this year yoga is hot.
^

13 Sentence Fragments

In advertisements, you will find **sentence fragments** in frequent use:

> Our Lifetime Guarantee may come as a shock. *Or a strut. Or a muffler.* Because once you pay to replace them, Toyota's Lifetime Guarantee covers parts and labor on any dealer-

---

bedfordstmartins.com/easywriter For exercises, go to **Exercise Central** and click on **Sentence Fragments**.

installed muffler, shock, or strut for as long as you own your Toyota! So if anything should ever go wrong, your Toyota dealer will fix it. *Absolutely free.*

— TOYOTA ADVERTISEMENT

As complete sentences, the information in the three italicized fragments would be less clever and far less memorable.

Sentence fragments are groups of words that are punctuated as sentences but lack some element necessary to an **independent clause**. Although you will often see and hear sentence fragments, you will seldom, if ever, want to use them in academic or professional writing, where some readers will regard them as errors.

13a Phrase fragments

A **phrase** is a group of words that lacks a **subject**, a **verb**, or both. When a **verbal phrase**, a **prepositional phrase**, a **noun phrase**, or an **appositive phrase** is punctuated like a sentence, it becomes a fragment. To revise a phrase fragment, attach it to an independent clause, or make it a separate sentence.

▸ **NBC is broadcasting the debates. ~~With~~ *with* discussions afterward.**

The second word group is a prepositional phrase, not a sentence. The editing combines the phrase with an independent clause.

▸ **The town's growth is controlled by zoning laws. ~~A~~ *a* strict set of regulations for builders and corporations.**

A strict set of regulations for builders and corporations is an appositive phrase renaming the noun *zoning laws*. The editing attaches the fragment to the sentence containing that noun.

▸ **Kamika stayed out of school for three months after Linda was born. *She did so to* ~~To~~ recuperate and to take care of her baby.**

To recuperate and to take care of her baby includes verbals, not verbs. The revision — adding a subject (*she*) and a verb (*did*) — turns the fragment into a separate sentence.

Fragments beginning with transitions. If you introduce an example or explanation with a transitional word or phrase like *also, for example, such as,* or *that,* be certain you write a sentence, not a fragment.

▶ Joan Didion has written on many subjects/. ~~Such~~ as the Hoover Dam and migraine headaches.

> The second word group is a phrase, not a sentence. The editing combines it with an independent clause.

13b Compound-predicate fragments

A fragment occurs when one part of a **compound predicate** lacks a subject but is punctuated as a separate sentence. Such a fragment usually begins with *and, but,* or *or.* You can revise it by attaching it to the independent clause that contains the rest of the **predicate**.

▶ They sold their house/. ~~And~~ moved into an apartment.

13c Clause fragments

A **dependent clause** contains both a subject and a verb, but it cannot stand alone as a sentence; it depends on an independent clause to complete its meaning. A dependent clause usually begins with a **subordinating conjunction**, such as *after, because, before, if, since, though, unless, until, when, where, while, who, which,* or *that.* You can usually combine dependent-clause fragments with a nearby independent clause.

▶ When I decided to work part-time/. I gave up a lot of my earning potential.

If you cannot smoothly attach a clause to a nearby independent clause, try deleting the opening subordinating word and turning the dependent clause into a sentence.

▶ Most injuries in automobile accidents occur in two
    An
ways. ~~When an~~ occupant either is hurt by something inside the car or is thrown from the car.

Sentence
Style

Writing

Sentence
Grammar

Sentence Style

Punctuation/
Mechanics

Language

Multilingual
Writers

Research

Documentation

14 Consistency and Completeness

If you listen carefully to the conversations around you, you will hear inconsistent and incomplete structures all the time. For instance, when an interviewer asked actor Orlando Bloom whether he had been intimidated when cast in the film version of *The Lord of the Rings*, Bloom's response included this statement:

> "Can you imagine for me, coming out of drama school, being thrown into a group of actors like Ian McKellen, Ian Holm, and Christopher Leeyes, it was incredibly daunting."

Bloom's sentence begins one way but then takes off in another direction. The mixed structure posed no problem for the interviewer, but a sentence such as this can be confusing to a reader.

14a Consistent grammatical patterns

Beginning a sentence with one grammatical pattern and then switching to another one confuses readers.

MIXED   The fact that I get up at 5:00 am, a wake-up time that explains why I'm always tired in the evening.

The sentence starts out with a **subject** (*The fact*) followed by a **dependent clause** (*that I get up at 5:00 AM*). The sentence needs a **predicate** to complete the **independent clause**, but instead it moves to another **phrase** followed by a dependent clause (*a wake-up time that explains why I'm always tired in the evening*), and a **fragment** results.

REVISED   The fact that I get up at 5:00 AM explains why I'm always tired in the evening.

Deleting *a wake-up time that* changes the rest of the sentence into a predicate.

REVISED   I get up at 5:00 AM, a wake-up time that explains why I'm always tired in the evening.

Deleting *The fact that* turns the beginning of the sentence into an independent clause.

14b Matching subjects and predicates

Another kind of mixed structure, called faulty predication, occurs when a subject and predicate do not fit together grammatically or simply do not make sense together.

▶ A characteristic that I admire is ~~a person who is generous.~~
                                              generosity.
                                              ^

  A person is not a characteristic.

▶ The rules of the corporation ~~expect~~ employees to be on
                                   require that
                                   ^
  time.

  Rules cannot expect anything.

Is when, is where, the reason . . . is because.   Although you will often hear these expressions in everyday use, such constructions are inappropriate in academic or professional writing.

▶ A stereotype is ~~when someone characterizes~~ a group.
                    an unfair characterization of
                    ^   ^
  ~~unfairly.~~

▶ Spamming is ~~where companies send~~ electronic junk mail.
                the practice of sending
                ^

▶ ~~The reason~~ I like to play soccer ~~is~~ because it provides
  aerobic exercise.

14c Consistent compound structures

Sometimes writers omit certain words in compound structures. If the omitted word does not fit grammatically with other parts of the compound, the omission can be inappropriate.

▶ His skills are weak, and his performance only average.
                                          is
                                          ^

  The omitted verb *is* does not match the verb in the other part of the compound (*are*), so the writer needs to include it.

bedfordstmartins.com/easywriter For exercises, go to **Exercise Central** and click on **Consistency and Completeness.**

14d Complete, consistent, and clear comparisons

When you compare two or more things, the comparison must be complete, logically consistent, and clear.

▶ I was embarrassed because my parents were so
  from my friends' parents.
  different.
         ^

Adding *from my friends' parents* completes the comparison.

                                            the one by
▶ Woodberry's biography is better than Fields.
                                        ^
The original sentence illogically compares a book with a person.

UNCLEAR   Aneil always felt more affection for his brother
          than his sister.

CLEAR   Aneil always felt more affection for his brother
          than his sister did.

CLEAR   Aneil always felt more affection for his brother
          than he did for his sister.

15 Coordination and Subordination

You may notice a difference between your spoken and your written language. In speech, people tend to use *and* and *so* as all-purpose connectors.

He enjoys psychology, and the course requires a lot of work.

The meaning of this sentence may be perfectly clear in speech, which provides clues with voice, facial expressions, and gestures. But in writing, the sentence could have more than one meaning.

Although he enjoys psychology, the course requires a lot of work.

---

bedfordstmartins.com/easywriter For exercises, go to **Exercise Central** and click on **Coordination and Subordination**.

He enjoys psychology although the course requires a lot of work.

The first sentence links two ideas with a **coordinating conjunction**, *and*; the other two sentences link ideas with a **subordinating conjunction**, *although*. A coordinating conjunction gives the ideas equal emphasis, and a subordinating conjunction emphasizes one idea more than another.

15a Relating equal ideas

When you want to give equal emphasis to different ideas in a sentence, link them with a coordinating conjunction (*and, but, for, nor, or, so, yet*) or a semicolon.

▶ **They acquired horses, *and* their ancient nomadic spirit was suddenly free of the ground.**

There is perfect freedom in the mountains, *but* it belongs to the eagle and the elk, the badger and the bear.

— N. Scott Momaday, *The Way to Rainy Mountain*

Coordination can help make explicit the relationship between two separate ideas.

▶ **My son watches *The Simpsons* religiously;̶ ̶Forced to** *forced*

choose, he would probably take Homer Simpson over

his sister.

Connecting these two sentences with a semicolon strengthens the connection between two closely related ideas.

When you connect ideas in a sentence, make sure that the relationship between the ideas is clear.

▶ **Watching television is a common way to spend leisure**
time, and̶ it makes viewers apathetic. *but*

What does being a common form of leisure have to do with making viewers apathetic? Changing *and* to *but* better relates the two ideas.

15b Distinguishing main ideas

Subordination allows you to distinguish major points from minor points or to bring in supporting details. If, for instance, you put your main idea in an **independent clause**, you might then put any less significant ideas in **dependent clauses**, **phrases**, or even single words. The following sentence shows the subordinated point in italics:

▶ **Mrs. Viola Cullinan was a plump woman** *who lived in a three-bedroom house somewhere behind the post office.*

— MAYA ANGELOU, "My Name Is Margaret"

The dependent clause adds important information about Mrs. Cullinan, but it is subordinate to the independent clause.

Notice that the choice of what to subordinate rests with the writer and depends on the intended meaning. Angelou might have given the same basic information differently.

▶ **Mrs. Viola Cullinan,** *a plump woman,* **lived in a three-bedroom house somewhere behind the post office.**

Subordinating the information about Mrs. Cullinan's size to that about her house would suggest a slightly different meaning, of course. As a writer, you must think carefully about what you want to emphasize and must subordinate information accordingly.

Subordination also establishes logical relationships among ideas. These relationships are often specified by subordinating conjunctions.

SOME COMMON SUBORDINATING CONJUNCTIONS

after	if	though
although	in order that	unless
as	once	until
as if	since	when
because	so that	where
before	than	while
even though	that	

The following sentence is shown with the subordinate clause italicized and the subordinating word underlined.

> She usually rested her smile until late afternoon <u>when</u> *her women friends dropped in and Miss Glory, the cook, served them cold drinks on the closed-in porch.*

— MAYA ANGELOU, "My Name Is Margaret"

Using too many coordinate structures can be monotonous and can make it hard for readers to recognize the most important ideas. Subordinating lesser ideas can help highlight the main ideas.

> Many people come home tired in the evening, so they turn on the TV to relax. ~~They~~ *Though they* may intend to watch just the news, ~~but then~~ a game show comes on next, ~~and~~ *which* they decide to watch ~~it~~ for just a short while, ~~and~~ *Eventually,* they get too comfortable to get up, and they end up spending the whole evening in front of the TV.

The editing uses subordination to make clear to the reader that some of the ideas are more important than others.

Determining what to subordinate

> *Although our* ~~Our~~ new boss can be difficult, ~~although~~ she has revived and maybe even saved the division.

The editing puts the more important information — that the new boss has saved part of the company — in an independent clause and subordinates the rest.

Avoiding excessive subordination

When too many subordinate clauses are strung together, readers may have trouble keeping track of the main idea expressed in the independent clause.

TOO MUCH SUBORDINATION

> Philip II sent the Spanish Armada to conquer England, which was ruled by Elizabeth, who had executed Mary because she was plotting to overthrow Elizabeth, who was a Protestant, whereas Mary and Philip were Roman Catholics.

REVISED

▶ **Philip II sent the Spanish Armada to conquer England, which was ruled by Elizabeth, a Protestant. She had executed Mary, a Roman Catholic like Philip, because Mary was plotting to overthrow her.**

Putting the facts about Elizabeth executing Mary into an independent clause makes key information easier to recognize.

16 Conciseness

You can see the importance of concise writing in directions, particularly those on medicines. Consider the following directions found on one common prescription drug:

Take one tablet daily. Some nonprescription drugs may aggravate your condition, so read all labels carefully. If any include a warning, check with your doctor.

Squeezing words onto a three-inch label is probably not your ordinary writing situation, but more often than not, you will want to write as concisely as you can.

16a Eliminating redundant words

Sometimes writers add words for emphasis, saying that something is large *in size* or red *in color* or that two ingredients should be combined *together.* The italicized words are redundant (unnecessary for meaning), as are the deleted words in the following examples.

▶ ~~Compulsory~~ Âttendance at assemblies is required.

▶ **The auction featured** ~~contemporary~~ **"antiques" made recently.**

▶ **Many different forms of hazing occur, such as physical** ~~abuse~~ **and mental abuse.**

bedfordstmartins.com/easywriter For exercises, go to **Exercise Central** and click on **Conciseness.**

16b Eliminating empty words

Words that contribute little or no meaning to a sentence include vague **nouns** like *area, kind, situation,* and *thing* as well as vague **modifiers** like *definitely, major, really,* and *very.* Delete such words or find a more specific way to say what you mean.

> ~~The housing situation~~ can ~~have a really significant~~
> $\overset{H}{}$ *strongly influence*
>
> ~~impact on the social aspect of~~ a student's life.
>   *social*

16c Replacing wordy phrases

Many common **phrases** can be reduced to a word or two with no loss in meaning.

WORDY	CONCISE
at all times	always
at that point in time	then
at the present time	now/today
due to the fact that	because
for the purpose of	for
in order to	to
in spite of the fact that	although
in the event that	if

16d Simplifying sentence structure

Using the simplest grammatical structures can tighten and strengthen your sentences considerably.

> Kennedy, who was only the second Roman Catholic to be nominated for the presidency by a major party, had to handle the religion issue ~~in a delicate manner.~~ *delicately.*

Using strong verbs. *Be* **verbs** (*is, are, was, were, been*) often result in wordiness.

> A high-fat, high-cholesterol diet ~~is bad for~~ your heart. *harms*

Avoiding expletives. Sometimes **expletive** constructions such as *there is, there are,* and *it is* introduce a topic effectively; often, however, your writing will be better without them.

▶ ~~There are m~~any people ~~who~~ fear success because they
^M^ ^∧^
believe they do not deserve it.

▶ ~~It is necessary for p~~residential candidates to perform
^P^ ^need^
well on television.
^∧^

Using active voice.   Some writing situations call for the
passive **voice**, but it is always wordier than the active —
and often makes for dull or even difficult reading (7e).

▶ ~~In Gower's research, it was~~ found that pythons often
^Gower^
dwell in trees.
^∧^

17   Parallelism

If you look and listen, you will see parallel grammatical
structures in everyday use. Bumper stickers often use parallelism to make their messages memorable (*Don't follow
me; I'm lost too*), as do song lyrics and jump-rope rhymes. In
addition to creating pleasing rhythmic effects, parallelism
helps clarify meaning.

17a   Items in a series or list

All items in a series should be in parallel form — all **nouns**,
all **verbs**, all **prepositional phrases**, and so on. Parallelism
makes a series both graceful and easy to follow.

▶ In the eighteenth century, armed forces could fight *in
open fields* and *on the high seas*. Today, they can clash
on the ground anywhere, *on the sea*, *under the sea*, and *in
the air*.

> — DONALD SNOW AND EUGENE BROWN,
> *The Contours of Power*

▶ bedfordstmartins.com/easywriter For exercises, go to **Exercise Central** and
click on **Parallelism**.

The parallel structure of the phrases, and of the sentences themselves, highlights the contrast between the eighteenth century and today.

▶ The quarter horse skipped, pranced, and ~~was sashaying~~ *sashayed* onto the track.

▶ The children ran down the hill, skipped over the lawn, and *jumped* into the swimming pool.

▶ The duties of the job include babysitting, housecleaning, and ~~preparation of~~ *preparing* meals.

Items in a list, in a formal outline, and in headings should be parallel.

▶ Kitchen rules: (1) Coffee to be made only by library staff. (2) Coffee service to be closed at 4:00 PM. (3) Doughnuts to be kept in cabinet. (4) ~~No faculty members should handle coffee materials.~~ *Coffee materials not to be handled by faculty.*

17b Paired ideas

Parallel structures can help you pair two ideas effectively. The more nearly parallel the two structures are, the stronger the connection between the ideas will be.

▶ I type in one place, but I write all over the house.

— TONI MORRISON

▶ Writers are often more interesting on the page than they are in ~~person.~~ *the flesh.*

In these examples, the parallel structures help readers see an important contrast between two ideas or acts.

With conjunctions. When you link ideas with *and, but, or, nor, for, so,* or *yet,* try to make the ideas parallel in structure. Always use the same structure after both parts of a **correlative conjunction**: *either . . . or, both . . . and, neither . . . nor, not . . . but, not only . . . but also, just as . . . so,* and *whether . . . or.*

▶ Consult a friend in your class or ~~who is~~ good at math.
  ^ *who is*

▶ The wise politician promises the possible and
  ~~should accept~~ the inevitable.
  ^ *accepts*

▶ I wanted not only to go away to school but also to
  New England.
  ^ *live in*

17c Words necessary for clarity

In addition to making parallel elements grammatically similar, be sure to include any words — **prepositions**, **articles**, verb forms, and so on — that are necessary for clarity.

▶ We'll move to a city in the Southwest or Mexico.
  ^ *in*

  To a city in Mexico or to Mexico in general? The editing clarifies the meaning.

18 Shifts

A shift in writing is an abrupt change of some sort that results in inconsistency. Sometimes a writer will shift deliberately, as Dave Barry does in noting he "would have to say that the greatest single achievement of the American medical establishment is nasal spray." Barry's shift in tone from the serious (the American medical establishment) to the banal (nasal spray) makes us laugh, as Barry wishes us to. Unintentional shifts, on the other hand, can be jolting and confusing to readers.

18a Shifts in tense

If the **verbs** in a passage refer to actions occurring at different times, they may require different **tenses**. Be careful, however, not to change tenses for no reason.

---

bedfordstmartins.com/easywriter For exercises, go to **Exercise Central** and click on **Shifts**.

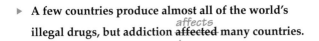
▶ A few countries produce almost all of the world's
                                affects
  illegal drugs, but addiction ~~affected~~ many countries.
                                  ^

18b Shifts in voice

Do not shift between the **active voice** (she *sold* it) and the
passive voice (it *was sold*) without a reason. Sometimes a
shift in voice is justified, but often it only confuses readers.

                                         me
▶ Two youths approached ~~me,~~ and ~~I was~~ asked for my

  wallet.

    The original sentence shifts from the active (*youths approached*)
    to the passive (*I was asked*), so it is unclear who asked for the
    wallet. Making both verbs active clears up the confusion.

18c Shifts in point of view

Unnecessary shifts in point of view between first **person**
(*I* or *we*), second person (*you*), and third person (*he, she, it,
one,* or *they*), or between **singular** and **plural subjects** can
be very confusing to readers.

   You
▶ ~~One~~ can do well on this job if you budget your time.
  ^
    Is the writer making a general statement or giving advice to
    someone? Eliminating the shift eliminates this confusion.

▶ Nurses receive much less pay than doctors, even
              nurses have
  though ~~a nurse has~~ the primary responsibility for daily
          ^
  patient care.

    The writer had no reason to shift from third-person plural
    (*nurses*) to third-person singular (*a nurse*).

18d Shifts between direct and indirect discourse

When you quote someone's exact words, you are using
direct discourse: *She said, "I'm an editor."* When you report
what someone says without repeating the exact words, you

are using **indirect discourse**: *She said she was an editor.* Shifting between direct and indirect discourse in the same sentence can cause problems, especially with questions.

▸ Bob asked what ^he^ could ~~he~~ do to help~~?~~.

The editing eliminates an awkward shift by reporting Bob's question indirectly. It could also be edited to quote Bob directly: *Bob asked, "What can I do to help?"*

18e Shifts in tone and diction

Watch out for shifts in your tone (overall attitude toward a topic or audience) and diction (choice of words). These shifts can confuse readers and leave them wondering what your real attitude is.

INCONSISTENT TONE

> The question of child care forces a society to make profound decisions about its values. If some conservatives had their way, June Cleaver would still be in the kitchen baking cookies for Wally and the Beaver and waiting for Ward to bring home the bacon, but with only one income, the Cleavers would be lucky to afford hot dogs.

REVISED

> The question of child care forces a society to make profound decisions about its values. Some conservatives believe that women with young children should not work outside the home, but many mothers are forced to do so for financial reasons.

The shift in diction from formal to informal makes readers wonder whether the writer is presenting a serious analysis or a humorous satire. As revised, the passage makes more sense because the words are consistently formal.

Punctuation/
Mechanics

Writing

Sentence
Grammar

Sentence Style

Punctuation/
Mechanics

Language

Multilingual
Writers

Research

Documentation

19 Commas

It's hard to go through a day without encountering directions of some kind, and commas often play a crucial role in how you interpret instructions. See how important the comma is in the following directions for making hot cereal:

> Add Cream of Wheat slowly, stirring constantly.

That sentence tells the cook to *add the cereal slowly.* If the comma came before the word *slowly,* however, the cook might add all of the cereal at once and *stir slowly.*

19a To set off introductory elements

In general, use a comma after any word, **phrase**, or **clause** that precedes the **subject** of the sentence.

▶ **In Fitzgerald's novel, the color green takes on great symbolic qualities.**

▶ **Sporting a pair of specially made running shoes, Brendan prepared for the race.**

▶ **To win the game, Connor needed skill and luck.**

▶ **Pen poised in anticipation, Logan waited for the test to begin.**

▶ **Since my mind was not getting enough stimulation, I decided to read some good literature.**

Some writers omit the comma after a short introductory element that does not seem to require a pause after it. However, you will never be wrong if you use a comma.

---

bedfordstmartins.com/easywriter For exercises, go to **Exercise Central** and click on **Commas**.

19b To separate clauses in compound sentences

A comma usually precedes a **coordinating conjunction** (*and, but, or, nor, for, so,* or *yet*) that joins two **independent clauses** in a **compound sentence**.

▶ **The climbers must reach the summit today, or they will have to turn back.**
         ∧

With very short clauses, you can sometimes omit the comma if there is no chance the sentence will be misread without it.

▶ **She saw her chance and she took it.**

Use a semicolon rather than a comma when the clauses are long and complex or contain their own commas.

▶ **When these early migrations took place, the ice was still confined to the lands in the far north; but eight hundred thousand years ago, when man was already established in the temperate latitudes, the ice moved southward until it covered large parts of Europe and Asia.**

— ROBERT JASTROW, *Until the Sun Dies*

19c To set off nonrestrictive elements

Nonrestrictive elements are clauses, phrases, and words that do not limit, or restrict, the meaning of the words they modify. Since such elements are not essential to the meaning of a sentence, they should be set off from the rest of the sentence with commas. **Restrictive elements**, on the other hand, *do* limit meaning; they should *not* be set off with commas.

RESTRICTIVE   Drivers *who have been convicted of drunken driving* should lose their licenses.

In the preceding sentence, the clause *who have been convicted of drunken driving* is essential to the meaning because it limits the word it modifies, *Drivers*, to only those drivers who have been convicted of drunken driving. Therefore, it is *not* set off with commas.

NONRESTRICTIVE   The two drivers involved in the accident,
                      who have been convicted of drunken driving,
                      should lose their licenses.

In this sentence, however, the clause *who have been convicted of drunken driving* is not essential to the meaning because it does not limit what it modifies, *The two drivers involved in the accident,* but merely provides additional information about these drivers. Therefore, the clause *is* set off with commas.

To decide whether an element is restrictive or nonrestrictive, mentally delete the element, and see if the deletion changes the meaning of the rest of the sentence or makes it unclear. If the deletion *does* change the meaning, you should probably not set the element off with commas. If it *does not* change the meaning, the element probably requires commas.

Adjective and adverb clauses.   An **adjective clause** that begins with *that* is always restrictive; do not set it off with commas. An adjective clause beginning with *which* may be either restrictive or nonrestrictive; however, some writers prefer to use *which* only for nonrestrictive clauses, which they set off with commas. An **adverb clause** that follows a main clause does *not* usually require a comma to set it off unless the adverb clause expresses contrast.

NONRESTRICTIVE CLAUSES

▶ **I borrowed books from the rental library of Shakespeare and Company,** *which was the library and bookstore of Sylvia Beach at 12 rue de l'Odeon.*

— ERNEST HEMINGWAY, *A Moveable Feast*

The adjective clause describing Shakespeare and Company is not necessary to the meaning of the independent clause and therefore is set off with a comma.

▶ **The park became a popular gathering place, although nearby residents complained about the noise.**

The adverb clause *although nearby residents complained about the noise* expresses the idea of contrast; therefore, it is set off with a comma.

RESTRICTIVE CLAUSES

▶ **The claim *that men like seriously to battle one another to some sort of finish* is a myth.**

> — JOHN MCMURTRY, "Kill 'Em! Crush 'Em! Eat 'Em Raw!"

The adjective clause is necessary to the meaning of the sentence because it explains which claim is a myth; therefore, the clause is not set off with commas.

▶ **The man/who rescued Jana's puppy/won her eternal gratitude.**

The adjective clause *who rescued Jana's puppy* is necessary to the meaning because it identifies the man, so it takes no commas.

Phrases. **Participial phrases** may be restrictive or nonrestrictive. **Prepositional phrases** are usually restrictive, but sometimes they are not essential to the meaning of a sentence and thus are set off with commas.

NONRESTRICTIVE PHRASES

▶ **The bus drivers, rejecting the management offer, remained on strike.**

Using commas around the participial phrase makes it nonrestrictive, telling us that all of the drivers remained on strike.

RESTRICTIVE PHRASES

▶ **The bus drivers/rejecting the management offer/ remained on strike.**

If the phrase *rejecting the management offer* limits the meaning of *The bus drivers*, the commas should be deleted. The revised sentence says that only some of the bus drivers, the ones who rejected the offer, remained on strike, implying that the other drivers went back to work.

Appositives. An **appositive** is a **noun** or **noun phrase** that renames a nearby noun. When an appositive is not essential to identify what it renames, it is set off with commas.

NONRESTRICTIVE APPOSITIVES

▶ **Savion Glover, the award-winning dancer, taps like poetry in motion.**

Savion Glover's name identifies him; the appositive *the award-winning dancer* provides extra information.

RESTRICTIVE APPOSITIVES

▶ **Mozart's opera /*The Marriage of Figaro* / was considered revolutionary.**

The phrase *The Marriage of Figaro* is essential to the meaning of the sentence because Mozart wrote more than one opera. Therefore, it is *not* set off with commas.

19d To separate items in a series

You may see a series with no comma after the next-to-last item, particularly in newspaper writing. Occasionally, however, omitting the comma can cause confusion, and you will never be wrong if you include it.

▶ **He has plundered our seas, ravaged our coasts, burnt our towns, and destroyed the lives of our people.**

— Declaration of Independence

▶ **The long, twisting, muddy road led to a shack in the woods.**

▶ **Diners had a choice of broccoli, green beans, peas, and carrots.**

Without the comma after *peas,* you wouldn't know if there were three choices (the third being a *mixture* of peas and carrots) or four.

19e To set off parenthetical and transitional expressions

Parenthetical expressions add comments or information. Because they often interrupt the flow of a sentence, they are usually set off with commas.

▶ **Some studies, incidentally, have shown that chocolate, of all things, helps prevent tooth decay.**

Transitions (such as *as a result*), **conjunctive adverbs** (such as *however*), and other expressions used to connect parts of sentences are usually set off with commas.

▶ **Ozone is a by-product of dry cleaning, for example.**

19f To set off contrasting elements, interjections, direct address, and tag questions

▶ **I asked you, *not your brother*, to sweep the porch.**

▶ **My God, who wouldn't want a wife?**   — JUDY BRADY,
    "I Want a Wife"

▶ **Remember, *sir*, that you are under oath.**

▶ **The governor did not veto the unemployment bill, *did she*?**

19g To set off parts of dates and addresses

Dates.   Use a comma between the day of the week and the month, between the day of the month and the year, and between the year and the rest of the sentence, if any.

▶ **The attacks on the morning of Tuesday, September 11, 2001, took the United States by surprise.**

Do not use commas with dates in inverted order or with dates consisting of only the month and the year.

▶ **She dated the letter** *26 August 2004.*

▶ **Thousands of Germans swarmed over the wall in** *November 1989.*

Addresses and place names. Use a comma after each part of an address or a place name, including the state if there is no ZIP code. Do not precede a ZIP code with a comma.

▶ **Forward my mail to the Department of English, The Ohio State University, Columbus, Ohio 43210.**

▶ **Portland, Oregon, is much larger than Portland, Maine.**

19h To set off quotations

Commas set off a quotation from words used to introduce or identify the source of the quotation. A comma following a quotation goes *inside* the closing quotation mark.

▶ **A German proverb warns, "Go to law for a sheep, and lose your cow."**

▶ **"All I know about grammar," said Joan Didion, "is its infinite power."**

Do not use a comma after a question mark or an exclamation point.

▶ **"Out, damned spot!" cries Lady Macbeth.**

Do not use a comma to introduce a quotation with *that* or when you do not quote a speaker's exact words.

▶ **The writer of Ecclesiastes concludes that "all is vanity."**

▶ **Patrick Henry declared that he wanted either liberty or death.**

19i Unnecessary commas

Excessive use of commas can spoil an otherwise fine sentence.

Around restrictive elements. Do not use commas to set off restrictive elements — elements that limit, or define, the meaning of the words they modify or refer to (see 19c).

▶ **I don't let my children watch TV shows/that are violent.**

The *that* clause restricts the meaning of *TV shows*, so the comma should be omitted.

▶ **The actor/Russell Crowe/might win the award.**

Between subjects and verbs, verbs and objects or complements, and prepositions and objects. Do not use a comma between a subject and its **verb**, a verb and its **object** or **complement**, or a **preposition** and its object.

▶ **Watching movies late at night/allows me to relax.**

▶ **Parents must decide/how much TV their children may watch.**

▶ **The winner of/the trophy for community service stepped forward.**

In compound constructions. In compound constructions other than compound sentences, do not use a comma before or after a coordinating conjunction that joins the two parts (see 19b).

▶ **Improved health care/and more free trade were two goals of the Clinton administration.**

The *and* joins parts of a compound subject, which should not be separated by a comma.

▶ **Mark Twain trained as a printer,/and worked as a steamboat pilot.**

The *and* joins parts of a compound predicate, which should not be separated by a comma.

In a series. Do not use a comma before the first or after the last item in a series.

▶ **The auction included,/furniture, paintings, and china.**

▶ **The swimmer took slow, elegant, powerful,/strokes.**

20 Semicolons

If you've ever pored over the fine print at the bottom of an ad for a big sale, looking for the opening hours or the address of the store nearest you, then you've seen plenty of semicolons in action. Here's an example from a Bloomingdale's ad:

> Store Hours — SUN., 12–6; MON. through FRI., 10–9:30; SAT., 10–8.

The semicolons separate the information for each day's hours. Semicolons create a pause stronger than that of a comma but not as strong as the full pause of a period.

20a To link independent clauses

Though a comma and a **coordinating conjunction** often join **independent clauses** (see 19b), semicolons provide writers with subtler ways of signaling closely related clauses. The clause following a semicolon often restates an idea expressed in the first clause; it sometimes expands on or presents a contrast to the first.

---

 bedfordstmartins.com/easywriter For exercises, go to **Exercise Central** and click on **Semicolons.**

▶ **Immigration acts were passed; newcomers had to prove, besides moral correctness and financial solvency, their ability to read.**

— MARY GORDON,
"More Than Just a Shrine"

Gordon uses a semicolon to join the two clauses, giving the sentence an abrupt rhythm that suits the topic: laws that imposed strict requirements.

If two independent clauses joined by a coordinating conjunction contain commas, you may use a semicolon instead of a comma before the conjunction to make the sentence easier to read.

▶ **Every year, whether the Republican or the Democratic party is in office, more and more power drains away from the individual to feed vast reservoirs in far-off places; and we have less and less say about the shape of events which shape our future.**

— WILLIAM F. BUCKLEY JR.,
"Why Don't We Complain?"

20b To link independent clauses joined by conjunctive adverbs or transitions

A semicolon — not a comma — should link independent clauses joined by a **conjunctive adverb** such as *however* or *therefore* or a **transition** such as *as a result* or *for example*. Using a comma in this construction creates a **comma splice** (see Chapter 12).

▶ **The circus comes as close to being the world in microcosm as anything I know; in a way, it puts all the rest of show business in the shade.**

— E. B. WHITE, "The Ring of Time"

▶ **Every kid should have access to a computer/; further-**
⠀⠀⠀⠀⠀⠀⠀⠀⠀⠀⠀⠀⠀⠀⠀⠀⠀⠀⠀⠀⠀⠀⠀⠀⠀⠀⠀⠀⠀⠀⠀^
more, access to the Internet should be free.

20c To separate items in a series containing other punctuation

Ordinarily, commas separate items in a series (see 19d). But when the items themselves contain commas or other punctuation, semicolons make the sentence clearer.

▶ **Anthropology encompasses archaeology, the study of ancient civilizations through artifacts;̷ linguistics, the study of the structure and development of language;̷ and cultural anthropology, the study of language, customs, and behavior.**

20d Misused semicolons

Use a comma, not a semicolon, to separate an independent clause from a **dependent clause** or **phrase**.

▶ **The police found fingerprints;̷ which they used to identify the thief.**

▶ **The new system would encourage students to register for courses online;̷ thus streamlining registration.**

Use a colon, not a semicolon, to introduce a series or list.

▶ **The tour includes visits to the following art museums;̷ the Prado, in Madrid; the Louvre, in Paris; and the van Gogh, in Amsterdam.**

21 End Punctuation

Periods, question marks, and exclamation points often appear in advertising to create special effects:

Millions of pictures will be taken this holiday.
Will your smile be ready?
You can have whiter teeth in just three days!

End punctuation tells us how to read each sentence — as a matter-of-fact statement, a question for the reader, or an enthusiastic exclamation.

21a Periods

Use a period to close sentences that make statements or give mild commands.

▶ **All books are either dreams or swords.**

— AMY LOWELL

▶ **Don't use a fancy word if a simpler word will do.**

— GEORGE ORWELL, "Politics and the English Language"

A period also closes **indirect questions**, which report rather than ask questions.

▶ **I asked how old the child was.**

In American English, periods are used with most abbreviations. However, more and more abbreviations are appearing without periods.

Mr.	MD	BCE *or* B.C.E.
Ms.	PhD	AD *or* A.D.
Sen.	Jr.	PM *or* p.m.

Some abbreviations rarely if ever appear with periods. These include the postal abbreviations of state names, such as *FL* and *TN*, and most groups of initials (*GE, CIA, AIDS, YMCA, UNICEF*). If you are not sure whether a particular abbreviation should include periods, check a dictionary or follow the style guidelines you are using for a research paper. (For more about abbreviations, see Chapter 26.)

Do not use an additional period when a sentence ends with an abbreviation that has its own period.

▶ **The social worker referred me to John Pintz Jr.**/

 bedfordstmartins.com/easywriter For exercises, go to **Exercise Central** and click on **End Punctuation**.

21b Question marks

Use question marks to close sentences that ask direct questions.

▶ **How is the human mind like a computer, and how is it different?**

— KATHLEEN STASSEN BERGER and ROSS A. THOMPSON,
The Developing Person through Childhood and Adolescence

Question marks do not close indirect questions, which report rather than ask questions.

▶ **She asked whether I opposed his nomination?.**
                                              ∧

21c Exclamation points

Use an exclamation point to show surprise or strong emotion. Use these marks sparingly because they can distract your readers or suggest that you are exaggerating.

▶ **In those few moments of geologic time will be the story of all that has happened since we became a nation. And what a story it will be!**

— JAMES RETTIE, "But a Watch in the Night"

▶ **This university is so large, so varied, that attempting to tell someone everything about it would take three years!.**
                                                                    ∧

22   Apostrophes

The little apostrophe can sometimes make a big difference in meaning. If you saw a note on a vacationing friend's refrigerator asking you to put out the cat's food, how many

---

⊙ bedfordstmartins.com/easywriter For exercises, go to **Exercise Central** and click on **Apostrophes.**

cats would you expect to be feeding? One, of course, and so you'd put out enough food for one cat. If your friend had slipped up with that apostrophe, however, and meant *cats'* instead of *cat's* — well, there would be some hungry cats around.

22a To signal possessive case

The **possessive case** denotes ownership or possession. Add an apostrophe and -*s* to form the possessive of most **singular nouns**, including those that end in -*s*, and of **indefinite pronouns** (see 8d). The possessive forms of **personal pronouns** do not take apostrophes: *yours, his, hers, its, ours, theirs.*

▶ The *bus's* fumes overpowered her.

▶ George *Lucas's* movies have been wildly popular.

▶ *Anyone's* guess is as good as mine.

Plural nouns. To form the possessive case of **plural** nouns not ending in -*s*, add an apostrophe and -*s*. For plural nouns ending in -*s*, add only the apostrophe.

▶ Robert Bly helped to popularize the *men's* movement.

▶ The *clowns'* costumes were bright green and orange.

Compound nouns. For **compound nouns**, make the last word in the group possessive.

▶ Both her *daughters-in-law's* birthdays fall in July.

Two or more nouns. To signal individual possession by two or more owners, make each noun possessive.

▶ Great differences exist between *Angela Bassett's* and *Oprah Winfrey's* films.

Bassett and Winfrey appeared in different films.

To signal joint possession, make only the last noun possessive.

▶ *MacNeil and Lehrer's* television program focused on current issues.

MacNeil and Lehrer participated in the same program.

22b To signal contractions

Contractions are two-word combinations formed by leaving out certain letters, which are replaced by an apostrophe.

it is, it has/it's   I would, I had/I'd   will not/won't

Contractions are common in conversation and informal writing. Academic and professional work, however, often calls for greater formality.

Apostrophes also signal omissions in some common phrases.

rock and roll   class of 1997
rock 'n' roll   class of '97

Distinguishing *its* and *it's*.   *Its* is a **possessive pronoun** — the possessive form of *it*. *It's* is a contraction for *it is* or *it has*.

▶ This disease is unusual; *its* symptoms vary from person to person.

▶ *It's* a difficult disease to diagnose.

22c To form certain plurals

Use an apostrophe and -*s* to form the plural of numbers, letters, symbols, and words referred to as words. Italicize numbers, letters, and words referred to as terms, but do not italicize the plural ending.

▶ The gymnasts need marks of *8*'s and *9*'s to qualify for the finals.

▶ The computer prints *e*'s whenever there is an error in the program.

▶ I marked special passages with a series of three ***'s.

▶ The five *Shakespeare*'s in the essay were spelled five different ways.

You can omit the apostrophe before the *-s* for the plural of years (*2020s*). However, when the century is omitted before a decade, an apostrophe marks the omission (*fashion of the '80s*).

23 Quotation Marks

"Hilarious!" "A great family movie!" "A must see!" Claims of this kind leap out from most movie ads, always set off by quotation marks. In fact, the quotation marks are a key component of such statements; they make the praise more believable by indicating that it comes from people other than the movie promoter. Quotation marks identify a speaker's exact words or the titles of short works.

23a To signal direct quotation

▸ **President Bush referred to an "axis of evil" in his speech.**

▸ **She smiled and said, "Son, this is one incident that I will never forget."**

Use quotation marks to enclose the words of each speaker within running dialogue. Mark each shift in speaker with a new paragraph.

> "But I can see you're bound to come," said the father. "Only we ain't going to catch us no fish, because there ain't no water left to catch 'em in."
> "The river!"
> "All but dry."
>
> — EUDORA WELTY, "Ladies in Spring"

---

 bedfordstmartins.com/easywriter For exercises, go to **Exercise Central** and click on **Quotation Marks.**

Single quotation marks.   Single quotation marks enclose
a quotation within a quotation. Open and close the quoted
passage with double quotation marks, and change any
quotation marks that appear *within* the quotation to single
quotation marks.

▶ **Baldwin says, "The title 'The Uses of the Blues' does
not refer to music; I don't know anything about
music."**

Long quotations.   To quote a long passage, set the quotation off by starting it on a new line and indenting it from
the left margin. This format, known as block quotation,
does not require quotation marks.

MLA documentation style (see Chapter 42) requires you
to format a prose passage of more than four typed lines as a
block quotation. The block should be indented one inch, or
ten spaces. In APA style (see Chapter 43), block quotation is
used for a quotation of forty words or more, and the block is
indented five spaces. *The Chicago Manual of Style* (see Chapter 44) recommends setting off quotations of eight lines or
more, or more than one hundred words. *The CBE Manual*
(see Chapter 45) endorses the use of block quotations but
does not provide precise guidelines for when to use them.
The following example illustrates MLA style.

> In "Suspended," Joy Harjo tells of her first awareness of jazz as
> a child:
>
> > My rite of passage into the world of humanity occurred
> > then, via jazz. The music made a startling bridge
> > between the familiar and strange lands, an appropriate
> > vehicle, for though the music is predominantly west
> > African in concept, with European associations, jazz
> > was influenced by the Creek (or Muscogee) people, for
> > we were there when jazz was born. I recognized it,
> > that humid afternoon in my formative years, as a way
> > to speak beyond the confines of ordinary language. I
> > still hear it. (84)

Quoting poetry.   When quoting poetry, if the quotation is
brief (fewer than four lines), you should include it within
your text if you are using MLA style. Separate the lines of
the poem with slashes, each preceded and followed by a

space, in order to tell the reader where one line of the poem ends and the next begins.

> In one of his best-known poems, Robert Frost remarks, "Two roads diverged in a yellow wood, and I — / I took the one less traveled by / And that has made all the difference."

To quote more than three lines of poetry, indent the block one inch (or ten spaces) from the left margin. Do not use quotation marks. Take care to follow the spacing, capitalization, punctuation, and other features of the original poem.

> The duke in Robert Browning's poem "My Last Duchess" is clearly a jealous, vain person, whose arrogance is illustrated through this statement:
>
>> She thanked men, — good! but thanked
>> Somehow — I know not how — as if she ranked
>> My gift of a nine-hundred-years-old name
>> With anybody's gift.

FOR MULTILINGUAL WRITERS

Quoting in American English

Remember that the way you mark quotations in American English (" ") may not be the same as in other languages. In French, for example, quotations are marked with *guillemets* (« »), while in German, quotations take split-level marks („ "). American English and British English offer opposite conventions for double and single quotation marks. Writers of British English use single quotation marks first and, when necessary, double quotation marks for quotations within quotations. If you are writing for an American audience, be careful to follow the U.S. conventions governing quotation marks: double quotation marks first and, when necessary, single quotation marks within double.

23b To enclose titles of short works and definitions

Use quotation marks to enclose the titles of short poems, short stories, articles, essays, songs, sections of books, and episodes of television and radio programs. Quotation marks also enclose definitions.

▶ The essay "Big and Bad" analyzes some reasons for the popularity of SUVs.

▶ In social science, the term *sample size* means "the number of individuals being studied in a research project."

— KATHLEEN STASSEN BERGER and ROSS A. THOMPSON,
The Developing Person through Childhood and Adolescence

23c With other punctuation

Periods and commas go *inside* closing quotation marks.

▶ "Don't compromise yourself," said Janis Joplin. "You are all you've got."

Colons, semicolons, and footnote numbers go *outside* closing quotation marks.

▶ I felt one emotion after finishing "Eveline": sorrow.

▶ Tragedy is defined by Aristotle as "an imitation of an action that is serious and of a certain magnitude."[1]

Question marks, exclamation points, and dashes go *inside* if they are part of the quoted material, *outside* if they are not.

▶ The cashier asked, "Would you like to super-size that?"

▶ What is the theme of "The Birth-Mark"?

23d Misused quotation marks

Do not use quotation marks for **indirect quotations** — those that do not use someone's exact words.

▶ Mother smiled and said that ⁄"she was sure she would never forget the incident."⁄

Do not use quotation marks just to add emphasis to particular words or phrases.

▶ The hikers were startled by the appearance of a ⁄"gigantic"⁄ grizzly bear.

Do not use quotation marks around slang or colloquial language; they create the impression that you are apologizing for using those words. If you have a good reason to use slang or a colloquial term, use it without quotation marks.

▶ **After our twenty-mile hike, we were completely exhausted and ready to ⫽turn in.⫽**

24 Other Punctuation

Parentheses, brackets, dashes, colons, slashes, and ellipses are all around us. Pick up the television listings, for instance, and you will find these punctuation marks in abundance, helping viewers preview programs in a clear and efficient way.

⑦⑧ **College Football** *3:30* 501019/592361 — Northwestern Wildcats at Ohio State Buckeyes. The Buckeyes are looking for their 20th straight win over Northwestern. (Live) [Time approximate.]

These marks of punctuation can signal relationships among sentence parts, create particular rhythms, and help readers follow your thoughts.

24a Parentheses

Use parentheses to enclose material that is of minor or secondary importance in a sentence — material that supplements, clarifies, comments on, or illustrates what precedes or follows it.

▶ **Inventors and men of genius have almost always been regarded as fools at the beginning (and very often at the end) of their careers.**

— FYODOR DOSTOYEVSKY

---

 bedfordstmartins.com/easywriter For exercises, go to **Exercise Central** and click on **Other Punctuation**.

▶ **My research indicated problems with the flat tax (a single-rate tax with no deductions).**

Parentheses are also used to enclose textual citations and numbers or letters in a list.

▶ **Freud and his followers have had a most significant impact on the ways abnormal functioning is understood and treated (Joseph, 1991).**

— RONALD J. COMER, *Abnormal Psychology*

The in-text citation in this sentence shows the style of the American Psychological Association (APA).

▶ **Five distinct styles can be distinguished: (1) Old New England, (2) Deep South, (3) Middle American, (4) Wild West, and (5) Far West or Californian.**

— ALISON LURIE, *The Language of Clothes*

With other punctuation. A period may be placed either inside or outside a closing parenthesis, depending on whether the parenthetical text is part of a larger sentence. A comma, if needed, is always placed *outside* a closing parenthesis (and never before an opening one).

▶ **Gene Tunney's single defeat in an eleven-year career was to a flamboyant and dangerous fighter named Harry Greb ("The Human Windmill"), who seems to have been, judging from boxing literature, the dirtiest fighter in history.**

— JOYCE CAROL OATES, "On Boxing"

24b Brackets

Use brackets to enclose parenthetical elements in material that is itself within parentheses. Also use brackets to enclose explanatory words or comments that you are inserting into a quotation.

▶ **Eventually, the investigation had to examine the major agencies (including the National Security Agency [NSA]) that were conducting covert operations.**

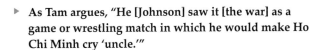

▶ **As Tam argues, "He [Johnson] saw it [the war] as a game or wrestling match in which he would make Ho Chi Minh cry 'uncle.'"**

The bracketed words clarify the words *he* and *it* in the original quotation.

In the quotation in the following sentence, the artist Gauguin's name is misspelled. The bracketed word *sic,* which means "so," tells readers that the person being quoted — not the writer who has picked up the quotation — made the mistake.

▶ **One admirer wrote, "She was the most striking woman I'd ever seen — a sort of wonderful combination of Mia Farrow and one of Gaugin's [*sic*] Polynesian nymphs."**

24c Dashes

Use dashes to insert a comment or to highlight material in a sentence.

▶ **The pleasures of reading itself — who doesn't remember? — were like those of Christmas cake, a sweet devouring.**

— EUDORA WELTY, "A Sweet Devouring"

A single dash can be used to emphasize material at the end of a sentence, to mark a sudden change in tone, to indicate hesitation in speech, or to introduce a summary or an explanation.

▶ **In the twentieth century it has become almost impossible to moralize about epidemics — except those which are transmitted sexually.**

— SUSAN SONTAG, *AIDS and Its Metaphors*

▶ **In walking, the average adult person employs a motor mechanism that weighs about eighty pounds — sixty pounds of muscle and twenty pounds of bone.**

— EDWIN WAY TEALE

Dashes give more emphasis than parentheses to the material they enclose or set off. Most word-processing software allows a dash to be created by typing two hyphens

(--) with no spaces before, between, or after. Many word-processing programs automatically convert two typed hyphens into a solid dash (—). Use dashes carefully, not only because they are somewhat informal but also because too many create a jerky, disconnected effect that can make it hard for readers to follow your thought.

24d Colons

Use a colon to introduce an explanation, an example, an appositive, a series, a list, or a quotation.

▶ **At the baby's one-month birthday party, Ah Po gave him the Four Valuable Things: ink, inkslab, paper, and brush.**

— MAXINE HONG KINGSTON, *China Men*

▶ **We began a series of workshops on nonviolence, and we repeatedly asked ourselves: "Are you able to accept blows without retaliation?"**

— MARTIN LUTHER KING JR., "Letter from Birmingham Jail"

Colons are also used after salutations in formal letters; with numbers indicating hours, minutes, and seconds; with ratios; with biblical chapters and verses; with titles and subtitles; and in bibliographic entries.

▶ **Dear Dr. Chapman:**
▶ **4:59 PM**
▶ **a ratio of 5:1**
▶ *The Joy of Insight: Passions of a Physicist*
▶ **Boston: Bedford/St. Martin's, 2006**

Misused colons. Do not put a colon between a **verb** and its **object** or **complement** (unless the object is a quotation), between a **preposition** and its object, or after such expressions as *such as, especially,* and *including.*

▶ **Some natural fibers are⫶ cotton, wool, silk, and linen.**

▶ **In poetry, additional power may come from devices such as⫶ simile, metaphor, and alliteration.**

24e Slashes

Use slashes to mark line divisions between two or three lines of poetry quoted within text. When using a slash to separate lines of poetry (see 23a), precede and follow it with a space.

▶ **Shakespeare's Sonnet 29 states, "For thy sweet love rememb'red such wealth brings / That then I scorn to change my state with kings."**

Use a slash to separate alternatives, parts of fractions, and Internet addresses.

▶ **Then there was Daryl, the cabdriver/bartender.**

— JOHN L'HEUREUX, *The Handmaid of Desire*

▶ **1/2**

▶ **http://www.bedfordstmartins.com/easywriter**

24f Ellipses

Ellipses, or ellipsis points, are three equally spaced dots. Ellipses are usually used to indicate that something has been omitted from a quoted passage. Just as you should carefully use quotation marks around any material that you quote directly from a source, so you should carefully use ellipses to indicate that you have left out part of a quotation that otherwise appears to be a complete sentence. Ellipses have been used in the following example to indicate two omissions — one in the middle of the first sentence and one at the end of the second sentence.

ORIGINAL TEXT

> Much male fear of feminism is the fear that, in becoming whole human beings, women will cease to mother men, to provide the breast, the lullaby, the continuous attention associated by the infant with the mother. Much male fear of feminism is infantilism — the longing to remain the mother's son, to possess a woman who exists purely for him.

— ADRIENNE RICH

WITH ELLIPSES

> As Adrienne Rich argues, "Much male fear of feminism is the fear that . . . women will cease to mother men, to provide the breast, the lullaby, the continuous attention associated by the infant with the mother. Much male fear of feminism is infantilism — the longing to remain the mother's son. . . ."

When you omit the last part of a quoted sentence, add a period after the ellipses — for a total of four dots. Be sure a complete sentence comes before and after the four dots. If your shortened quotation ends with a source citation (such as a page number, a name, or a title), place the documentation source in parentheses after the three ellipsis points and the closing quotation mark but before the period.

▶ **Packer argues, "The Administration is right to reconsider its strategy . . . " (34).**

You can also use ellipses to indicate a pause or a hesitation in speech in the same way that you can use a dash for that purpose.

▶ **Then the voice, husky and familiar, came to wash over us — "The winnah, and still heavyweight champeen of the world . . . Joe Louis."**

— MAYA ANGELOU, *I Know Why the Caged Bird Sings*

24g Online punctuation

Some fairly new uses of punctuation marks in electronic communication can add emphasis and set off the titles of works. When italics and underlining are unavailable, use asterisks to help create special emphasis.

▶ **Her homepage *must* be updated.**

Use the underscore symbol before and after the title of a full-length work.

▶ **Have you read Bill Gates's _The Road Ahead_?**

You may want to use angle brackets to set off email addresses and addresses on the World Wide Web from the rest of your text.

▶ **Visit us on the Web at <bedfordstmartins.com>.**

25 Capitalization

Capital letters are a key signal in everyday life. Look around any store to see their importance: you can shop for Levi's or *any* blue jeans, for Coca-Cola or *any* cola, for Kleenex or *any* tissue. In each of these instances, the capital letter indicates the name of a particular brand.

25a The first word of a sentence

With very few exceptions, capitalize the first word of a sentence. If you are quoting a full sentence, capitalize its first word unless you are introducing the quotation with *that*.

▸ **Kennedy said, "Let us never negotiate out of fear."**

▸ **The study's lead author emphasized that "the trial results were promising but not yet confirmed."**

Capitalization of a nonquoted sentence following a colon is optional.

▸ **Gould cites the work of Darwin: The [*or* the] theory of natural selection incorporates the principle of evolutionary ties among all animals.**

Capitalize a sentence within parentheses unless the parenthetical sentence is inserted into another sentence.

▸ **Gould cites the work of Darwin. (Other researchers cite more recent evolutionary theorists.)**

▸ **Gould cites the work of Darwin (see page 150).**

When citing poetry, follow the capitalization of the original poem. Though most poets capitalize the first word of each line in a poem, some do not.

▶ **Morning sun heats up the young beech tree leaves and almost lights them into fireflies**

— JUNE JORDAN, "Aftermath"

25b Proper nouns and proper adjectives

Capitalize **proper nouns** (those naming specific persons, places, and things) and most **adjectives** formed from proper nouns. All other nouns are **common nouns** and are not capitalized unless they are used as part of a proper noun: *a street,* but *Elm Street.*

Capitalized nouns and adjectives include personal names; nations, nationalities, and languages; months, days of the week, and holidays (but not of the year); geographical names; structures and monuments; ships, trains, aircraft, and spacecraft; organizations, businesses, and government institutions; academic institutions and courses; historical events and eras; and religions, their deities, followers, and sacred writings. For trade names, follow the capitalization you see in company advertising or on the product itself.

PROPER	COMMON
Alfred Hitchcock, Hitchcockian	a director
Brazil, Brazilian	a nation, a language
Pacific Ocean	an ocean
Challenger	a spaceship
Library of Congress	a federal agency
World Wide Web	a homepage, a site
Political Science 102	a political science course
the Qur'an	a prayer book
Catholicism, Catholics	a religion
Cheerios, eBay	cereal, an auction site

FOR MULTILINGUAL WRITERS

Learning English Capitalization

Capitalization systems vary considerably. Arabic, Chinese, and Hebrew, for example, do not use capital letters at all. English may be the only language to capitalize the first-person singular pronoun (*I*), but Dutch and German capitalize some forms of the second-person pronoun (*you*) — and German also capitalizes all nouns.

25c Titles before proper names

When used alone or following a proper name, most titles are not capitalized. One common exception is the word *president,* which many writers capitalize whenever it refers to the President of the United States.

Professor Lisa Ede	my history professor
Dr. Teresa Ramirez	Teresa Ramirez, our doctor

25d Titles of works

Capitalize most words in titles of books, articles, speeches, stories, essays, plays, poems, documents, films, paintings, and musical compositions. Do not capitalize **articles** (*a, an, the*), **prepositions**, **conjunctions**, and the *to* in an **infinitive** unless they are the first or last words in a title or subtitle.

Walt Whitman: A Life	Declaration of Independence
"As Time Goes By"	*The Producers*
"Crazy in Love"	*Harry Potter and the Sorcerer's Stone*

25e Compass directions

Capitalize compass directions only if the word designates a specific geographical region.

▶ **John Muir headed west, motivated by the desire to explore.**

▶ **Water rights are an increasingly contentious issue in the West.**

25f Family relationships

Capitalize family relationships only if the word is used as part of a name or as a substitute for the name.

▶ **When she was a child, my mother shared a room with my aunt.**

▶ **I could always tell when Mother was annoyed with Aunt Rose.**

26 Abbreviations and Numbers

Any time you open up a telephone book, you see an abundance of abbreviations and numbers, as in the following movie theater listing from the Berkeley, California, telephone book:

Oaks Theater   1875 Solano Av   Brk

Abbreviations and numbers allow writers to present detailed information in a small amount of space.

26a Abbreviations

Certain titles, including those indicating academic degrees, are normally abbreviated when used before or after a person's name.

Ms. Susanna Moller   Henry Louis Gates Jr.
Mr. Mark Otuteye   Karen Lancry, MD

Religious, academic, and government titles should be spelled out in academic writing but can be abbreviated in other writing when they appear before a full name.

Rev. Fleming Rutledge   Reverend Rutledge
Prof. Jaime Mejía   Professor Mejía
Sen. Barack Obama   Senator Obama

Business, government, and science terms.   As long as you can be sure your readers will understand them, use common abbreviations such as *PBS, NASA,* and *DNA.* If an abbreviation may be unfamiliar, spell out the full term the first time you use it, and give the abbreviation in parentheses; after that, you can use the abbreviation by itself. Use abbreviations such as *Co., Inc., Corp.,* and *&* only if they are part of a company's official name.

● bedfordstmartins.com/easywriter For exercises, go to **Exercise Central** and click on **Abbreviations and Numbers.**

▶ **The Comprehensive Test Ban (CTB) Treaty was first proposed in the 1950s. For those nations signing it, the CTB would bring to a halt all nuclear weapons testing.**

▶ **Sears, Roebuck & Co. was the only large** ~~corp.~~ *corporation* **in town.**

With numbers. The following abbreviations are acceptable with specific years and times.

> 399 BC ("before Christ") or 399 BCE ("before the common era")
> AD 49 (*anno Domini,* Latin for "year of our Lord") or 49 CE ("common era")
> 11:15 AM (*or* a.m.)
> 9:00 PM (*or* p.m.)

Symbols such as % and $ are acceptable with figures (*$11*) but not with words (*eleven dollars*). Units of measurement can be abbreviated in charts and graphs (*4 in.*) but not in the body of a paper (*four inches*).

In notes and source citations. Some abbreviations required in notes and in source citations are not appropriate in the body of a paper.

cf.	compare (*confer*)
e.g.	for example (*exempli gratia*)
et al.	and others (*et alia*)
etc.	and so forth (*et cetera*)
i.e.	that is (*id est*)
N.B.	note well (*nota bene*)

In addition, except in notes and source citations, do not abbreviate such terms as *chapter, page,* and *volume* or the names of months, states, cities, or countries. Two exceptions are *Washington, D.C.,* and *U.S.,* which is acceptable as an **adjective** but not as a **noun**: *U.S. borders* but *in the United States.*

26b Numbers

If you can write out a number in one or two words, do so. Use figures for longer numbers.

▶ **Her screams were ignored by** ~~38~~ *thirty-eight* **people.**

▶ A baseball is held together by ~~two hundred sixteen~~ red
stitches.

216

If one of several numbers *of the same kind* in the same sentence requires a figure, you should use figures for all the numbers in that sentence.

▶ An audio system can range in cost from ~~one hundred dollars~~ to $2,599.

$100

When a sentence begins with a number, either spell out the number or rewrite the sentence.

▶ ~~119~~ years of CIA labor cost taxpayers sixteen million dollars.

One hundred nineteen

Most readers find it easier to read figures than three-word numbers; thus, the best solution may be to rewrite this sentence: *Taxpayers spent sixteen million dollars for 119 years of CIA labor.*

In general, use figures for the following:

ADDRESSES	23 Main Street; 175 Fifth Avenue
DATES	September 17, 1951; 6 June 1983; 4 BCE; the 1860s
DECIMALS AND FRACTIONS	65.34; $8\frac{1}{2}$
PERCENTAGES	77 percent (*or* 77%)
EXACT AMOUNTS OF MONEY	$7,348; $1.46 trillion; $2.50; thirty-five (*or* 35) cents
SCORES AND STATISTICS	an 8–3 Red Sox victory; an average age of 22
TIME OF DAY	6:00 AM (*or* a.m.)

27 Italics

The slanted type known as *italics* is more than just a pretty typeface. Indeed, italics give words special meaning or emphasis. In the sentence "Many people read *People* on the subway every day," the italics (and the capital letter) tell us that *People* is a publication. You may use your computer to produce italic type; if not, underline words that you would otherwise italicize.

27a For titles

In general, use italics for titles of long works; use quotation marks for shorter works (see 23b).

BOOKS	*Harry Potter and the Half-Blood Prince*
CHOREOGRAPHIC WORKS	Agnes de Mille's *Rodeo*
FILMS AND VIDEOS	*The Return of the King*
LONG MUSICAL WORKS	*Brandenburg Concertos*
LONG POEMS	*The Bhagavadgita*
MAGAZINES AND JOURNALS	*Ebony, New England Journal of Medicine*
NEWSPAPERS	the Cleveland *Plain Dealer*
PAINTINGS AND SCULPTURE	Georgia O'Keeffe's *Black Iris*
PAMPHLETS	Thomas Paine's *Common Sense*
PLAYS	*Caroline, or Change*
RADIO SERIES	*All Things Considered*
RECORDINGS	*The Ramones Leave Home*
SOFTWARE	*Quicken*
TELEVISION SERIES	*Desperate Housewives*
WEB SITES	*Salon*

Do not italicize titles of sacred books, such as the Bible and the Qur'an; public documents, such as the Constitution and the Magna Carta; or your own papers.

27b For words, letters, and numbers used as terms

▶ **On the back of his jersey was the famous *24*.**

▶ **One characteristic of some New York speech is the absence of postvocalic *r* — for example, pronouncing the word *four* as "fouh."**

27c For non-English words

Italicize words from other languages unless they have become part of English — like the French "bourgeois" or the Italian "pasta," for example. If a word is in an English dictionary, it does not need italics. Always italicize Latin genus and species names.

▶ **At last one of the phantom sleighs gliding along the street would come to a stop, and with gawky haste Mr. Burness in his fox-furred *shapka* would make for our door.**

— VLADIMIR NABOKOV, *Speak, Memory*

▶ **The caterpillars of *Hapalia,* when attacked by the wasp *Apanteles machaeralis,* drop suddenly from their leaves and suspend themselves in air by a silken thread.**

— STEPHEN JAY GOULD, "Nonmoral Nature"

27d For aircraft, spacecraft, ships, and trains

Spirit of St. Louis   Amtrak's *Silver Star*
Discovery   U.S.S. *Iowa*

---

 bedfordstmartins.com/easywriter For exercises, go to **Exercise Central** and click on **Italics.**

27e For emphasis

Italics can help create emphasis in writing, but use them sparingly for this purpose. It is usually better to create emphasis with sentence structure and word choice.

▶ **Great literature and a class of literate readers are nothing new in India. What is new is the emergence of a gifted generation of Indian writers** *working in English.*

— SALMAN RUSHDIE

28 Hyphens

Hyphens show up every time you make a left-hand turn, wear a T-shirt, visit a self-service gas station, get one-on-one tutoring, listen to hip-hop, or eat Tex-Mex food. Sometimes the dictionary will tell you whether to hyphenate a word. Other times you will have to apply some general rules.

28a In compound nouns and verbs

Some **compound nouns** and **verbs** are one word, some are separate words, and some require hyphens. Consult a dictionary to be sure.

ONE WORD	rowboat, textbook, homepage
SEPARATE WORDS	high school, parking meter, shut up
WITH HYPHENS	city-state, sister-in-law, cross-fertilize

28b In compound adjectives

Hyphenate most **compound adjectives** before a **noun**. Do not hyphenate compound adjectives that follow a noun.

a *well-liked* boss
a *six-foot* plank

Our boss is *well liked.*
The plank is *six feet* long.

Never hyphenate an *-ly* **adverb** and an adjective.

▶ **They used a widely/distributed mailing list.**

Use suspended hyphens in a series of compound adjectives.

▶ **Each student did the work him- or herself.**
          ^

28c In fractions and numbers

Hyphenate spelled-out fractions and numbers from twenty-one to ninety-nine.

two-sevenths   thirty-five

28d With prefixes and suffixes

Most words containing a **prefix** or **suffix** are written without hyphens: *antiwar, gorillalike.* Here are some exceptions:

BEFORE CAPITALIZED WORDS   pro-Democratic, non-Catholic

WITH FIGURES   pre-1960, post-1945

WITH *ALL-, EX-,* AND *SELF-*   all-state, ex-partner, self-possessed

WITH *-ELECT*   mayor-elect

FOR CLARITY   re-cover, anti-inflation, troll-like

Re-cover means "cover again"; the hyphen distinguishes it from *recover,* meaning "get well." In *anti-inflation* and *troll-like,* the hyphens separate double and triple letters.

Language

Writing

Sentence
Grammar

Sentence Style

Punctuation/
Mechanics

Language

Multilingual
Writers

Research

Documentation

People today often communicate instantaneously across vast distances and cultures. Businesspeople complete multinational transactions, students take online classes at distant universities, and grandparents check in with family members across multiple time zones. You may already find yourself writing to (or with) people from other cultures, language groups, and countries. In this era of rapid global communication, you must know how to write effectively to the world.

29a Thinking about what you consider "normal"

More than likely, your judgments about what is "normal" are based on assumptions that you are not aware of. Most of us tend to see our own way as the "normal" or right way to do things. If your ways seem inherently right, then perhaps you assume that other ways are somehow less than right. To communicate effectively with people across cultures, recognize the norms that guide your own behavior and how those norms differ from those of other people.

- Know that most ways of communicating are influenced by cultural contexts and differ widely from one culture to the next.

- Notice the ways that people from cultures other than your own communicate, and be open to them.

- Pay attention to and respect the differences among individuals within a culture. Don't assume that all members of a community behave in the same way or value the same things.

29b Considering meaning

All writers face challenges in trying to communicate across space, languages, and cultures. You can address these challenges by working to be sure that you understand what others say — and that they understand you. In such situations, take care to be explicit about the meanings of the words you use. In addition, don't hesitate to ask people to explain a point if you're not absolutely sure you understand, and invite responses by asking whether you're making yourself clear.

29c Considering your own authority as a writer

Writers communicating across cultures often encounter audiences who have differing attitudes about authority and about the relationship between the writer and the people being addressed. In the United States, students are often asked to establish authority in their writing — by drawing on personal experience, by reporting on research, or by taking a position for which they can offer strong evidence and support. But some cultures position student writers as novices, whose job is to learn from others who have greater authority. When you write, think carefully about your audience's expectations and attitudes toward authority.

- Whom are you addressing, and what is your relationship to him or her?
- What knowledge are you expected to have? Is it appropriate for you to demonstrate that knowledge — and if so, how?
- What is your goal — to answer a question? to make a point? to agree? something else?
- What tone is appropriate? If in doubt, show respect: politeness is rarely if ever inappropriate.

29d Considering your responsibility to your audience

In the United States, Canada, and Great Britain, many audiences expect a writer to get to the point as directly as possible and to articulate that point efficiently and unambiguously. But audiences in some other cultures find such writing blunt and ineffective, preferring a more subtle or indirect style. Thus, you must think carefully about whether audience members expect the writer to make the meaning of a text explicitly clear or whether the audience will take more responsibility for figuring out what is being said. You should consider what your audience members already know about the subject and look for cues about what they expect or need you to provide.

29e Considering what counts as evidence

Every writer should think carefully about how to use evidence in writing and pay attention to what counts as evidence to members of particular cultures. Are facts, concrete examples, or firsthand experience convincing to the intended audience? Is the testimony of experts weighed heavily as evidence? What people are considered trustworthy experts, and why? Will the audience value citations from religious or philosophical texts, proverbs, or everyday wisdom? Are there other sources that would be considered strong evidence? If analogies are used as support, which kinds are most powerful?

Once you determine what counts as evidence in your own thinking and writing, think about where you learned to use and value this kind of evidence. You can ask these same questions about the use of evidence by members of other cultures.

29f Considering organization

The organizational patterns that you find pleasing are likely to be deeply embedded in your own culture. Many U.S. readers expect a well-organized piece of writing to use the following structure: introduction and thesis, necessary background, overview of the parts, systematic presentation of evidence, consideration of other viewpoints, and conclusion. However, in cultures that value indirection, subtlety, or repetition, writers tend to prefer different organizational patterns. When writing for world audiences, think about how you can organize material to get your message across effectively. Consider where to state your thesis or main point (at the beginning, at the end, somewhere else, or not at all) and whether to use a straightforward organization or to employ digressions to good effect.

29g Considering style

Effective style varies broadly across cultures and depends on the rhetorical situation — purpose, audience, and so on. Even so, there is one important style question to consider when writing across cultures: what level of formality is most appropriate? In most writing to a general audience in the United

States, a fairly informal style is often acceptable, even appreciated. Many cultures, however, tend to value a more formal approach. When in doubt, err on the side of formality in writing to people from other cultures, especially to your elders or to those in authority. Use appropriate titles (*Dr. Moss, Professor Mejía*); avoid slang and informal structures, such as **sentence fragments**; use complete words and sentences (even in email); and use first names only if invited to do so.

30 Language That Builds Common Ground

The supervisor who refers to her staff as "team members" (rather than as "my staff" or as "subordinates") has chosen language intended to establish common ground with people who are important to her. Your own language can work to build common ground if you carefully consider the sensitivities and preferences of others and if you watch for words that betray your assumptions, even though you have not directly stated them.

30a Stereotypes and unstated assumptions

To some extent, we all think in terms of stereotypes, and sometimes they can be helpful in making generalizations. Stereotyping any individual on the basis of generalizations about a group, however, can lead to inaccurate and even hurtful conclusions. Careful writers want to make sure that language doesn't stereotype any group or individual.

Other unstated assumptions that enter into thinking and writing can destroy common ground by ignoring the differences between others and ourselves. For example, a student in a religion seminar who uses *we* to refer to Christians and *they* to refer to members of other religions had better be sure that everyone in the class is Christian, or some students may feel left out of the discussion.

---

 bedfordstmartins.com/easywriter For exercises, go to **Exercise Central** and click on **Language That Builds Common Ground.**

Sometimes assumptions even lead writers to call special attention to a group affiliation when it is not relevant to the point, as in *a woman bus driver, a Jewish doctor, a lesbian politician,* or *an elderly but still active homeowner.*

30b Assumptions about gender

Powerful and often invisible gender-related words affect our thinking and our behavior. Consider the traditional use of *man* and *mankind* to refer to people of both sexes and the use of *he, him, his,* and *himself* to refer to people of unknown sex. Because such usage ignores half the human race, it hardly helps a writer build common ground. Sexist language — words and **phrases** that stereotype or ignore members of either sex or that unnecessarily call attention to gender — can usually be revised fairly easily. There are several alternatives to using masculine **pronouns** to refer to persons of unknown sex:

▶ A ~~lawyer~~ Lawyers must pass the bar exam before ~~he~~ they can practice.

▶ A lawyer must pass the bar exam before he or she can practice.

▶ A lawyer must pass the bar exam before ~~he can practice~~ practicing.

Try to eliminate common sexist **nouns** from your writing.

INSTEAD OF	TRY USING
anchorman, anchorwoman	anchor
businessman	businessperson, business executive
congressman	member of Congress, representative
fireman	firefighter
male nurse	nurse
man, mankind	humans, human beings, humanity, the human race, humankind
policeman, policewoman	police officer
woman engineer	engineer

30c Assumptions about race and ethnicity

In building common ground, writers must watch for any words that ignore differences not only among individual members of a race or ethnic group but also among subgroups. Writers must be aware, for instance, of the many nations to which American Indians belong and of the diverse places from which Americans of Spanish-speaking ancestry come.

Preferred terms.   Identifying preferred terms is sometimes not an easy task, for they can change often and vary widely.

- The word *colored*, for example, was once widely used in the United States to refer to Americans of African ancestry. By the 1950s, the preferred term had become *Negro;* in the 1960s, *black* came to be preferred by most, though certainly not all, members of that community. Then, in the late 1980s, some leaders of the community urged that *black* be replaced by *African American.*

- The word *Oriental*, once used to refer to people of East Asian descent, is now often considered offensive.

- Once widely preferred, the term *Native American* is being challenged by those who argue that the most appropriate way to refer to indigenous peoples is by the specific name of the tribe or pueblo, such as *Chippewa, Crow,* or *Tlinget.* If you do not know a specific name, it's probably wise to use the term *American Indian* or *indigenous peoples.*

- Among Americans of Spanish-speaking descent, the preferred terms of reference are many: *Chicano/Chicana, Hispanic, Latin American, Latino/Latina, Mexican American, Dominican,* and *Puerto Rican,* to name but a few.

Clearly, then, ethnic terminology changes often enough to challenge even the most careful writers. The best advice may be to consider your words carefully, to listen for the way members of groups refer to themselves (or ask them their preferences), and to check in a current dictionary for any term you're unsure of.

31 Varieties of Language

English comes in many varieties that differ from one another in pronunciation, vocabulary, rhetoric, and grammar. Whether you order a hero, a poor boy, a hoagie, a submarine, a grinder, or a *cubano* reflects such differences.

31a Standard varieties of English

The variety of English often referred to as "standard" or "standard academic" is taught prescriptively in schools, represented in this and all other textbooks, used in the national media, and written and spoken widely by those wielding the most social and economic power. As the language used in business and most public institutions, standard English is a variety you will want to be completely familiar with. Standard English, however, is only one of many effective varieties of English and itself varies according to purpose and audience, from the very formal style used in academic writing to the informal style characteristic of casual conversation.

31b Ethnic varieties of English

Whether you are an American Indian or trace your ancestry to Europe, Asia, Africa, Latin America, or elsewhere, you have an ethnic heritage that probably lives on in the English language. See how one Hawaiian writer uses an ethnic variety of English to paint a picture of young teens hearing a scary "chicken skin" story about sharks from their grandmother.

> "— So, rather dan being rid of da shark, da people were stuck with many little ones, for dere mistake."
>
> Then Grandma Wong wen' pause, for dramatic effect, I guess, and she wen' add, "Dis is one of dose times. . . . Da time of da sharks."
>
> Those words ended another of Grandma's chicken skin stories. The stories she told us had been passed on to her by her grandmother, who had heard them from her grandmother. Always skipping a generation.
>
> — RODNEY MORALES, "When the Shark Bites"

Notice how the narrator uses both standard and ethnic varieties of English — presenting information necessary to the story line mostly in standard English and using a local, ethnic variety to represent spoken language, which helps us hear the characters talk.

In this example, Morales's use of local, ethnic English demonstrates that he is a member of the community whose language he is representing, a strategy that builds credibility with others in the community. Take care, however, in using the language of communities other than your own. When used inappropriately, such language can backfire, destroying your credibility and alienating your audience.

31c Occupational varieties of English

From the fast-food business to taxi driving, from art to zoology, every job has its own special variety of English. Here is an example from the computer world about how Extensible Markup Language (XML) is changing the way databases are created and making them more sophisticated:

> Most database servers are on a collision course with XML. The move to XML is a natural tie-in with a new approach to computing — deploying database-enabled Web applications running on application servers in place of stand-alone Windows programs. XML is causing database vendors to rethink their direction from the ground up, and the SQL language itself could well be on the way out in a few years, potentially to be replaced by an XML-based language called XML Query, now in development.
>
> — TIMOTHY DYCK, "Clash of the Titans"

The writer here uses technical abbreviations (*XML, SQL*) as well as ordinary words that have special meanings, such as *database-enabled*. Remember to consider your audience when you use occupational varieties of English; will everyone understand the work-related terms?

31d Regional varieties of English

Using regional language is an effective way to evoke a character or place. Look at the following piece of dialogue from an essay about Vermont:

> "There'll be some fine music on the green tonight, don't ya know?"
> "Well, I sure do want to go."
> "So don't I!"

Here, the regional English creates a homespun effect and captures the flavor of the language used in a particular place.

FOR MULTILINGUAL WRITERS

Recognizing Global Varieties of English

English is used in many countries around the world, resulting in many global varieties. You may, for example, have learned a British variety. British English differs somewhat from U.S. English in certain vocabulary (*bonnet* for *hood* of a car), syntax (*to hospital* rather than *to the hospital*), spelling (*centre* rather than *center*), and, of course, pronunciation. If you have learned a global variety of English, you will want to recognize the ways in which it differs from the U.S. standard.

32 Diction

One restaurant's *down-home beef stew with spuds* may be similar to another restaurant's *boeuf bourguignon with butter-creamed potatoes*. Both describe beef dishes, but in each case, the words say something about how the beef is prepared as well as something about the restaurant serving it. Considering diction means choosing words that are clear and appropriate for your purpose, topic, and audience.

32a Appropriate levels of formality

In an email or letter to a friend or close associate, informal language is often appropriate. For most academic and professional writing, however, more formal language is appropriate, since you are addressing people you do not know well.

EMAIL TO SOMEONE YOU KNOW WELL

Myisha is great — hire her if you can!

LETTER OF RECOMMENDATION TO SOMEONE YOU DO NOT KNOW

I am pleased to recommend Myisha Fisher. She will bring good ideas and extraordinary energy to your organization.

---

 bedfordstmartins.com/easywriter For exercises, go to **Exercise Central** and click on **Diction**.

Slang and colloquial language. Slang, or extremely informal language, is often confined to a relatively small group and changes very quickly, though some slang gains wide use (*yuppie, bummer*). Colloquial language, such as *a lot*, *in a bind*, or *snooze*, is less informal, more widely used, and longer lasting than most slang.

Writers who use slang and colloquial language run the risk of not being understood or of not being taken seriously. If you are writing for a general audience about arms-control negotiations and you use the term *nukes*, some readers may not know what you mean, and others may be irritated by what they see as a frivolous reference to a deadly serious subject.

Jargon. Jargon is the special vocabulary of a trade or profession that enables members to speak and write concisely to one another. Jargon should usually be reserved for an audience that will understand the terms.

> Conservative shares, especially those that pay dividend yields above 2.5%, have generally been strong performers over the past two years.
>
> — JEAN CHATZKY, *Money*

If Chatzky were not writing for a specialized audience (investors who read *Money* magazine), other language would be called for.

Pompous language, euphemisms, and doublespeak. Stuffy or pompous language is unnecessarily formal for the purpose, audience, or topic. It often gives writing an insincere or unintentionally humorous tone, making a writer's ideas seem insignificant or even unbelievable.

POMPOUS

▶ Pursuant to the August 9 memorandum regarding petroleum supply exigencies, it is incumbent upon us to endeavor to make maximal utilization of telephonic communication in lieu of personal visitation.

REVISED

▶ As of August 9, petroleum shortages require us to use the telephone whenever possible rather than make personal visits.

Euphemisms are words and **phrases** that make unpleasant ideas seem less harsh. *Your position is being eliminated* seeks to soften the blow of being fired or laid off. Although euphemisms can sometimes appeal to an audience by showing that you are considerate of people's feelings, they can also sound insincere or evasive.

Doublespeak is language used to hide or distort the truth. During massive layoffs in the business world, companies may describe a job-cutting policy as *employee repositioning, deverticalization,* or *rightsizing.* The public — and particularly those who lose their jobs — recognize such terms as doublespeak.

FOR MULTILINGUAL WRITERS

Avoiding Fancy Diction

In writing academic English, which is fairly formal, you may be inclined to use the biggest and newest English words that you know. Though your intention is good — to put new words to good use — resist the temptation to use flowery or high-flown diction in your college writing. Academic writing calls first of all for clear, concise prose.

32b Denotation and connotation

The words *maxim, epigram, proverb, saw, saying,* and *motto* all carry roughly the same denotation, or dictionary meaning. Because of their different connotations, however, *proverb* would be appropriate in reference to a saying from the Bible, *saw* in reference to wisdom handed down anonymously, *epigram* in reference to a witty statement.

Note the differences in connotation among the following three statements:

▶ **Students Against Racism (SAR) erected a temporary barrier on the campus oval, saying the structure symbolized "the many barriers to those discriminated against by university policies."**

▶ **Left-wing agitators threw up an eyesore right on the oval to try to stampede the university into giving in to their demands.**

▶ **Supporters of human rights for all students challenged the university's investment in racism by erecting a protest barrier on campus.**

The first statement is the most neutral, merely stating facts (and quoting the assertion about university policy to represent it as someone's opinion); the second, by using words with negative connotations (*agitators, eyesore, stampede*), is strongly critical; the third, by using words with positive connotations (*supporters of human rights*) and presenting assertions as facts (*the university's investment in racism*), gives a favorable slant to the protest.

32c General and specific diction

Effective writers balance general words (those that name groups or classes) with specific words (those that identify individual and particular things). Abstractions, which are types of general words, refer to things we cannot perceive through our five senses. Specific words are often concrete, naming things we can see, hear, touch, taste, or smell.

GENERAL	LESS GENERAL	SPECIFIC	MORE SPECIFIC
book	dictionary	abridged dictionary	my 2002 edition of the *American Heritage College Dictionary*

ABSTRACT	LESS ABSTRACT	CONCRETE	MORE CONCRETE
culture	visual art	painting	van Gogh's *Starry Night*

32d Figurative language

Figurative language, or figures of speech, paints pictures in readers' minds, allowing readers to "see" a point readily and clearly. Far from being a frill, such language is crucial to understanding.

Similes, metaphors, and analogies. Similes use *like, as, as if,* or *as though* to make explicit the comparison between two seemingly different things.

▶ **The comb felt as if it was raking my skin off.**

— MALCOLM X, "My First Conk"

Metaphors are implicit comparisons, omitting the *like, as, as if,* or *as though* of similes.

▶ **Before the pen of Jefferson etched across the pages of history the majestic words of the Declaration of Independence, we were here.**

— MARTIN LUTHER KING JR., "Letter from Birmingham Jail"

Analogies compare similar features of two dissimilar things; they explain something unfamiliar by relating it to something familiar.

▶ **The mouse genome . . . [is] the Rosetta Stone for understanding the language of life.**

— TOM FRIEND

Clichés and mixed metaphors. A cliché is an overused figure of speech, such as *busy as a bee.* By definition, we use clichés all the time, especially in speech, and many serve usefully as shorthand for familiar ideas. But if you use clichés to excess in your writing, readers may conclude that what you are saying is not very new or is even insincere.

Mixed metaphors make comparisons that are inconsistent.

▶ **The lectures were like brilliant comets streaking through the night sky,** ~~showering~~ *dazzling* **listeners with** ~~a torrential rain~~ *flashes* **of insight.**

The images of streaking light and heavy precipitation are inconsistent; in the revised sentence, all of the images relate to light.

Multilingual
Writers

Writing

Sentence
Grammar

Sentence Style

Punctuation/
Mechanics

Language

Multilingual
Writers

Research

Documentation

33 U.S. Academic Conventions

Before Xiao Ming Li, now a college teacher, first came to the United States, she had been a good writer in China — both in English and in Chinese. When she became a college student in the United States, however, she struggled to figure out what her teachers expected of her writing. Although she used appropriate words and sentence grammar, her instructors seemed to expect her to write in a whole new way. Xiao actively tackled the question of how to write effectively "U.S.A. style" by seeking help from writing-center tutors and instructors.

Of course, even the variety of English often referred to as "standard" covers a wide range of styles (see Chapter 31). But you can learn the basic style called for most often in U.S. college writing — a style based on certain expectations about what readers and writers should do.

33a Understanding expectations about readers

U.S. college instructors expect you to respond to class readings and to offer informed opinions on what the readings say. Such highly active reading may seem unusual or even impolite to you, but it shows instructors that you are engaged with the text and the class.

College instructors expect you to understand the overall content of a piece and be able to summarize it. In addition, you should understand each sentence, make connections among sentences and paragraphs, notice repeated themes or images, and figure out how the parts contribute to the entire piece. You should also go beyond content to notice organizational patterns, use of sources, and the choice of words.

As an engaged reader, you should note an author's attitude and assumptions and be able to speculate on how these may have affected the author's thinking. Be careful to

---

 bedfordstmartins.com/easywriter For sample "U.S.A. style" essays, click on **Student Writing.**

distinguish between the author's own stance and the author's reports of opposing arguments.

33b Understanding expectations about writers

Establishing authority.   In some cultures, what students write is supposed to reflect — not differ from — what they are learning. In contrast, instructors in the United States typically view students as writers who create new knowledge based on their own thinking and on what others have said. In U.S. academic writing, assume that your opinions count (as long as they are informed and thoughtful) and that your audience expects you to present them. Draw conclusions based on your reading and offer those conclusions.

You can build your authority by citing the works of others, being careful to document your sources in the appropriate style. You may be used to relying on sources without mentioning them; while that is an old and time-honored tradition in some cultures, in U.S. academic writing, it almost always results in a charge of misuse of sources or even of plagiarism. Your instructors expect you to acknowledge every source you use, even if you are only paraphrasing or summarizing it rather than quoting it directly.

Being direct.   U.S. college instructors usually expect you to get to your main point quickly and to be direct throughout a paper. U.S. academic writing prepares readers for what is coming next, provides definitions, and includes topic sentences.

To achieve directness in your writing, avoid overqualifying your statements — instead of saying *I think the facts reveal,* come right out and say *The facts reveal.* Avoid digressions and be sure that any anecdote relates directly to your main point. Make your **transitions** from point to point obvious and clear, and make sure that the first **sentence** of a new paragraph reaches back to the paragraph before and then looks forward to what is to come. Sometimes you may want to use summary statements between sections, especially if your paper is longer than two or three pages.

34 Nouns and Articles

Everyday life is filled with **nouns**: orange *juice*, the morning *news*, a *bus* to work, *meetings*, *pizza*, *email*, *Diet Coke*, *errands*, *dinner* with *friends*, a *chapter* in a good *book*. No matter what your first language is, it includes nouns. In English, **articles** (*a* book, *an* email, *the* news) often accompany nouns.

34a Count and noncount nouns

Nouns in English can be either **count nouns** or **noncount nouns**. Count nouns refer to distinct individuals or things that can be directly counted: *a doctor, an egg, a child; doctors, eggs, children.* Noncount nouns refer to masses, collections, or ideas that cannot be directly counted: *milk, rice, courage.* They can be quantified only broadly or with a preceding **phrase**: *a glass of milk, three grains of rice, a little courage.*

Count nouns usually have **singular** and **plural** forms: *tree, trees.* Noncount nouns usually have only a singular form: *grass.*

COUNT	NONCOUNT
people (plural of *person*)	humanity
tables, chairs, beds	furniture
letters	mail
pebbles	gravel
suggestions	advice

Some nouns can be either count or noncount, depending on meaning.

COUNT   Before video games, children played with *marbles.*

NONCOUNT   The palace floor was made of *marble.*

When you learn a noun in English, you need to learn whether it is count, noncount, or both. Print and online resources such as the *Cambridge Advanced Learner's Dictionary*, the *Oxford Advanced Learner's Dictionary*, the *Collins Cobuild English Dictionary*, Dave's ESL Café

⊙ bedfordstmartins.com/easywriter For exercises, go to **Exercise Central** and click on **Nouns and Articles.**

(www.eslcafe.com), ESL go.com (www.eslgo.com), ESLflow (www.eslflow.com), or English-Zone.com (www.english-zone.com) can help.

34b Articles

The **definite article** *the* and the **indefinite articles** *a* and *an* can be challenging to multilingual speakers. Many languages have nothing directly comparable to them, and languages that do have articles differ from English in the details of their use.

Using *the*. Use the definite article *the* with nouns whose identity is known or is about to be made known to readers. The necessary information for identification can come from the **noun phrase** itself, from elsewhere in the text, from context, from general knowledge, or from a **superlative**.

▶ Let's meet at ^{the}fountain in front of Dwinelle Hall.

> The phrase *in front of Dwinelle Hall* identifies the specific fountain.

▶ A fire that started in a restaurant spread to a toy store.
  ~~Store~~ The store was saved, although it suffered water damage.

> The word *store* is preceded by *the,* which directs our attention to the previous sentence, where the store is identified.

▶ She asked him to shut ^{the}door when he left her office.

> The context indicates that she is referring to her office door.

▶ ~~Pope~~ The pope is expected to visit Africa in October.

> Since there is never more than one living pope, his identity is clear.

▶ Will is now ^{the}best singer in the choir.

> The superlative *best* identifies the noun *singer.*

Using *a* or *an*. Use the indefinite articles *a* and *an* only with singular count nouns. Use *a* before a consonant sound: *a car.* Use *an* before a vowel sound: *an uncle.* Pay attention to sounds rather than to spelling: *a house, an hour, a university.*

    A or *an* tells readers they do not have enough information to identify what the noun refers to. Compare the following sentences:

▸ I need *a* new *parka* for the winter.

▸ I saw *a parka* that I liked, but it wasn't heavy enough.

The parka in the first sentence is hypothetical. Since it is indefinite to the writer, it is indefinite to the reader and is used with *a*, not *the*. The second sentence refers to a specific, actual parka, but since the writer cannot expect the reader to know which one, it is used with *a* rather than *the*.

    If you want to speak of an indefinite quantity rather than an indefinite thing, use *some* with a noncount noun or a plural count noun.

▸ This stew needs *some* more *salt*.

▸ I saw *some plates* that I liked at the department store.

No article.   Noncount and plural count nouns can be used without an article to make generalizations:

▸ In this world nothing is certain but *death* and *taxes*.

— BENJAMIN FRANKLIN

Franklin refers not to a particular death or specific taxes but to death and taxes in general, so no article is used with *death* or with *taxes*.

    English differs from many other languages — Greek, Spanish, and German, for example — that use the definite article to make generalizations. In English, a sentence like *The ants live in colonies* can refer only to particular, identifiable ants, not to ants in general.

35   Verbs and Verb Phrases

When we must act, **verbs** tell us what to do — from the street signs that say *stop* or *yield* to email commands such as *send* or *delete*. If you speak Russian or Arabic, you might not find anything wrong with the **sentence** *Where Main Street?* But unlike sentences in those and many other languages, English sentences must have a verb: *Where is Main Street?*

35a Verb phrases

Verb phrases can be built up out of a **main verb** and one or more **auxiliary verbs**, such as *My cat is drinking milk* or *My cat has been drinking milk*. Verb phrases have strict rules of order. If you try to rearrange the words in these sentences, you will find that most alternatives are impossible. You cannot say, for example, *My cat has drinking been milk*.

AUXILIARY AND MAIN VERBS. In *My cat may have been drinking milk*, the main verb *drinking* is preceded by three auxiliaries: *may, have,* and *been. May* is a **modal**, which must be followed by a **base form** (*have*). *Have* indicates a **perfect tense**, and it must be followed by a **past participle** (*been*). *Been* (or any other form of *be*), when it is followed by a **present participle** (such as *drinking*), indicates a **progressive tense**. When a form of *be* is followed by a past participle, as in *My cat may have been bitten by a dog,* it indicates **passive voice** (7e).

Auxiliaries must be in the following order: modal + perfect *have* + progressive *be* + passive *be*. Note that few sentences use all of these auxiliaries.

       MOD   PERF   PROG MAIN

▸ Sonya *must have been studying* for the test today.

Only one modal is permitted in a verb phrase.

          will be able to speak
▸ Soon she ~~will can speak~~ Czech quite well.
          ^

Every time you use an auxiliary, you should be careful to put the next word in the appropriate form.

Modal + base form. Use the base form of the verb after the modals *can, could, will, would, shall, should, may, might,*

---

 bedfordstmartins.com/easywriter For exercises, go to **Exercise Central** and click on **Verbs and Verb Phrases.**

and *must*: *Alice <u>can read</u> Latin.* In many other languages, modals like *can* or *must* are followed by the **infinitive** (*to* + base form). Do not substitute an infinitive for the base form in English.

▶ **Alice can ~~to~~ read Latin.**

PERFECT *HAVE, HAS,* OR *HAD* + PAST PARTICIPLE. To form the perfect tenses, use *have, has,* or *had* with a past participle: *Everyone <u>has gone</u> home. They <u>have been</u> working all day.*

PROGRESSIVE *BE* + PRESENT PARTICIPLE. A progressive form of the verb is signaled by two elements, a form of the auxiliary *be* (*am, is, are, was, were, be,* or *been*) and the *-ing* form of the next word: *The children are studying.* Be sure to include both elements.

▶ **The children ^{are} studying science.**
     ^

▶ **The children are ~~study~~ ^{studying} science.**
                      ^

Some verbs are rarely used in progressive forms. These are verbs that express unchanging conditions or mental states rather than deliberate actions: *believe, belong, hate, know, like, love, need, own, resemble, understand.*

PASSIVE *BE* + PAST PARTICIPLE. Use *am, is, are, was, were, being, be,* or *been* with a past participle to form the passive voice.

▶ **Tagalog *is spoken* in the Philippines.**

Notice that the word following the progressive *be* (the present participle) ends in *-ing,* but the word following the passive *be* (the past participle) never ends in *-ing.*

PROGRESSIVE   Meredith *is* <u>studying</u> music.

PASSIVE   Natasha *was* <u>taught</u> by a famous violinist.

If the first auxiliary in a verb phrase is a form of *be* or *have,* it must show either present or past tense and must agree with the subject: *Meredith has played in an orchestra.*

Notice that a modal auxiliary never changes form to agree with the subject.

▶ Michiko ~~cans~~ play two instruments.
   ‸ *can*

35b Infinitives and gerunds

Knowing whether to use an infinitive (*to read*) or a **gerund** (*reading*) in a sentence may be a challenge to multilingual writers.

INFINITIVE

▶ My adviser urged me *to apply* to several colleges.

GERUND

▶ Her *writing* a strong letter of recommendation made a big difference.

In general, infinitives tend to represent intentions, desires, or expectations, while gerunds tend to represent facts. The infinitive in the first sentence conveys the message that the act of applying was desired but not yet accomplished, while the gerund in the second sentence calls attention to the fact that a letter was actually written.

The association of intention with infinitives and facts with gerunds can often help you decide whether to use an infinitive or a gerund when another verb immediately precedes it.

INFINITIVES

▶ Kumar *expected to get* a good job after graduation.

▶ Last year, Fatima *decided to become* a math major.

▶ The strikers have *agreed to go* back to work.

GERUNDS

▶ Jerzy *enjoys going* to the theater.

▶ We *resumed working* after our coffee break.

▶ Kim *appreciated getting* candy from Sean.

A few verbs can be followed by either an infinitive or a gerund. With some, such as *begin* and *continue,* the choice makes little difference in meaning. With others, however, the difference in meaning is striking.

▶ **Carlos was working as a medical technician, but he** *stopped to study* **English.**

The infinitive indicates that Carlos left his job because he intended to study English.

▶ **Carlos** *stopped studying* **English when he left the United States.**

The gerund indicates that Carlos actually studied English but then stopped.

The distinction between fact and intention is a tendency, not a rule, and other rules may override it. Always use a gerund — not an infinitive — directly following a **preposition**.

▶ **This fruit is safe for** ~~to eat.~~
                              eating.
                              ^

You can also remove the preposition and keep the infinitive.

▶ **This fruit is safe** ~~for~~ **to eat.**

35c Conditional sentences

English distinguishes among many different types of conditional sentences — sentences that focus on questions of truth or likelihood and that are introduced by *if* or its equivalent. Each of the following examples makes different assumptions about the likelihood that what is stated in the *if* **clause** is true; each then draws the corresponding conclusion in the **main clause.**

▶ **If you** *practice* **(or** *have practiced***) writing often, you** *learn* **(or** *have learned***) what your main problems are.**

This sentence assumes that what is stated in the *if* clause may well be true; the alternatives in parentheses indicate that any tense that is appropriate in a simple sentence may be used in both the *if* clause and the main clause.

▶ **If you *practice* writing for the rest of this term, you *will* (or *may*) understand the process better.**

This sentence makes a prediction and again assumes that what is stated may well turn out to be true. Only the main clause uses the future tense (*will understand*) or some other modal that can indicate future time (*may understand*). The *if* clause must use the present tense, even though it too refers to the future.

▶ **If you *practiced* (or *were to practice*) writing every day, it *would* eventually *seem* easier.**

This sentence indicates doubt that what is stated will be put into effect. In the *if* clause, the verb is either past — actually, past subjunctive (see 7f) — or *were to* + the base form, though it refers to future time. The main clause contains *would* + the base form of the main verb.

▶ **If you *practiced* writing on Mars, you *would find* no one to read your work.**

This sentence considers an impossibility for now and the foreseeable future. Again, the past subjunctive is used in the *if* clause, although past time is not being referred to, and *would* + the base form is used in the main clause.

▶ **If you *had practiced* writing in ancient Egypt, you *would have used* hieroglyphics.**

This sentence shifts the impossibility back to the past; obviously you will never find yourself in ancient Egypt. But since past forms have been used in the preceding two situations, this one demands a form that is "more past": the past perfect in the *if* clause and *would* + the present perfect form of the main verb in the main clause.

---

36 Prepositions and Prepositional Phrases

If you were traveling by rail and asked for directions, it would not be helpful to be told to "take the Chicago train." You would need to know whether to take the train *to*

Chicago or the one *from* Chicago. Words such as *to* and *from,* which show the relations between other words, are **prepositions**. Not all languages use prepositions to show such relations, and English differs from other languages in the way prepositions are used.

36a Using the right preposition

Even if you usually know where to use prepositions, you may have difficulty from time to time knowing which preposition to use. Each of the most common prepositions, whether in English or in other languages, has a wide range of different applications, and this range never coincides exactly from one language to another. See, for example, how English speakers use *in* and *on.*

▶ The peaches are *in* the refrigerator.

▶ The peaches are *on* the table.

▶ Is that a diamond ring *on* your finger?

The Spanish translations of these sentences all use the same preposition (*en*), a fact that might lead you astray in English.

There is no easy solution to the challenge of using English prepositions idiomatically, but a few strategies can make it less troublesome.

Know typical examples. The **object** of the preposition *in* is often a container that encloses something; the object of the preposition *on* is often a horizontal surface that supports something touching it.

IN The peaches are *in* the refrigerator.

There are still some pickles *in* the jar.

ON The peaches are *on* the table.

---

 bedfordstmartins.com/easywriter For exercises, go to **Exercise Central** and click on **Prepositions and Prepositional Phrases.**

Learn related examples. Prepositions that are not used in typical ways may still show some similarities to typical examples.

IN   You shouldn't drive *in* a snowstorm.

Like a container, the falling snow surrounds and seems to enclose the driver.

ON   Is that a diamond ring *on* your finger?

A finger is not a horizontal surface, but it supports a ring that touches it.

Use your imagination. Create mental images that can help you remember figurative uses of prepositions.

IN   Michael is *in* love.

Imagine a warm bath — or a raging torrent — in which Michael is immersed.

ON   I've just read a book *on* computer science.

Imagine the book sitting on a shelf labeled "Computer Science."

Learn prepositions as part of a system. In identifying the location of a place or an event, the three prepositions *in, on,* and *at* can be used. *At* specifies the exact point in space or time; *in* is required for expanses of space or time within which a place is located or an event takes place; and *on* must be used with the names of streets (but not exact addresses) and with days of the week or month.

AT   There will be a meeting tomorrow *at* 9:30 AM
             at 160 Main Street.

IN   I arrived *in* the United States *in* January.

ON   The airline's office is *on* Fifth Avenue.

             I'll be moving to my new apartment *on* September 30.

36b Using two-word verbs

Some words that look like prepositions do not always function as prepositions. Consider the following sentences:

▶ The balloon rose *off* the ground.

▶ The plane took *off* without difficulty.

In the first sentence, *off* is a preposition that introduces the **prepositional phrase** *off the ground.* In the second sentence, *off* neither functions as a preposition nor introduces a prepositional phrase. Instead, it combines with *took* to form a two-word **verb** with its own meaning. Such a verb is called a **phrasal verb**, and the word *off*, when used in this way, is called an **adverbial particle**. Many prepositions can function as particles to form phrasal verbs.

The verb + particle combination that makes up a phrasal verb is a tightly knit entity that cannot usually be torn apart.

▶ The plane took *off* without difficulty. ~~off.~~

Exceptions include some phrasal verbs that are **transitive**, meaning that they take a **direct object**. Some of these verbs have particles that may be separated from the verb by the object.

▶ I *picked up my baggage* at the terminal.

▶ I *picked my baggage up* at the terminal.

If a **personal pronoun** is used as the direct object, it *must* separate the verb from its particle.

▶ I picked up *it* ~~it~~ at the terminal.

In some idiomatic two-word verbs, the second word is a preposition. With such verbs, the preposition can never be separated from the verb.

▶ We *ran into* our neighbor on the train. [not *ran our neighbor into*]

The combination *run + into* has a special meaning (find by chance). Therefore, *run into* is a two-word verb and *ran our neighbor into* is unacceptable.

37 Sentence Structure

Sound bites surround us, from Nike's "Just do it" to the "Got Milk?" ad campaign. These short, simple **sentences** may be memorable, but they don't tell us very much. Ordinarily, we need more elaborate sentences to convey meaning. English sentences are put together in particular ways that may differ from sentence patterns in other languages.

37a Expressing subjects and objects explicitly

With few exceptions, English demands that an explicit **subject** accompany an explicit **predicate** in every sentence. Though you might write *Went from Yokohama to Nagoya* on a postcard, in most varieties of spoken and written English, you must explicitly state who went.

In fact, every **dependent clause** must have an explicit subject.

▸ They took the Acela Express to Boston because $\overset{it}{\underset{\wedge}{was}}$

fast.

English even requires a kind of "dummy" subject to fill the subject position in certain kinds of sentences:

▸ *It* is raining.

▸ *There* is a strong wind.

Speakers of some languages, such as Spanish, might be inclined to leave out dummy subjects. In English, however, *it* and *there* are indispensable.

▸ $\overset{It\ is}{\underset{\wedge}{\text{Is}}}$ raining.

▸ $\overset{There\ is}{\underset{\wedge}{\text{Has}}}$ a strong wind.

---

 bedfordstmartins.com/easywriter For exercises, go to **Exercise Central** and click on **Clauses and Sentences**.

Transitive verbs typically require that **objects** — and sometimes other information — also be explicitly stated. It is not enough to say *Tell!* even if it is clear what is to be told to whom. You must say, for example, *Tell me the story* or *Tell her your name.*

37b Keeping words in appropriate order

In general, you should not move subjects, **verbs**, or objects out of their normal positions in a sentence. In the following sentence, each element is in an appropriate place:

```
SUBJECT VERB OBJECT    ADVERB
  |     |    |          |
```
▶ Mario left Venice reluctantly.

This sentence would also be acceptable as *Mario reluctantly left Venice* or as *Reluctantly, Mario left Venice,* but note that only the **adverb** can be moved.

If you speak Turkish, Korean, Japanese, or another language in which the verb must come last, you should make a special effort not to write such a sentence as *Mario Venice reluctantly left,* which is not acceptable in English.

If you speak Russian or another language that permits a great deal of freedom in word order, you must remember never to interchange the position of subject and object (*Venice left Mario reluctantly* is not acceptable English). In general, also avoid separating the verb from its object (*Mario left reluctantly Venice*).

Research

Writing

Sentence
Grammar

Sentence Style

Punctuation/
Mechanics

Language

Multilingual
Writers

Research

Documentation

38 Conducting Research

Your employer asks you to recommend the best software for a project. You need to plan a week's stay in Tokyo. Your instructor assigns a term project about a musician. Each of these situations calls for research, for examining various kinds of sources — and each calls for you to assess the data you collect, synthesize your findings, and come up with an original recommendation or conclusion. Many tasks that call for research require that your work culminate in a written document that refers to and lists the sources you used.

38a Beginning the research process

For academic research assignments, once you have a topic, you need to move as efficiently as possible to analyze the research assignment, articulate a research question to answer, and form a hypothesis. Then, after preliminary research, you can refine your hypothesis into a working thesis and begin your research in earnest.

Considering the context for a research project. Ask yourself what the *purpose* of the project is — perhaps to describe, survey, analyze, persuade, explain, classify, compare, or contrast. Then consider your *audience*. Who will be most interested, and what will they need to know? What assumptions might they hold? What response do you want from them?

You should also examine your own *stance* or *attitude* toward your topic. Do you feel curious, critical, confused, or some other way about it? What influences have shaped your stance?

For a research project, consider how many and what *kinds of sources* you need to find. What kinds of evidence will convince your audience? What visuals — charts, photographs, and so on — might you need? Would it help to do field research, such as interviews, surveys, or observations?

Finally, consider practical matters, such as how long your project will be, how much time it will take, and when it is due.

Formulating a research question and hypothesis. After analyzing your project's context, work from your general topic to a research question and a hypothesis.

TOPIC	Farming
NARROWED TOPIC	Small family farms in the United States
ISSUE	Making a living from a small family farm
RESEARCH QUESTION	How can small family farms in the United States successfully compete with big agriculture?
HYPOTHESIS	Small family farmers can succeed by growing specialty products that consumers want and by participating in farmers' markets and community-supported agriculture programs that forge relationships with customers.

After you have explored sources to test your hypothesis and sharpened it by reading, writing, and talking with others, you can refine it into a working thesis.

WORKING THESIS	Although recent data show that small family farms are more endangered than ever, some enterprising farmers have reversed the trend by growing specialized products and connecting with consumers through farmers' markets and community-supported agriculture programs.

Planning research. Once you have formulated a hypothesis, determine what you already know about your topic and try to remember where you got your information. Consider the kinds of sources you expect to consult and the number you think you will need, how current they should be, and where you might find them.

38b Kinds of sources

Keep in mind some important differences among types of sources.

Print versus Internet sources. Some Internet sources are electronic versions of printed texts, but most Internet sources do not have a print equivalent. Why is this distinction important? If you use a scholarly book or journal — probably published first in print and then online — you can be fairly sure that the text was sent out to experts for review before it was published. Many other print publishers also obtain reviews or check facts before publication. However, for most materials published only on the Internet, reviewing and editorial oversight depend solely on the author of the text. As a result, you need to know whether a source exists only in electronic form and, if so, how much you can trust it.

Also, Internet sources are generally less stable than print sources. Since such sources can easily be changed or deleted, make a copy (either print or electronic) so that you have a record of the original.

Since most print sources do not exist online and vice versa, be careful not to limit the type of research you do. If you use only Internet sources, for example, you will miss out on valuable sources available only in print.

Primary versus secondary sources. Another difference in sources is between primary sources, or firsthand knowledge, and secondary sources, information available from the research of others. Primary sources are basic sources of raw information, including experiments, surveys, or interviews you conduct; notes from your field research; objects of art you examine; literary works you read; and eyewitness accounts, photographs, news reports, and historical documents. Secondary sources are descriptions or interpretations of primary sources, such as researchers' reports, book reviews, and biographies. Most research projects draw on both primary and secondary sources.

Scholarly versus popular sources. While nonacademic sources like popular magazines can help you get started on a research project, you will generally want to depend more on authorities in a field, whose work usually appears in scholarly journals. The following lists of features will help you distinguish scholarly journals from popular magazines:

SCHOLARLY	POPULAR
Cover may list contents of issue	Cover features a color picture
Title often contains the word *Journal*	*Journal* usually does not appear in title
Source found at the library	Source found at grocery stores, newsstands, and so on
Few commercial advertisements	Lots of advertisements
Authors identified with academic credentials	Authors are journalists or reporters, not experts
Summary or abstract appears on first page of article; articles are fairly long	No summary or abstract; articles are fairly short
Articles have bibliographies	No bibliographies included

Older versus current sources.   Most research projects can benefit from both older, historical sources and more current ones. However, if you are examining a recent scientific discovery, you will want to depend primarily on contemporary sources.

38c Kinds of searches

Even when you have a general idea of what kinds of sources exist and which kinds you need for your research project, you still have to locate these sources. The library and the Internet give you a variety of search options.

Online library resource searches.   Your library's computers hold resources that are accessible to students only through the library's system. Most college libraries subscribe to databases — electronic collections of information, such as indexes to journal and magazine articles, texts of news stories and legal cases, lists of sources on particular topics, and compilations of statistics — that students can access for free. Many of these databases — such as Lexis-Nexis, *MLA Bibliography,* and ERIC — have been screened or compiled by scholars.

Catalog and database searches.   Library catalogs and databases usually index their contents not only by author and title but also by subject heading. When you search by subject, you need to use the exact subject words. (For books, most libraries use the Library of Congress Subject Headings, or LCSH.) When you search using **keywords**, on the other hand, you can search for any term in any field of the electronic record. Keyword searching is less restrictive, but it requires you to choose your search terms carefully to get the best results.

Internet searches.   Most Internet search tools, such as Yahoo! and Google, allow you to search for sources using either subject categories or keywords. A subject directory allows you to choose a broad category like "Art" and then to click on increasingly narrow categories like "Movies" or "Thrillers" until you reach a point where you are given a list of Web sites or the opportunity to do a keyword search. The second option, a search engine, allows you to start right off with a keyword search. Because the Internet contains more material than even the largest library catalog or database, using a search engine requires even more care in the choice of keywords.

38d Library resources

The library — including the staff, especially reference librarians — can be one of a researcher's best friends. Your college library houses a great number of print materials and gives you access to electronic catalogs and databases. To learn about your library, visit its Web site; make an appointment with a librarian; or participate in a tour, tutorial, or workshop.

Consulting reference works.   Consulting general reference works is a good way to get an overview of a topic, to identify subtopics, to find more specialized sources, and to identify useful keywords for electronic searches. Researchers often consult encyclopedias; biographical resources; and almanacs, yearbooks, news digests, and atlases.

Using the library catalog. The library catalog lists all of the library's books, periodical holdings, and subscriptions. Most libraries have an electronic catalog you can access easily. Besides identifying a book's author, title, subject, and publication information, each catalog entry also lists a call number — the book's identification number. Once you have printed out the catalog entry for the book or written down the call number, look for a library map or shelving plan to tell you where your book is housed. Browse through the books around the area for other items related to your topic.

Using indexes. Various indexes can help you locate information about books, reviews, or periodicals.

- Book indexes (such as *Books in Print* and *Cumulative Book Index*) can help you locate complete bibliographic information on a book when you know only a piece of it, such as the author's last name or the title, and can alert you to other works by an author or on a particular subject.

- Review indexes (such as *Book Review Digest* and *Index to Book Reviews in the Humanities*) allow you to check the relevance of a source or get an overview of its contents.

- Periodical indexes are guides to articles published in newspapers, magazines, and scholarly journals. General indexes of periodicals list articles from general-interest magazines (such as *Time*), newspapers, or a combination of these. Specialized indexes — which often list articles in scholarly journals — and abstracts help researchers find detailed information. Most of these indexes are now available as electronic databases.

38e Internet research

It's possible to find any and all information on the Web, from scholarly articles to banal statements to outright misinformation, so use information from the Web with great care.

Using Web browsers. Web browsers, such as Netscape Navigator and Internet Explorer, give you access to powerful search tools but also provide help in organizing and keeping track of your research. You can track your searches over more than one session by finding out how to use the browser's HISTORY function, which will help you retrace your steps to a source. Save the URLs for sites you want to return to by using the BOOKMARK (in Netscape) or FAVORITES (in Internet Explorer) function.

Using keywords, Boolean operators, and quotation marks. Using a search engine can result in millions of "hits" if you don't choose your keywords — names, titles, concepts — carefully. Most search engines offer options (sometimes on a separate advanced-search page) for narrowing searches. These options let you combine keywords, search for an exact phrase, or exclude items containing particular keywords.

Many library catalogs and some search engines also allow you to refine your search using the **Boolean operators** *AND, NOT,* and *OR* as well as parentheses and quotation marks. The Boolean operators work this way:

- **AND** LIMITS YOUR SEARCH. If you enter the terms *Hollywood AND heroes*, the search engine will retrieve only those items that contain both those terms.

- **NOT** ALSO LIMITS YOUR SEARCH. If you enter the terms *Hollywood NOT heroes*, the search tool will retrieve every item that contains *Hollywood* except those that also contain the term *heroes*.

- **OR** EXPANDS YOUR SEARCH. If you enter the terms *Hollywood OR heroes*, the search tool will retrieve every item that contains the term *Hollywood* and every item that contains the term *heroes*.

- **PARENTHESES CUSTOMIZE YOUR SEARCH FURTHER.** Entering *Oscar AND (Halle Berry OR Morgan Freeman)*, for example, will locate items that mention either of those actors in connection with the Academy Awards.

You can also place quotation marks around a phrase to narrow your search; they indicate that all the words in the phrase must appear together in that exact order.

Online discussion. The Internet allows you to find and communicate with groups of people who share your research interest — be it organic farming or heroes in the movies. Such interest groups can be found through listservs (also called discussion lists) or Usenet newsgroups. To make citing the source easier, always use archived versions of postings to such lists when available.

38f Field research

For many research projects, you will need to collect field data. Consider *where* you can find relevant information, *how* to gather it, and *who* might be your best providers of information.

Interviews. Some information is best obtained by asking direct questions of other people. If you can talk with an expert — in person, on the telephone, or via the Internet — you may get information you cannot obtain through any other kind of research.

1. Determine your exact purpose, and be sure it relates to your research question and your hypothesis.
2. Set up the interview well in advance. Specify how long it will take, and if you wish to tape-record the session, ask permission to do so.
3. Prepare a written list of factual and open-ended questions. If the interview proceeds in a direction that seems fruitful, do not feel that you have to ask all of your prepared questions.
4. Record the subject, date, time, and place of the interview.
5. Thank those you interview, either in person or in a letter or email.

Observation. Trained observers report that making a faithful record of an observation requires intense concentration and mental agility.

1. Determine the purpose of the observation, and be sure it relates to your research question and hypothesis.
2. Brainstorm about what you are looking for, but don't be rigidly bound to your expectations.
3. Develop an appropriate system for recording data. Consider using a split notebook or page: on one side, record your observations directly; on the other, record your thoughts or interpretations.
4. Record the date, time, and place of observation.

Opinion surveys. Surveys usually depend on questionnaires. On any questionnaire, the questions should be clear and easy to understand and designed so that you can analyze the answers easily. Questions that ask respondents to say *yes* or *no* or to rank items on a scale are particularly easy to tabulate.

1. Write out your purpose, and determine the kinds of questions to ask.

2. Figure out how to reach respondents.
3. Draft questions that call for short, specific answers.
4. Test the questions on several people, and revise questions that seem unfair, ambiguous, or too hard or time consuming.
5. For a questionnaire that is to be mailed, draft a cover letter. Provide an addressed, stamped return envelope, and be sure to state a deadline.
6. On the final version of the questionnaire, leave adequate space for answers.
7. Proofread the questionnaire carefully.

39 Evaluating Sources and Taking Notes

All research builds on the careful and sometimes inspired use of sources — that is, on research done by others. Since you want the information you glean from sources to be reliable and persuasive, you must evaluate each potential source carefully.

39a Evaluating the usefulness and credibility of potential sources

Use these guidelines to assess the usefulness of a source.

- YOUR PURPOSE. What will this source add to your research project? Does it help you support a major point, demonstrate that you have thoroughly researched your topic, or help establish your own credibility through its authority?

- RELEVANCE. Is the source closely related to your research question? You may need to read beyond the title and opening paragraph to check for relevance.

- PUBLISHER'S CREDENTIALS. What do you know about the publisher of the source you are using? For example, is it a major newspaper known for integrity in reporting, or is it a tabloid? Is it a popular magazine or a journal sponsored by a professional or scholarly organization?

- AUTHOR'S CREDENTIALS. Is the author an expert on the topic? An author's credentials may be presented in the article,

bedfordstmartins.com/easywriter For additional help, click on **The St. Martin's Tutorial on Avoiding Plagiarism.** For tips on working with quotations, paraphrases, and summaries, click on **Taking Notes.**

book, or Web site, or you can search the Internet for information on the author.

- **DATE OF PUBLICATION.** Recent sources are often more useful than older ones, particularly in the sciences. However, in some fields, the most authoritative works may be the older ones. The publication dates of Internet sites can often be difficult to pin down. And even for sites that include the dates of posting, remember that the material posted may have been composed some time earlier. Most reliable will be those sites that regularly list the dates of updating.

- **ACCURACY OF SOURCE.** How accurate and complete is the information in the source? How thorough is the bibliography or list of works cited that accompanies the source? Can you find other sources that corroborate what your source is saying?

- **STANCE OF SOURCE.** Identify the source's point of view or stance on the issue(s) involved, and scrutinize it carefully. What does the author or sponsoring group want to make happen — to convince you of an idea? sell you something? call you to action in some way?

- **CROSS-REFERENCING.** Is the source cited in other works? If you see your source cited by others, looking at how they cite it and what they say about it can provide additional clues to its credibility. For Web sources, check for links to other sources. How reliable and credible are these other sources?

- **LEVEL OF SPECIALIZATION.** General sources can be helpful as you begin your research, but you may then need the authority or currentness of more specialized sources. On the other hand, extremely specialized works may be very hard to understand.

- **AUDIENCE OF SOURCE.** Was the source written for the general public? specialists? advocates or opponents?

As you look at potential sources, be sure to evaluate Internet sources with special scrutiny. Remember that much of the material on the Internet does not go through an editorial or review process. For more on evaluating sources, see the source maps on pp. 178–181.

39b Reading and interpreting sources

As you read and take notes on your sources, keep in mind that you will need to present data and sources to other readers so that they can understand the point you are making.

(continued on p. 182)

SOURCE MAP EVALUATING ARTICLES

Determine the relevance of the source.

1 Look for an abstract, which provides a summary of the entire article. Is this source directly related to your research? Does it provide useful information and insights? Will your readers consider it persuasive support for your thesis?

Determine the credibility of the publication.

2 Consider the publication's title. Words in the title such as *Journal, Review,* and *Quarterly* may indicate that the periodical is a scholarly source. Most research projects rely on authorities in a particular field, whose work usually appears in scholarly journals. For more on distinguishing between scholarly and popular sources, see 38b.

3 Try to determine the publisher or sponsor. This journal is published by Johns Hopkins University Press. Academic presses such as this one generally review articles carefully before publishing them and bear the authority of their academic sponsors.

Determine the credibility of the author.

4 Evaluate the author's credentials. In this case, they are given in a note, which indicates that the author is a college professor and has written at least two books on related topics.

Determine the currency of the article.

5 Look at the publication date and think about whether your topic and your credibility depend on your use of very current sources.

Determine the accuracy of the article.

6 Look at the sources cited by the author of the article. Here, they are documented in footnotes. Ask yourself whether the works the author has cited seem credible and current. Are any of these works cited in other articles you've considered?

In addition, consider the following questions:

- What is the article's stance or point of view? What are the author's goals? What does the author want you to know or believe?

- How does this source fit in with your other sources? Does any of the information it provides contradict or challenge other sources?

HUMAN RIGHTS QUARTERLY

2

Prisons and Politics in Contemporary Latin America

Mark Ungar*

ABSTRACT

Despite democratization throughout Latin America, massive human rights abuses continue in the region's prisons. Conditions have become so bad that most governments have begun to enact improvements, including new criminal codes and facility decongestion. However, once in place, these reforms are undermined by chaotic criminal justice systems, poor policy administration, and rising crime rates leading to greater detention powers for the police. After describing current prison conditions in Latin America and the principal reforms to address them, this article explains how political and administrative limitations hinder the range of agencies and officials responsible for implementing those changes.

I. INTRODUCTION

Prison conditions not only constitute some of the worst human rights violations in contemporary Latin American democracies, but also reveal fundamental weaknesses in those democracies. Unlike most other human rights problems, those in the penitentiary system cannot be easily explained with authoritarian legacies or renegade officials. The systemic killing, overcrowding, disease, torture, rape, corruption, and due process abuses all occur under the state's twenty-four hour watch. Since the mid-1990s,

* *Mark Ungar* is Associate Professor of Political Science at Brooklyn College, City University of New York. Recent publications include the books *Elusive Reform: Democracy and the Rule of Law in Latin America* (Lynne Rienner, 2002) and *Violence and Politics: Globalization's Paradox* (Routledge, 2001) as well as articles and book chapters on democratization, policing, and judicial access. He works with Amnesty International USA and local rights groups in Latin America.

Human Rights Quarterly 25 (2003) 909–934 © 2003 by The Johns Hopkins University Press

5

4

915

...la, the ...ped to ...ency in ...ar from ...humber ...s form ...)—with ...he riots ...gan in ...spread ...he PCC ...eaders. ...security ...ordable ..., some ...r airless ...iving in ...e in the ...cility of ...ntra el ...cells of ...water, ...ats and ...eapons ...ne and ...officials, ...uard in ...bution. ...otesting ...hy of El

...4).
...997.
...rison (19
...n La Paz

...e as high
...ate house
three or four, says the prisons "are collapsing" because of insufficient budgets to train personnel. "Things fall apart and stay that way." Interview, Luis A. Lara Roche, Warden of Retén de la Planta, Caracas, Venezuela, 19 May 1995. At El Dorado prison in Bolívar state, there is one bed for every four inmates, cells are infested with vermin, and inmates lack clean bathing water and eating utensils.

14. *La Crisis Penitenciaria*, El Nacional (Caracas), 2 Sept. 1988, at D2. On file with author.

6

Determine the credibility of the sponsoring organization.

1 Consider the URL, specifically the top-level domain name. (For example, *.edu* may indicate that the sponsor is an accredited college or university; *.org* may indicate it's a nonprofit organization.) Ask yourself whether such a sponsor might be biased about the topic you're researching.

2 Look for an *About* page or a link to the homepage for background information on the sponsor, including a mission statement. What is the sponsoring organization's stance or point of view? Does the mission statement seem biased or balanced? Does the sponsor seem to take other points of view into account? What is the intended purpose of the site? Is this site meant to inform? Or is it trying to persuade, advertise, or accomplish something else?

Determine the credibility of the author.

3 Evaluate the author's credentials. On this Web page, the author's professional affiliation is indicated in his email address, but other information about him isn't provided. You will often have to look elsewhere — such as at other sites on the Web — to find out more about an author. When you do, ask yourself if the author seems qualified to write about the topic.

Determine the currency of the Web source.

4 Look for the date that indicates when the information was posted or last updated. Here, the date is given at the beginning of the press release.

5 Check to see if the sources referred to are also up to date. This author cites sources from October 2004. Ask yourself if, given your topic, an older source is acceptable or if only the most recent information will do.

Determine the accuracy of the information.

6 How complete is the information in the source? Examine the works cited by the author. Are sources for statistics included? Do the sources cited seem

credible? Is a list of additional resources provided? Here, the author cites the U.S. Forest Service and the U.S. Fish & Wildlife Service, but he does not give enough information to track down these sources. Ask yourself whether you can find a way to corroborate what a source is saying.

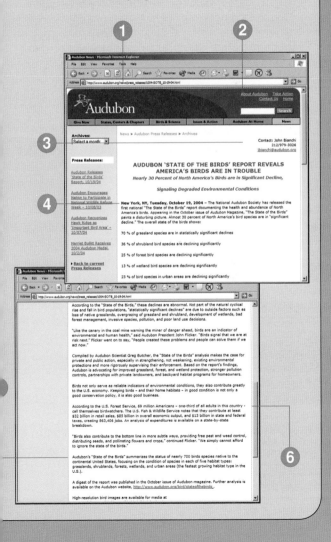

To do so, you'll need to interpret your sources, which entails synthesizing — grouping similar pieces of data together, looking for patterns or trends, and identifying the main points of the data — and drawing inferences — making conclusions on your own that follow logically from the data given.

39c Taking notes

While note-taking methods vary from one researcher to another, for each note you should (1) record enough information to help you recall the major points of the source; (2) put the information in the form in which you are most likely to incorporate it into your research project; and (3) note all the information you will need to cite the source accurately, including a subject heading and a label saying what type of note it is — paraphrase, summary, or quotation. Keep a running list that includes citation information for each source in an electronic file or on note cards that you can rearrange and alter as your project takes shape. This working bibliography will simplify the process of documenting sources for your final project.

Quoting

Quoting involves bringing a source's exact words into your text. Use an author's exact words when the wording is so memorable or expresses a point so well that you cannot improve or shorten it without weakening it, when the author is a respected authority whose opinion supports your own ideas, or when an author challenges or disagrees profoundly with others in the field. Here are guidelines for quoting:

- Copy quotations carefully, with punctuation, capitalization, and spelling exactly as in the original. (23a)
- Enclose the quotation in quotation marks. (23a)
- Use brackets if you introduce words of your own into the quotation or make changes in it. (24b)
- Use ellipses if you omit words from the quotation. (24f)
- If you later incorporate the quotation into your research project, copy it from the note precisely, including brackets and ellipses.
- Record the author's name, shortened title, and page number(s) on which the quotation appeared. For online

sources without page numbers, record the paragraph, screen, or other section number(s) if indicated.

- Make sure you have a corresponding working-bibliography entry with complete source information.

- Label the note with a subject heading, and identify it as a quotation.

QUOTATION NOTE

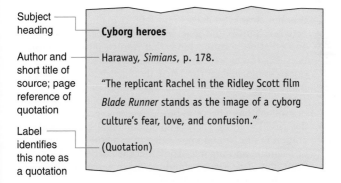

Subject heading

Author and short title of source; page reference of quotation

Label identifies this note as a quotation

Cyborg heroes

Haraway, *Simians*, p. 178.

"The replicant Rachel in the Ridley Scott film *Blade Runner* stands as the image of a cyborg culture's fear, love, and confusion."

(Quotation)

Paraphrasing

When you paraphrase, you put an author's material (including major and minor points, usually in the order they are presented) into *your own words and sentence structures*. If you wish to cite some of the author's words within the paraphrase, enclose them in quotation marks. Here are guidelines for paraphrasing:

- Include all main points and any important details from the original source in the same order in which the author presents them.

- State the meaning in your own words and sentence structures. If you want to include any language from the original, enclose it in quotation marks.

- Save for another note your own comments, elaborations, or reactions.

- Record the author, shortened title, and page number(s) on which the original material appeared. For online sources without page numbers, record the paragraph, screen, or other section number(s) if indicated.

- Make sure you have a corresponding working-bibliography entry.

- Label the note with a subject heading, and identify it as a paraphrase to avoid confusion with a summary.
- Recheck to be sure that the words and sentence structures are your own and that they express the author's meaning accurately.

The following examples of paraphrases resemble the original either too little or too much.

ORIGINAL

It is not clear who makes and who is made in the relation between human and machine. It is not clear what is mind and what body in machines that resolve into coding practices. In so far as we know ourselves in both formal discourse (for example, biology) and in daily practice (for example, the homework economy in the integrated circuit), we find ourselves to be cyborgs, hybrids, mosaics, chimeras. Biological organisms have become biotic systems, communications devices like others. There is no fundamental, ontological separation in our formal knowledge of machine and organism, of technical and organic. The replicant Rachel in the Ridley Scott film *Blade Runner* stands as the image of a cyborg culture's fear, love, and confusion.

— DONNA J. HARAWAY, *Simians, Cyborgs, and Women*

UNACCEPTABLE PARAPHRASE: STRAYING FROM THE AUTHOR'S IDEAS

Haraway's point is that we can no longer be sure of the distinction between humans and machines. In fact, she argues that we are all already combinations — part body, part mind, part machine. On the other hand, Haraway could be completely wrong: the cyborg metaphor doesn't always work.

Note that this paraphrase starts off well enough, but it moves away from paraphrasing the original to inserting the writer's ideas into the paraphrase of Haraway's text.

UNACCEPTABLE PARAPHRASE: USING THE AUTHOR'S WORDS

As Haraway explains, in a high-tech culture like ours, *who makes and who is made, what is mind or body, becomes unclear.* When we look at ourselves in relation to the real or the mechanical world, we must admit we are cyborgs, and even *biological organisms* are now *communications systems.* Thus our beings can't be separated from machines. A fine example of this cyborg image is Rachel in Ridley Scott's *Blade Runner.*

Because the italicized phrases are either borrowed from the original without quotation marks or changed only superficially, this paraphrase plagiarizes (40d).

UNACCEPTABLE PARAPHRASE: USING THE AUTHOR'S
SENTENCE STRUCTURES

> As Haraway explains, it is unclear who is the maker and who is the made. It is unclear what in the processes of machines might be the mind and what the body. Thus in order to know ourselves at all, we must recognize ourselves to be cyborgs. Biology then becomes just another device for communicating. As beings, we can't separate the bodily from the mechanical anymore. Thus Rachel in Ridley Scott's *Blade Runner* becomes the perfect symbol of cyborg culture.

Although this paraphrase is not overly reliant on the words of the original, it does follow the sentence structures too closely and might still be considered plagiarism (40d). A paraphrase must represent your own interpretation of the material and thus must show your own thought patterns.

ACCEPTABLE PARAPHRASE

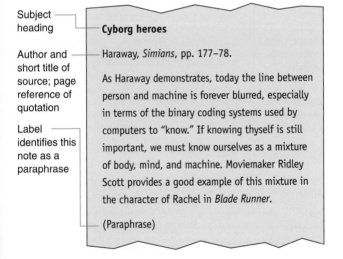

Subject heading — **Cyborg heroes**

Author and short title of source; page reference of quotation — Haraway, *Simians*, pp. 177–78.

As Haraway demonstrates, today the line between person and machine is forever blurred, especially in terms of the binary coding systems used by computers to "know." If knowing thyself is still important, we must know ourselves as a mixture of body, mind, and machine. Moviemaker Ridley Scott provides a good example of this mixture in the character of Rachel in *Blade Runner*.

Label identifies this note as a paraphrase —

(Paraphrase)

Summarizing

A summary is a significantly shortened version of a passage or even a whole chapter or work that captures main ideas *in your own words*. Unlike a paraphrase, a summary uses just enough information to record the points you wish to emphasize. Here are some guidelines for summarizing accurately.

- Include just enough information to recount the main points you want to cite. A summary is usually far shorter than the original.

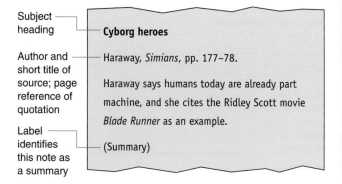
- Use your own words. If you include any language from the original, enclose it in quotation marks.
- Record the author, shortened title, and page number(s) on which the original material appeared. For online sources without page numbers, record the paragraph, screen, or other section number(s) if indicated.
- Make sure you have a corresponding working-bibliography entry.
- Label the note with a subject heading, and identify it as a summary to avoid confusion with a paraphrase.
- Recheck to be sure you have captured the author's meaning and that the words are entirely your own.

ACCEPTABLE SUMMARY

Subject heading — **Cyborg heroes**

Author and short title of source; page reference of quotation — Haraway, *Simians*, pp. 177–78.

Haraway says humans today are already part machine, and she cites the Ridley Scott movie *Blade Runner* as an example.

Label identifies this note as a summary — (Summary)

Annotating sources

Sometimes you may photocopy or print out a source you intend to use. In such cases, you can annotate the photocopies or printouts with your thoughts and questions and highlight interesting quotations and key terms.

FOR MULTILINGUAL WRITERS

Identifying Sources

While some language communities and cultures expect audiences to recognize the sources of important documents and texts, thereby eliminating the need to cite them directly, conventions for writing in North America call for careful attribution of any quoted, paraphrased, or summarized material. When in doubt, explicitly identify your sources.

If you take notes in a computer file, you may be able to copy online sources electronically, paste them into the file, and annotate them there, perhaps even using software designed for this purpose. Try not to rely too heavily on copying or printing out whole pieces, however; you still need to read the material very carefully. And resist the temptation to treat copied material as notes, an action that could lead to inadvertent plagiarizing. (In a computer file, using a different color for text pasted from a source will help prevent this problem.)

40 Integrating Sources and Avoiding Plagiarism

In some ways, there is really nothing new under the sun, in writing and research as well as in life. Whatever writing you do has been influenced by what you have already read and experienced. As you work on your research project, you will need to know how to integrate and acknowledge the work of others. And all writers need to understand current definitions of plagiarism (which have changed over time and differ from culture to culture) as well as the concept of intellectual property — those works protected by copyright and other laws — so that they can give credit where credit is due.

40a Integrating quotations, paraphrases, and summaries

Integrate source materials into your writing with care to ensure that the integrated materials make grammatical and logical sense.

Integrating quotations. Because your research project is primarily your own work, limit your use of quotations to those necessary to your thesis or memorable for your readers.

Short quotations should run in with your text, enclosed by quotation marks. Longer quotations should be set off

---

 bedfordstmartins.com/easywriter For additional help, click on **The St. Martin's Tutorial on Avoiding Plagiarism.** For tips on using sources and considering your own intellectual property, click on **Additional Resources.**

from the text (see 23a). Integrate all quotations into the text so that they flow smoothly and clearly into the surrounding sentences. Be sure that the sentence containing the quotation is grammatically complete, especially if you incorporate a quotation into your own words.

SIGNAL PHRASES
Introduce the quotation with a signal phrase or signal **verb**, such as those underlined in these examples.

> <u>As Eudora Welty notes</u>, "learning stamps you with its moments. Childhood's learning," <u>she continues</u>, "is made up of moments. It isn't steady. It's a pulse" (9).

> In her essay, <u>Haraway strongly opposes</u> those who condemn technology outright, <u>arguing</u> that we must not indulge in a "demonology of technology" (181).

Choose a signal verb that is appropriate to the idea you are expressing and that accurately characterizes the author's viewpoint. Other signal verbs include words such as *acknowledges, agrees, asserts, believes, claims, concludes, describes, disagrees, lists, objects, offers, remarks, reports, reveals, says, suggests,* and *writes.*

When you write about literary and artistic works, generally follow the Modern Language Association (MLA) style, used in the examples in this chapter, and put verbs in signal phrases in the **present tense**. For papers on history and some other areas of the humanities that use *Chicago* style, use the present tense. The **past tense** is acceptable in *Chicago* style if you wish to emphasize that an author's point was made in the past.

If you are writing for the social sciences using the style of the American Psychological Association (APA) to describe research results, use verbs in the past tense or the **present perfect tense** (*the study <u>showed</u>, the study <u>has shown</u>*) in your signal phrase. When explaining the implications of research, use the present tense (*for future research, these findings <u>suggest</u>*).

When you write in the natural sciences using the Council of Science Editors (CSE) style, in general use the present tense for research reports and the past tense to describe specific experimental methods or observations, or to cite research published in the past.

BRACKETS AND ELLIPSES
In direct quotations, enclose in brackets any words you change or add, and indicate any deletions with ellipsis points (see 42a).

> "There is something wrong in the [Three Mile Island] area," one farmer told the Nuclear Regulatory Commission after the plant accident ("Legacy" 33).

> Economist John Kenneth Galbraith pointed out that "large corporations cannot afford to compete with one another. . . . In a truly competitive market someone loses" (Key 17).

Be careful that any changes you make in a quotation do not alter its meaning. Use brackets and ellipses sparingly; too many make for difficult reading and might suggest that you have removed some of the context for the quotation.

Integrating paraphrases and summaries. Introduce paraphrases and summaries clearly, usually with a signal phrase that includes the author of the source, as the underlined words in this example indicate.

> In her book *That's Not What I Meant!* <u>linguistics expert Deborah Tannen illustrates</u> how communication between women and men breaks down <u>and then suggests</u> that an awareness of what she calls "genderlects" can help all speakers realize that there are many ways to communicate with others and that these differing styles of communication have their own validity (298).

Because paraphrases and summaries put the author's ideas into your own words and sentence structures, they do not appear in quotation marks. Therefore, it is essential that you indicate the source of a summary or paraphrase, including the author's name and other information required by the documentation style you are using.

40b Integrating visuals

Choose visuals that convey information more efficiently than words alone could do. If you use visuals (such as graphs, cartoons, maps, photographs, charts, tables, or time lines), integrate them smoothly into your text.

Insert each visual as close as possible after the relevant text, making sure that the text refers to the visual by number before the visual appears (*As Figure 3 demonstrates* . . .). Number and title tables and figures according to the documentation system you are using, and label each visual clearly and consistently. Explain or comment on the relevance of the visual. If you are posting your project on a Web site, make sure you have permission to use any visuals that are covered by copyright. (See Chapter 4 for more on using visuals.)

40c Knowing which sources to acknowledge

As you carry out research, it is important to understand the distinction between materials that require acknowledgment (in in-text citations, footnotes, or endnotes; and in the list of works cited or bibliography) and those that do not.

Materials that do not require acknowledgment. You do not usually need to cite a source for the following:

- Common knowledge — facts that most readers already know.
- Facts available in a wide variety of sources, such as encyclopedias, almanacs, or textbooks.
- Your own findings from field research. You should, however, acknowledge people you interview as individuals rather than as part of a survey.

Materials that require acknowledgment. You should cite all of your other sources to be certain to avoid plagiarism. Follow the documentation style required (see Chapters 42–45), and list the source in a bibliography or list of works cited. Be especially careful to cite the following:

- Sources for quotations, paraphrases, and summaries that you include.
- Facts not widely known or arguable assertions.
- All visuals from any source, including your own artwork, photographs you have taken, and graphs or tables you create from data found in a source.
- Any help provided by a friend, an instructor, or another person.

40d Avoiding plagiarism

Academic integrity accounts for our being able to trust those sources we use and to demonstrate that our own work is equally trustworthy. Plagiarism is especially damaging to academic integrity, whether it involves inaccurate or incomplete acknowledgment of sources in citations — sometimes called unintentional plagiarism — or deliberate plagiarism that is intended to pass off one writer's work as another's.

Whether it is intentional or not, plagiarism can have serious consequences. Students caught plagiarizing may fail the course or be expelled. Others who have plagiarized, even inadvertently, have had degrees revoked or have been stripped of positions or awards.

Unintentional plagiarism. If your paraphrase is too close to the wording or sentence structure of a source (even if you identify the source); if after a quotation you do not identify the source (even if you include the quotation marks); or if you fail to indicate clearly the source of an idea that you did not come up with on your own, you may be accused of plagiarism, even if your intent was not to plagiarize. This inaccurate or incomplete acknowledgment of sources often results either from carelessness or from not learning how to borrow material properly in the first place.

Take responsibility for your research and for acknowledging all sources accurately. To guard against unintentional plagiarism, photocopy sources and identify the needed quotations right on the copy. You can also insert footnotes or endnotes into the text as you write.

Deliberate plagiarism. Deliberate plagiarism — handing in an essay written by a friend or purchased or downloaded from an essay-writing company; cutting and pasting passages directly from source materials without marking them with quotation marks and acknowledging their sources; failing to credit the source of an idea or concept in your text — is what most people think of when they hear the word *plagiarism*. This form of plagiarism is particularly troubling because it represents dishonesty and deception: those who intentionally plagiarize present someone else's hard work as their own and claim knowledge they really don't have, thus deceiving their readers.

FOR MULTILINGUAL WRITERS

Thinking about Plagiarism as a Cultural Concept

Many cultures do not recognize Western notions of plagiarism, which rest on a belief that writers can own their language and ideas. Indeed, in many cultures and communities, using the words and ideas of others without attribution is considered a sign of deep respect as well as an indication of knowledge. In academic writing in the United States, however, you should credit all materials except those that are common knowledge, that are available in a wide variety of sources, or that are your own creations or your own findings from field research.

Deliberate plagiarism is also fairly simple to spot: your instructor will be well acquainted with your writing and likely to notice any sudden shifts in the style or quality of your work. In addition, by typing a few words from a project into a search engine, your instructor can identify "matches" very easily.

41 Drafting, Revising, and Editing

When you are working on a research project, there comes a time to draw the strands of your research together and articulate your conclusions in writing.

41a Drafting your text

To group the information you have collected, try arranging your notes and visuals to identify connections, main ideas, and possible organization. You may also want to develop a working outline, a storyboard, or an idea map, or you can plot out a more detailed organization in a formal outline.

For almost all research writing, drafting should begin well before the deadline in case you need to gather more information or do more drafting. Begin drafting wherever you feel most confident. If you have an idea for an introduction, begin there. If you are not sure how you want to introduce the project but do know how you want to approach one point, begin with that, and return to the introduction later.

If you will be doing most of your drafting with a word-processing program, take advantage of its outlining and formatting tools.

Working title and introduction. The title and introduction set the stage for what is to come. Ideally, the title announces the subject in an intriguing or memorable way. The introduction should draw readers in and provide any

---

bedfordstmartins.com/easywriter If you're using **Comment** in your course, you and your classmates can take part in peer-reviewing activities online.

background they will need to understand your discussion. You may want to open with a question, explain how you will answer it, and end with your explicit thesis statement.

Conclusion. A good conclusion helps readers know what they have learned. One effective strategy is to begin with a reference to your thesis and then expand to a more general conclusion that reminds readers why your discussion is significant. Or you may want to remind readers of your main points. Try to conclude with something that will have an impact — but guard against sounding preachy.

41b Revising your draft

Once you've completed your draft, reread it slowly. As you do so, reconsider the project's purpose and audience, your stance and thesis, and the evidence you have gathered. Next, ask others to read and respond to your draft. Asking specific questions of your readers will result in the most helpful advice.

Once you get feedback, reread your draft very carefully, making notes for necessary changes and additions. Look closely at your support for your thesis, and gather additional information if necessary. Pay particular attention to how you have used both print and visual sources, and make sure you have full documentation for them.

41c Preparing a list of sources

Once you have a final draft with your source materials in place, you are ready to prepare your list of sources. Create an entry for each source used in your final draft, consulting your notes and working bibliography (see 39c).

FOR MULTILINGUAL WRITERS

Asking a Native Speaker to Review Your Draft

You may find it helpful to ask a native speaker to read over your draft and point out any words or patterns that are unclear or not idiomatic.

Then double-check your draft against your list of sources cited; be sure that you have listed every source mentioned in the in-text citations or notes and that you have not listed any sources not cited in your project. (For guidelines on documentation styles, see Chapters 42–45.)

41d Editing your text

Proofread the final version of your project carefully. Work with a hard copy, since reading onscreen often leads to inaccuracies. Proofread once for typographical and grammatical errors and once again to make sure you haven't introduced new errors. You may find that reading the final draft backwards helps you focus on details.

Documentation

Writing

Sentence
Grammar

Sentence Style

Punctuation/
Mechanics

Language

Multilingual
Writers

Research

Documentation

42 MLA Style

Many fields in the humanities ask students to follow Modern Language Association (MLA) style to format manuscripts and to document various kinds of sources. This chapter introduces MLA guidelines. For further reference, consult the *MLA Handbook for Writers of Research Papers,* Seventh Edition, 2009.

42a From assignment to thesis and support

Developing a strong thesis that states your goal clearly is crucial to writing an effective essay. Study your assignment carefully, focusing on key terms like *analyze, compare, discuss,* or *persuade.* What do such words mean in this context? (For more on beginning a research project, see Chapter 38a.) The examples in this section show how one student moved from an assignment to a strong thesis and began crafting an MLA-style essay.

Assignment. Before you begin, make sure you understand the requirements and limits of the assignment. What is the scope of the assignment: How many and what kinds of sources should you use? How long is your project supposed to be? When is it due?

For an introductory writing course, one student received the following assignment:

> Choose a subject of interest to you, and use it as the basis for a research essay that makes and substantiates a claim.

For this open-ended assignment, the student chose to focus on the effects of instant messaging on youth literacy as his topic.

Generating ideas about the assignment. Ask questions about the topic of your project. As you focus the questions by brainstorming, reading or rereading sources, talking with others, and considering what you know, you develop a starting point for your research. For his instant messaging topic, the student met with classmates to discuss their experiences with instant messaging. He also located IM users online who were willing to share chat logs with him.

Working thesis. A working thesis makes an important point about the main question your research poses (see 1c). After reading chat logs, taking extensive notes, and talking with others, the student wrote the following thesis:

> Instant messaging is a positive force in the development of youth literacy because it promotes regular contact with words, the use of a written medium for communication, and the development of an alternative form of literacy.

Evidence. Some assignments require you to respond carefully to a text or two, while others will require a variety of sources. As you work, consider what kinds of evidence you will need to convince readers of your view.

An assignment like the sample one allows for significant research into secondary sources (see 38b). This student found several newspaper articles on his topic. However, much of his work involved closely analyzing reports and a book on literacy in young people, and conducting field research to support his points. He gathered information from the sources that illustrated and supported his thesis, and then used these passages to make an informal outline of the points he wanted to make, along with quotations to support these points.

Sources. As you prepare your essay, take careful notes on the sources you use (see 39c). Be sure to introduce quotations with a signal phrase (see 40a) and to explain the significance of each quotation. Make sure each quotation supports your thesis. Be careful not to plagiarize when you paraphrase and summarize sources (see 40d). Finally, note that MLA style requires you to use the **present tense** when you write about literature and art (*Many photographs from Ellis Island depict tired and anxious immigrants gathered in the Great Hall*).

42b MLA manuscript format

The MLA recommends the following format for the manuscript of a research paper. However, check with your instructor before preparing your final draft.

---

 bedfordstmartins.com/easywriter To access the advice in this chapter online, click on **Documenting Sources.**

First page and title. The MLA does not require a title page. Type each of the following items on a separate line on the first page, beginning one inch from the top and flush with the left margin: your name, the instructor's name, the course name and number, and the date. Double-space between each item; then double-space again and center the title. Double-space between the title and the beginning of the text.

Margins and spacing. Leave one-inch margins at the top and bottom and on both sides of each page. Double-space the entire text, including set-off quotations, notes, and the list of works cited. Indent the first line of a paragraph one-half inch, or five spaces. Indent set-off quotations one inch, or ten spaces.

Page numbers. Include your last name and the page number on each page, one-half inch below the top and flush with the right margin.

Long quotations. To quote a long passage (more than four typed lines), set the quotation off by starting it on a new line and indenting each line one inch, or ten spaces, from the left margin. Do not enclose the passage in quotation marks (see 23a).

Headings. MLA style allows, but does not require, headings. Many students and instructors find them helpful. (See 4c for guidelines on using headings and subheadings.)

Visuals. Visuals (photographs, drawings, charts, graphs, and tables) should be placed as near as possible to the relevant text. (See 4d for guidelines on incorporating visuals into your text.) Tables should have a label and number (*Table 1*) and a clear caption. The label and caption should be aligned on the left, on separate lines. Give the source information below the table. All other visuals should be labeled *Figure* (abbreviated *Fig.*), numbered, and captioned. The label and caption should appear on the same line, followed by source information (see 5d). Remember to refer to each visual in your text, indicating how it contributes to the point(s) you are making.

The list of works cited. Start the list of works cited on a new page at the end of the paper. Number each page, continuing the page numbers of the text. Center the heading *Works Cited* an inch from the top of the page; do not underline or italicize it or enclose it in quotation marks. Double-space between the heading and the first entry, and double-space the entire list. Start each entry flush with the left margin; indent any subsequent lines one-half inch, or five spaces.

Alphabetize the list by the authors' (or editors') last names. If the author is unknown, alphabetize by the first major word of the title, disregarding *A, An,* or *The.* If a list has two or more works by the same author, use the author's name in only the first entry; in subsequent entries, instead of the name, use three hyphens followed by a period, and alphabetize the works by title.

42c In-text citations

MLA style requires documentation in the text for every quote, paraphrase, or summary, or for other material that is cited (see Chapter 40). In-text citations document material from other sources with both signal phrases and parenthetical references. Signal phrases introduce the material, often including the author's name. Keep your parenthetical references short, but include enough information in the parentheses to allow readers to locate the full citation in the list of works cited.

Place the parenthetical citation as near the relevant material as possible without disrupting the sentence. Note in the following examples where punctuation is placed in relation to the parentheses.

1. AUTHOR NAMED IN A SIGNAL PHRASE. Ordinarily, you can use the author's name in a signal phrase — to introduce the material — and cite the page number(s) in parentheses.

> Herrera indicates that Kahlo believed in a "vitalistic form of pantheism" (328).

To quote a long passage (more than four typed lines), place the page reference in parentheses one space after the final punctuation of the block quotation (see 23a).

2. AUTHOR NAMED IN PARENTHESES. When you do not mention the author in a signal phrase, include the author's last name before the page number(s) in the parentheses. Use no punctuation between the author's name and the page number(s).

> In places, Beauvoir "sees Marxists as believing in subjectivity" (Whitmarsh 63).

3. TWO OR THREE AUTHORS. Use all the authors' last names.

> Gortner, Hebrun, and Nicolson maintain that "opinion leaders" influence other people in an organization because they are respected, not because they hold high positions (175).

4. FOUR OR MORE AUTHORS. Use the first author's name and *et al.* ("and others"), or name all the authors.

As Belenky et al. assert, examining the lives of women expands
our understanding of human development (7).

5. ORGANIZATION AS AUTHOR. Give the group's full name if it is
brief or a shortened form if it is long.

Any study of social welfare involves a close analysis of "the
impacts, the benefits, and the costs" of its policies (Social
Research Corporation iii).

6. UNKNOWN AUTHOR. Use the full title if it is brief or a shortened form if it is long.

"Hype," by one analysis, is "an artificially engendered atmosphere
of hysteria" ("Today's Marketplace" 51).

7. AUTHOR OF TWO OR MORE WORKS. If your list of works cited
has more than one work by the same author, include the
title (if it is brief) or a shortened form of the title.

Gardner shows readers their own silliness in his description
of a "pointless, ridiculous monster, crouched in the shadows,
stinking of dead men, murdered children, and martyred cows"
(*Grendel* 2).

8. AUTHORS WITH THE SAME LAST NAME. Include the author's
first and last names in a signal phrase or first initial and last
name in a parenthetical reference.

Children will learn to write if they are allowed to choose their
own subjects, James Britton asserts, citing the Schools Council
study of the 1960s (37–42).

9. MULTIVOLUME WORK. Note the volume number first and
then the page number(s), with a colon and one space
between them.

Modernist writers prized experimentation and gradually even
sought to blur the line between poetry and prose, according to
Forster (3: 150).

If you name only one volume of the work in your list of works
cited, include only the page number in the parentheses.

10. LITERARY WORK. Because literary works are often available in many different editions, cite the page number(s) from the edition you used followed by a semicolon, and then give other identifying information that will lead readers to the passage in any edition. Indicate the act and/or scene in a play (*37; sc. 1*). For a novel, indicate the part or chapter (*175; ch. 4*).

> Dostoyevsky's character Mitya wonders aloud about the "terrible
> tragedies realism inflicts on people" (376; bk. 8, ch. 2).

For a poem, cite the part (if there is one) and line(s), separated by a period. If you are citing only line numbers, use the word *line(s)* in the first reference (*lines 33–34*).

> On dying, Whitman speculates, "All goes onward and outward,
> nothing collapses, / And to die is different from what anyone
> supposed, and luckier" (6.129–30).

For a verse play, give only the act, scene, and line numbers, separated by periods.

> As *Macbeth* begins, the witches greet Banquo as "Lesser than
> Macbeth, and greater" (1.3.65).

11. WORK IN AN ANTHOLOGY. Use the name of the author of the work, not the editor of the anthology, but use the page number(s) from the anthology.

> Narratives of captivity play a major role in early writing by
> women in the United States, as demonstrated by Silko (219).

12. SACRED TEXT. Give the title of the edition you used followed by locator information, such as the book, chapter, or verse, separated by a period. In your text, spell out the names of books. In parenthetical references, use abbreviations for books with names of five or more letters.

> He ignored the admonition "Pride goes before destruction, and
> a haughty spirit before a fall" (*New Oxford Annotated Bible*,
> Prov. 16.18).

13. INDIRECT SOURCE. Use the abbreviation *qtd. in* to indicate that you are quoting from someone else's report of a conversation, an interview, a letter, or the like.

Arthur Miller says, "When somebody is destroyed everybody finally contributes to it, but in Willy's case, the end product would be virtually the same" (qtd. in Martin and Meyer 375).

14. TWO OR MORE SOURCES IN ONE CITATION. Separate the information with semicolons.

Economists recommend that *employment* be redefined to include unpaid domestic labor (Clark 148; Nevins 39).

15. ENTIRE WORK OR ONE-PAGE ARTICLE. Include the reference in the text without any page numbers or parentheses.

Michael Ondaatje's poetic sensibility transfers beautifully to prose in *The English Patient*.

16. WORK WITHOUT PAGE NUMBERS. If a work has no page numbers or is only one page long, you may omit the page number. If a work uses paragraph numbers instead, use the abbreviation *par.* (or *pars.*).

Whitman considered their speech "a source of a native grand opera," in the words of Ellison (par. 13).

17. ELECTRONIC OR NONPRINT SOURCE. Give enough information for readers to locate the source in the list of works cited. Usually use the author or title under which you list the source. Omit the page number if the work lacks stable pagination.

As a *Slate* analysis has noted, "Prominent sports psychologists get praised for their successes and don't get grief for their failures" (Engber).

If the work you are citing has stable pagination, such as an article in PDF format, include the page number.

42d Explanatory and bibliographic notes

MLA style recommends explanatory notes for information or commentary that does not readily fit into your text but is needed for clarification or further explanation. In addition, MLA style permits bibliographic notes for information about a source. Use superscript numbers (1) in the text to refer readers to the notes, which may appear as endnotes (typed under the heading *Notes* on a separate page after the text but before the list of works cited) or as footnotes at the bottom of the page.

1. SUPERSCRIPT NUMBER IN TEXT

Stewart emphasizes the existence of social contacts in Hawthorne's life so that the audience will accept a different Hawthorne, one more attuned to modern times than the figure in Woodberry.[3]

2. NOTE

[3]Woodberry does, however, show that Hawthorne was often an unsociable individual. He emphasizes the seclusion of Hawthorne's mother, who separated herself from her family after the death of her husband, often even taking meals alone (28).

42e List of works cited

A list of works cited is an alphabetical list of the sources you have referred to in your essay. (If your instructor asks you to list everything you have read as background, call the list *Works Consulted*.)

Continued

Books. The basic format for a works-cited entry for a book is outlined on p. 208.

1. ONE AUTHOR

> Winchester, Simon. *The Meaning of Everything: The Story of the Oxford English Dictionary*. New York: Oxford UP, 2003. Print.

2. MORE THAN ONE AUTHOR. For two or three authors, list all the names. For four or more authors, either list all the names or give the first author listed on the title page, followed by a comma and *et al.* ("and others").

> Martineau, Jane, Desmond Shawe-Taylor, and Jonathan Bate. *Shakespeare in Art*. London: Merrell, 2003. Print.

3. ORGANIZATION AS AUTHOR

> Getty Trust Publications. *Seeing the Getty Center/Seeing the Getty Gardens*. Los Angeles: Getty Trust Publications, 2000. Print.

4. UNKNOWN AUTHOR

> *New Concise World Atlas*. New York: Oxford UP, 2003. Print.

5. TWO OR MORE BOOKS BY THE SAME AUTHOR

> Lorde, Audre. *A Burst of Light*. Ithaca: Firebrand, 1988.
>
> ---. *Sister Outsider*. Trumansburg: Crossing, 1984. Print.

6. EDITOR

> Wall, Cheryl A., ed. *Changing Our Own Words: Essays on Criticism, Theory, and Writing by Black Women*. New Brunswick: Rutgers UP, 1989. Print.

7. AUTHOR AND EDITOR

> James, Henry. *Portrait of a Lady*. Ed. Leon Edel. Boston: Houghton, 1963. Print.

8. WORK IN AN ANTHOLOGY

> Komunyakaa, Yusef. "Facing It." *The Seagull Reader*. Ed. Joseph Kelly. New York: Norton, 2000. 126-27. Print.

9. TWO OR MORE ITEMS FROM AN ANTHOLOGY

Estleman, Loren D. "Big Tim Magoon and the Wild West." Walker
391-404.

Salzer, Susan K. "Miss Libbie Tells All." Walker 199-212.

Walker, Dale L., ed. *Westward: A Fictional History of the American
West*. New York: Forge, 2003. Print.

10. TRANSLATION

Hietamies, Laila. *Red Moon over White Sea*. Trans. Borje Vahamaki.
Beaverton, ON: Aspasia, 2000. Print.

11. EDITION OTHER THAN THE FIRST

Walker, John A. *Art in the Age of Mass Media*. 3rd ed. London:
Pluto, 2001. Print.

12. MULTIVOLUME WORK

Ch'oe, Yong-Ho, Peter Lee, and William Theodore De Barry, eds.
Sources of Korean Tradition. Vol. 2. New York: Columbia UP,
2000. 2 vols. Print.

If you cite more than one volume, give the total number of
volumes after the title.

Ch'oe, Yong-Ho, Peter Lee, and William Theodore De Barry, eds.
Sources of Korean Tradition. 2 vols. New York: Columbia UP,
2000. Print.

13. PREFACE, FOREWORD, INTRODUCTION, OR AFTERWORD

Atwan, Robert. Foreword. *The Best American Essays 2002*.
Ed. Stephen Jay Gould. Boston: Houghton, 2002.
viii-xii. Print.

14. ENTRY IN A REFERENCE WORK

Kettering, Alison McNeil. "Art Nouveau." *World Book
Encyclopedia*. 2002 ed. Print.

"Traquair, Sir John Stewart." *Encyclopaedia Brittanica*. 11th ed.
1911. Print.

When using MLA style to cite a book by one author, include the following elements. Get this information from the book's title page and copyright page (on the reverse side of the title page), not from the book's cover or a library catalog.

1. *Author.* List the last name first, followed by a comma, first name, and middle initial (if given). Omit titles such as *MD*, *PhD*, or *Sir*; include suffixes after the name and a comma (*O'Driscoll, Gerald P., Jr.*). End with a period.

2. *Title.* Italicize the title and any subtitle; capitalize all major words (25d). End with a period.

3. *City of publication.* If more than one city is given, use the first one listed. For foreign cities that may be unfamiliar to your readers, add an abbreviation of the country or province (*Cork, Ire.*). Follow it with a colon.

4. *Publisher.* Give a shortened version of the publisher's name (*Harper* for *HarperCollins Publishers*; *Harcourt* for *Harcourt Brace*; *Oxford UP* for *Oxford University Press*). Follow it with a comma.

5. *Year of publication.* Consult the copyright page. If more than one copyright date is given, use the most recent one. End with a period.

6. *Medium of publication.* End with the medium (*Print*) and a period.

For a book by one author, use the following format:

Last name, First name. *Title of Book*. City: Publisher, Year. Medium.

A citation for the book on p. 209 would look like this:

AUTHOR, LAST
NAME FIRST   TITLE AND SUBTITLE, ITALICIZED

Twitchell, James B. *Living It Up: America's Love Affair with*

  Luxury. New York: Simon, 2002. Print.
                                              MEDIUM
                          PUBLISHER'S CITY AND NAME,
                          YEAR OF PUBLICATION
DOUBLE-SPACE;
INDENT ONE-HALF INCH,
OR FIVE SPACES

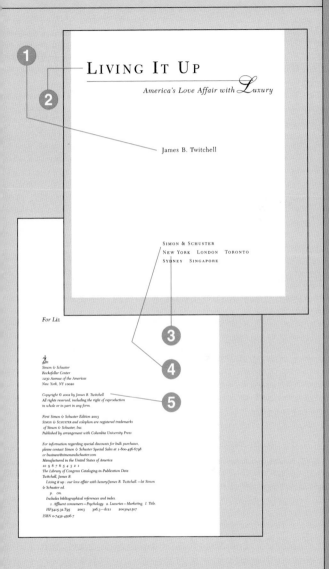

LIVING IT UP

America's Love Affair with Luxury

James B. Twitchell

SIMON & SCHUSTER
NEW YORK   LONDON   TORONTO
SYDNEY   SINGAPORE

For Liz

Simon & Schuster
Rockefeller Center
1230 Avenue of the Americas
New York, NY 10020

First Simon & Schuster Edition 2003
SIMON & SCHUSTER and colophon are registered trademarks
of Simon & Schuster, Inc.
Published by arrangement with Columbia University Press

For information regarding special discounts for bulk purchases,
please contact Simon & Schuster Special Sales at 1-800-456-6798
or business@simonandschuster.com
Manufactured in the United States of America
10 9 8 7 6 5 4 3 2 1
The Library of Congress Cataloging-in-Publication Data
Twitchell, James B.
    Living it up : our love affair with luxury/James B. Twitchell. —1st Simon
& Schuster ed.
        p.   cm.
    Includes bibliographical references and index.
    1. Affluent consumers—Psychology. 2. Luxuries—Marketing. I. Title.
    HF5415.32.T95   2003   306.3—dc21   2003041307
ISBN 0-7432-4506-7

For more on using MLA style to cite books, see pp. 206–10.
(For guidelines and models for using APA style, see pp. 241–43;
for *Chicago* style, see pp. 257–59; for CSE style, see pp. 272–74.)

15. BOOK THAT IS PART OF A SERIES

Nichanian, Marc, and Vartan Matiossian, eds. *Yeghishe Charents:
    Poet of the Revolution*. Costa Mesa: Mazda, 2003. Print.
    Armenian Studies Ser. 5.

16. REPUBLICATION

Scott, Walter. *Kenilworth*. 1821. New York: Dodd, 1956. Print.

17. PUBLISHER'S IMPRINT

Gilligan, Carol. *The Birth of Pleasure: A New Map of Love*. New
    York: Vintage-Random, 2003. Print.

18. TITLE WITHIN A TITLE

Mullaney, Julie. *Arundhati Roy's* The God of Small Things: *A
    Reader's Guide*. New York: Continuum, 2002. Print.

19. GOVERNMENT PUBLICATION

Kinsella, Kevin, and Victoria Velkoff. *An Aging World: 2001*. US
    Bureau of the Census. Washington: GPO, 2001. Print.

United States. Natl. Council on Disability. *Reconstructing Fair
    Housing*. Washington: Natl. Council on Disability, 2001.
    Print.

20. SACRED TEXT. If the version is not part of the title, list the
version after the title. If you are not citing a particular edition, do not include sacred texts in the works-cited list.

*Quran: The Final Testament (Authorized English Version) with
    Arabic Text*. Trans. Rashad Khalifa. Fremont: Universal Unity,
    2000. Print.

Periodicals. The basic format for a works-cited entry for
a periodical appears on p. 212.

21. ARTICLE IN A JOURNAL

Gigante, Denise. "The Monster in the Rainbow: Keats and the
    Science of Life." *PMLA* 117 (2002): 433–48. Print.

22. ARTICLE THAT SKIPS PAGES

Tyrnauer, Matthew. "Empire by Martha." *Vanity Fair* Sept. 2002:
    364+. Print.

23. ARTICLE IN A MAGAZINE. Give the month (if published monthly) or date (if weekly) of publication. Abbreviate the names of months except for May, June, and July.

Fonda, Daren. "Saving the Dead." *Life* Apr. 2000: 69-72. Print.

Gilgoff, Dan. "Unusual Suspects." *US News and World Report* 26
    Nov. 2001: 51. Print.

24. ARTICLE IN A NEWSPAPER

Vogel, Carol. "With Huge Gift, the Whitney Is No Longer a Poor
    Cousin." *New York Times* 3 Aug. 2002, late ed.: A1+. Print.

25. EDITORIAL OR LETTER TO THE EDITOR

Magee, Doug. "Soldier's Home." Editorial. *Nation* 26 Mar. 1988:
    400-01. Print.

26. REVIEW

Denby, David. "High Roller." Rev. of *The Aviator,* dir. Martin
    Scorsese. *New Yorker* 20 Dec. 2004: 186–87. Print.

27. UNSIGNED ARTICLE

"Performance of the Week." *Time* 6 Oct. 2003: 18. Print.

Electronic sources. The entry for most electronic sources may include up to six basic elements, as in the following list, but must always include the last two.

- **AUTHOR.** List the last name first, followed by a comma and the first name, and end with a period. If no author is given, begin the entry with the title.

- **TITLE.** Enclose the title of the document in quotation marks and end with a period inside the closing quotation mark. If you are citing an entire site or an online book, the title should be italicized. Capitalize all major words.

- **PRINT PUBLICATION INFORMATION.** Give any information the document provides about any previous or simultaneous publication in print.

- **ELECTRONIC PUBLICATION INFORMATION.** List all of the following items that you can find, with a period after each one: the title of the site, italicized, with all major

Include the following elements:

1 *Author.* List the last name first, followed by a comma, the first name, and the middle initial (if given). Omit titles such as *MD;* include suffixes after the name and a comma (*O'Driscoll, Gerald P., Jr.*). End with a period.

2 *Article title.* Enclose the title and any subtitle in quotation marks, and capitalize all major words (see 25d). The closing period goes inside the closing quotation mark.

3 *Periodical title.* Italicize the periodical title (excluding any initial *A, An,* or *The*), and capitalize all major words. For journals, give the volume number and issue number (if any).

4 *Date of publication.* For journals, list the year in parentheses followed by a colon. For monthly magazines, list the month and year. For weekly magazines and newspapers, list the day, month, and year. Abbreviate months except May, June, and July.

5 *Inclusive page number(s).* For page numbers up to 99, note all digits in the second number. For numbers above 99, note only the last two digits and any others that change in the second number (115–18, 1378–79, 296–301). Include section letters for newspapers, if relevant. End with a period.

6 *Medium of publication.* End with the medium of publication (*Print*) and a period.

For a journal article, use the following format:

Last name, First name. "Title of Article." *Journal* Volume number.
    Issue number (year): Page number(s). Medium.

For a newspaper article, use the following format:

Last name, First name. "Title." *Newspaper* Date, Edition (if any):
    Section number (if any): Page number(s) (including section
    letter, if any). Medium.

For a magazine article, use the following format:

Last name, First name. "Title of Article." *Magazine* Date:
    Page number(s). Medium.

A citation for the magazine article below would look like this:

AUTHOR, LAST
NAME FIRST

ARTICLE TITLE AND SUBTITLE,
IN QUOTATION MARKS

Hamilton, Anita. "All the Right Questions: Discussion Groups

Based on the Teachings of Socrates Are Reviving the Art

of Conversation." *Time* 5 Apr. 2004: 65–66. Print.

DOUBLE-SPACE;
INDENT ONE-HALF
INCH, OR FIVE
SPACES

PERIODICAL
TITLE,
ITALICIZED

DATE

INCLUSIVE PAGE
NUMBERS

MEDIUM

SOCIETY

INQUIRING MINDS: In
Seattle, participants
meet and talk in a
local coffeehouse

All the Right Questions

Discussion groups based on the teachings of
Socrates are reviving the art of conversation

By ANITA HAMILTON

THERE'S A BUZZ IN THE AIR AT THE El Diablo Coffee Co. in Seattle, and it's not just coming from the aroma of the shop's Cuban-style espresso drinks. On a recent Wednesday evening, as most patrons sat quietly reading books or tapping away on their laptop computers, about 15 people gathered in a circle discussing philosophy. "When is violence necessary?" asked one. "What is a well-lived life?" asked another, as the group enjoyed a well-caffeinated, intellectual high.

Known as a Socrates Café, the group at El Diablo is just one of 150 or so that meet in coffee shops, bookstores, libraries, churches and community centers across the country. Founded by Christopher Phil-

lips, a former journalist and teacher, the cafés are designed to get people talking about philosophical issues. Using a kind of Socratic method, they encourage people to develop their views by posing questions, being open to challenges and considering alternative answers. Adhering to Socrates' belief that the unexamined life is not worth living, the cafés focus on exchanging ideas, not using them to pummel other participants.

"Instead of just yelling back and forth, we take a few steps back and examine people's underlying values. People can ask why to their heart's content," says Phillips, whose most recent book, *Six Questions of Socrates* (Norton; 320 pages), came out earlier this year.

While a modern-day discussion group based on the teachings of a thinker from

the 5th century B.C. may seem quaintly outdated, Socrates Cafés have found a surprisingly large and diverse following. Meetings have been held everywhere from a Navajo Nation reservation in Ganado, Ariz., to an airplane terminal in Providence, R.I. Ongoing groups have formed in prisons, senior centers and homeless shelters. In recent months, international groups have popped up in Afghanistan, Finland and Spain. The common denominator? "People who get off on ideas come to this," says Fred Korn, 65, a retired philosophy professor, who attends the Wednesday-night meetings at El Diablo. "Outside of college, there's not a lot of opportunity to get together with people who want to talk about ideas," he says.

For Phillips, the dialogue groups are about much more than good conversation. "It's grass-roots democracy," he says. "It's only in a group setting that people can hash out their ideas about how we should act not just as an individual but as a society." To

For more on using MLA style to cite periodical articles, see
pp. 210–11. (For guidelines and models for using APA style, see
pp. 243–44; for *Chicago* style, see pp. 259–60; for CSE style, see
pp. 274–75.)

Services such as InfoTrac, EBSCOhost, ProQuest, and LexisNexis provide access to huge databases of electronic articles. When using MLA style to cite articles from databases, include the following elements:

① *Author.* Last name, comma, first name. End with a period.

② *Article title.* Enclose the title and any subtitle in quotation marks.

③ *Peridical title.* Italicize. Exclude any initial *A, An,* or *The.*

④ *Print publication information.* List the volume number and issue number (if any) separated by a period; the date of publication, including the day (if given), month, and year; and the inclusive page numbers.

⑤ *Name of database.* Italicize.

⑥ *Medium.* For an online database, use *Web.*

⑦ *Date of access.* Give the day, month, and year, then a period.

For an article from a database, use the following format:

[Citation format for the journal, magazine, or newspaper article —
see pp. 210-11]. *Name of Database.* Medium. Date accessed.

A citation for the article below would look like this:

CITATION INFORMATION FOR ARTICLE

Singer, P. W. "Outsourcing War." *Foreign Affairs* 84.2 (2005): 119- .

Academic Search Premier. Web. 10 June 2005.

ACCESS DATE

MEDIUM

NAME OF
DATABASE,
ITALICIZED

New Search | View Folder | Preferences | Help

EBSCO Research Databases

UNIV OF MISSOURI- COLUMBIA

Basic Search   Advanced Search   Choose Databases

Sign In to My EBSCOhost

Keyword   Publications   Subject Terms   Indexes   Cited References

Images

◀ 1 of 1 ▶   Result List | Refine Search   🖨 Print 📧 E-mail 💾 Save 📁 Add to folder   📁 Folder is empty.

Formats: 📑 Citation 📄 HTML Full Text

Choose Language ▼ Translate

Title: *Outsourcing War* , By: Singer, P. W., Foreign Affairs, 00157120, Mar/Apr2005, Vol. 84, Issue 2
Database: Academic Search Premier

Section: Essays

Outsourcing War

UNDERSTANDING THE PRIVATE MILITARY INDUSTRY

Contents

PRIVATE SECTOR
AND PUBLIC
INTEREST

FIVE OBSTRUCTIONS

CAVEAT EMPTOR–
AND RENTER

THE TALES of war, profit, honor, and greed that emerge from the private military industry often read like something out of a Hollywood screenplay. They range from action-packed stories of guns-for-hire fighting off swarms of insurgents in Iraq to the sad account of a private military air crew languishing in captivity in Colombia, abandoned by their corporate bosses in the United States. A recent African "rent-a-coup" scandal involved the son of a former British prime minister, and accusations of war profiteering have reached into the halls of the White House itself.

Incredible as these stories often sound, the private military industry is no fiction. Private companies are becoming significant players in conflicts around the world, supplying not merely the goods but also the services of war. Although recent well-publicized incidents from Abu Ghraib to Zimbabwe have shone unaccustomed light onto this new force in warfare, private military firms (PMFS) remain a poorly understood--and often unacknowledged-- phenomenon. Mystery, myth, and conspiracy theory surround them, leaving policymakers and the public in positions of dangerous ignorance. Many key questions remain unanswered, including, What is this industry and where did it come from? What is its role in the United States' largest current overseas venture, Iraq? What are the broader implications of that role? And how should policymakers respond? Only by developing a better understanding of this burgeoning industry can governments hope to get a proper hold on this newly powerful force in foreign policy. If they fail, the consequences for policy and democracy could be deeply destructive.

PRIVATE SECTOR AND PUBLIC INTEREST

PMFS are businesses that provide governments with professional services intricately linked to warfare; they

For more on using MLA style to cite articles from databases, see p. 216. (For guidelines and models for using APA style, see pp. 245–46; for *Chicago* style, see p. 261; for CSE style, see p. 277.)

words capitalized; the editor(s) of the site, preceded by
Ed.; the version number of the site, if given, preceded
by *Vers.*; and the name of the sponsoring institution or
organization.

- **DATE OF ACCESS.** Give the most recent date you accessed
  the source, with the name of the month abbreviated
  (except for May, June, and July).

- **URL.** Include a URL only if you think your readers will
  have difficulty finding your source without one. If you do
  include a URL, put it after the period following the date of
  access, enclose it in angle brackets, and put a period after
  the closing bracket.

Further guidelines for citing electronic sources can be
found in the *MLA Handbook for Writers of Research Papers*
and online at www.mla.org.

28. ARTICLE FROM AN ONLINE DATABASE OR A SUBSCRIPTION SERVICE.
For a work from an online database, provide all of the following elements that are available: the author's name; the
title of the work (in quotation marks); any print publication
information; the name of the online database, italicized; the
medium consulted (*Web*), and the date of access.

> Penn, Sean, and Jon Krakauer. *"Into the Wild* Script." *Internet*
> *Movie Script Database.* Web. 12 June 2008.

For a work from a library subscription service, include the
same information as for an online database: after the information about the work, give the name of the database, italicized; the medium consulted (*Web*); and the date of access.

> Collins, Ross F. "Cattle Barons and Ink Slingers: How Cow Country
> Journalists Created a Great American Myth." *American*
> *Journalism* 24.3 (2007): 7-29. *Communication and Mass*
> *Media Complete.* Web. 7 Feb. 2008.

For a work from a personal online subscription service
such as America Online, follow the guidelines in this chapter for the appropriate type of work. Then give the same
information as for an online database.

> Weeks, W. William. "Beyond the Ark." *Nature Conservancy* Mar.-Apr.
> 1999. *America Online.* Web. 2 Apr. 1999.

29. WORK FROM A WEB SITE. For basic information on citing a work from a Web site, see pp. 218–19. Include all of the following elements that are available: the author; the title of the document in quotation marks; the name of the Web site, italicized; the name of the publisher or sponsor (if none is available, use *N.p.*); the date of publication (if not available, use *n.d.*); the medium consulted (*Web*); and the date of access.

> "Hands Off Public Broadcasting." *Media Matters for America*. Media
>
> Matters for America, 24 May 2005. Web. 31 May 2005.

> Stauder, Ellen Keck. "Darkness Audible: Negative Capability
>
> and Mark Doty's 'Nocturne in Black and Gold.'" *Romantic*
>
> *Circles Praxis Series*. Ed. Orrin Wang. 2003. Web. 28 Sept. 2003.

Cite an entry from a blog as you would any document from a Web site, including the title of the blog, followed by the date of the posting.

> Parker, Randall. "Growth Rate for Electric Hybrid Vehicle Market
>
> Debated." *FuturePundit*. N.p. 20 May 2005. Web. 24 May
>
> 2005.

30. ENTIRE WEB SITE. Follow the guidelines for a specific work from the Web, but begin with the name of the editor(s), if any, and title of the site.

> Bernstein, Charles, Kenneth Goldsmith, Martin Spinelli, and
>
> Patrick Durgin, eds. *Electronic Poetry Corner*. SUNY Buffalo,
>
> 2003. Web. 26 Sept. 2006.

> *Weather.com*. Weather Channel Interactive, 2006. Web. 13 Mar.
>
> 2006.

For a personal Web site, include the name of the person who created the site; the title, italicized, or (if there is no title) a description such as *Home page*, not italicized; the publisher or sponsor of the site (if none, use *N.p.*); the date of the last update; the medium of publication (*Web*); and the date of access.

> Lunsford, Andrea A. Home page. Stanford U, 27 Mar. 2003. Web.
>
> 17 May 2006.

When using MLA style to cite a work from a Web site, include as many of the following elements as you can.

① *Author of the work.* List the last name first, a comma, the first name, and the middle initial (if given). End with a period. If no author is given, begin with the title.

② *Title of the work.* Enclose the title and any subtitle of the work in quotation marks.

③ *Title of the Web site.* Give the title of the entire site, italicized. Where there is no clear title, use *Home page* without italics.

④ *Name of the publisher or sponsoring organization.* The name often appears at the bottom of the home page. If no information is available, write *N.p.*

⑤ *Date of publication or latest update.* If no date is available, use *n.d.*

⑥ *Medium consulted.* Use *Web.*

⑦ *Date of access.* End with a period.

For a work from a Web site, use the following format:

Last name, First name. "Title of work." *Title of Web site*. Publisher
    or sponsoring organization, date. Medium. Access date.

A citation for the work on p. 219 would look like this:

AUTHOR OF WORK,   TITLE AND SUBTITLE OF WORK,
LAST NAME FIRST   IN QUOTATION MARKS

Jangfeldt, Bengt. "Joseph Brodsky: A Virgilian Hero, Doomed
    Never to Return Home." *Nobelprize.org*. Nobel Foundation,

                TITLE OF WEB SITE, ITALICIZED   SITE SPONSOR

    1 Dec. 1999. Web. 4 May 2005.

                MEDIUM
    PUBLICATION   ACCESS
    DATE   DATE

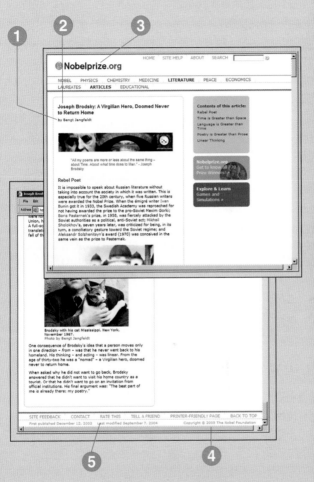

For more on using MLA style to cite Web documents, see p. 217. (For guidelines and models for using APA style, see p. 246; for *Chicago* style, see p. 260; for CSE style, see pp. 276–77.)

For a course site, include the name of the instructor, the title of the course in quotation marks, a description such as *Course home page*, the dates of the course, the department name, the institution, the medium consulted (*Web*), and the access information.

> Creekmur, Corey K., and Philip Lutgendorf. "Topics in Asian
>
> Cinema: Popular Hindi Cinema." Course home page. Fall
>
> 2004. Depts. of English, Cinema, and Comparative Literature.
>
> U of Iowa. Web. 13 Mar. 2007.

For a department Web site, give the department name, a description such as *Home page*, the institution, the medium (*Web*), and the access information.

> Dept. of English. Home page. Amherst Coll., n.d. Web. 5 Apr.
>
> 2006.

31. ONLINE BOOK. Cite an online book as you would a print book. After the print publication information, if any, give the title of the Web site or database, the medium (*Web*), and the date of access.

> Euripides. *The Trojan Women*. Trans. Gilbert Murray. New York:
>
> Oxford UP, 1915. Internet Sacred Text Archive. Web.
>
> 12 Oct. 2003.

32. PART OF AN ONLINE BOOK. Include the title of the part.

> "France." *Encyclopaedia Britannica Online*. 2003. Encyclopaedia
>
> Britannica. 13 Mar. 2003.
>
> Riis, Jacob. "The Genesis of the Gang." *The Battle with the Slum*.
>
> New York: Macmillan, 1902. *Bartleby.com: Great Books*
>
> *Online*. 2000. Web. 31 March 2005.

33. ARTICLE IN AN ONLINE JOURNAL, MAGAZINE, OR NEWSPAPER. Cite an online journal article as you would a print journal article (see models 27–28), using inclusive page numbers, if possible, or the first page number and a plus sign. If an online article does not have page numbers, use *n. pag.* Then end the entry with the medium consulted (*Web*) and the date of access.

Gallagher, Brian. "Greta Garbo Is Sad: Some Historical

    Reflections on the Paradoxes of Stardom in the American

    Film Industry, 1910-1960." *Images: A Journal of Film*

    and Popular Culture 3 (1997): n. pag. Web. 7 Aug. 2002.

For an online magazine or newspaper article, give the author, the title of the article in quotation marks, the name of the magazine or newspaper (italicized), the sponsor of the Web site, the date of publication, the medium consulted (*Web*), and the date of access.

Burt, Stephen. "Paper Trail: The True Legacy of Marianne Moore,

    Modernist Monument." *Slate*. Washingtonpost.Newsweek

    Interactive, 11 Nov. 2003. Web. 12 Nov. 2003.

Shea, Christopher. "Five Truths about Tuition." *New York Times*.

    New York Times, 9 Nov. 2003. Web. 11 Nov. 2003.

34. ONLINE EDITORIAL OR LETTER TO THE EDITOR. Include the word *Editorial* or *Letter* after the author (if given) and title (if any). Then follow with the name of the journal, magazine, or newspaper; the sponsor of the Web site; the date of publication; the medium consulted (*Web*); and the date of access.

Moore, Paula, "Go Vegetarian." Letter. *New York Times*. New York

    Times, 25 Feb. 2008. Web. 6 Mar. 2008.

35. ONLINE REVIEW. Give the reviewer's name and title of the review, if any; then add *Rev. of* and the title of the work being reviewed and the author, director, or other creator of the work. End with the name of the Web site, the sponsor of the site, the date of publication, the medium consulted (*Web*), and the date of access.

O'Hehir, Andrew. "The Nightmare in Iraq." Rev. of *Gunner Palace*,

    dir. Michael Tucker and Petra Epperlein. *Salon*. Salon Media

    Group, 4 Mar. 2005. Web. 24 Mar. 2005.

36. POSTING TO A DISCUSSION GROUP. Begin with the author's name and the title of the posting in quotation marks or, if

the posting has no title, use *Online posting* (not italicized or in quotation marks). Follow with the name of the Web site, the sponsor or publisher of the site (use *N.p.* if there is no sponsor), the date of publication, the medium (*Web*), and the date of access.

Daly, Catherine. "Poetry Slams." *Poetics Discussion List*. SUNY

Buffalo, 29 Aug. 2003. Web. 1 Oct. 2003.

37. EMAIL. Include the writer's name, the subject line of the message, a description that mentions the recipient, and the date of the message. (MLA style hyphenates *e-mail*.)

Harris, J. "Thoughts on Impromptu Stage Productions." Message

to the author. 16 July 2003. E-mail.

38. ENTRY IN A WIKI. Because wiki content is collectively edited, do not include an author. Include the title of the entry; the name of the wiki, italicized; the sponsor or publisher of the wiki (use *N.p.* if there is no sponsor); the date of the latest update; the medium (*Web*); and the date of access. Check with your instructor before using a wiki as a source. (The MLA does not provide guidelines on citing wikis; this model is based on the MLA's guidelines on citing short works from Web sites.)

"Fédération Internationale de Football Association." *Wikipedia*.

Wikimedia Foundation, 27 June 2006. Web. 27 June 2006.

39. CD-ROM. For a periodically revised CD-ROM, after the publication information for the text's print version, if any, include the term *CD-ROM*, the city of publication and name of the company or group producing it, and the electronic publication date.

Ashenfelter, Orley, and Kathryn Graddy. "Auctions and the Price of

Art." *Journal of Economic Literature* 41.3 (2003): 763-87.

CD-ROM. Nashville: Amer. Economic Assn., Sept. 2003.

If the CD-ROM is not regularly updated, cite it much like a book. Add the term *CD-ROM*.

Cambridge Advanced Learner's Dictionary. 3rd ed. Cambridge:

Cambridge UP, 2008. CD-ROM.

Other sources (including online versions). For online versions of sources listed here, use the appropriate model for the source and then end with the medium and date of access.

40. REPORT OR PAMPHLET

Allen, Katherine, and Lee Rainie. *Parents Online*. Washington: Pew Internet and Amer. Life Project, 2002. Print.

41. DISSERTATION

Yau, Rittchell Ann. *The Portrayal of Immigration in a Selection of Picture Books Published since 1970*. Diss. U of San Francisco, 2003. Print.

42. DISSERTATION ABSTRACT

Huang-Tiller, Gillian C. "The Power of the Meta-Genre: Cultural, Sexual, and Racial Politics of the American Modernist Sonnet." Diss. U of Notre Dame, 2000. *DAI* 61 (2000): 1401. Print.

43. UNPUBLISHED OR PERSONAL INTERVIEW

Freedman, Sasha. Personal interview. 10 Nov. 2003.

44. PUBLISHED INTERVIEW. Include the name of the interviewer after the label *Interview,* if relevant.

Ebert, Roger. Interview with Matthew Rothschild. *Progressive*. Progressive Magazine, Aug. 2003. Web. 5 Oct. 2003.

Taylor, Max. "Max Taylor on Winning." *Time* 13 Nov. 2000: 66. Print.

45. BROADCAST INTERVIEW

Gyllenhaal, Maggie. Interview by Terry Gross. *Fresh Air*. Natl. Public Radio. WBUR, Boston, 30 Sept. 2003. Radio.

46. UNPUBLISHED LETTER

Lanois, Sophia. Letter to the author. 25 Aug. 2003.

47. LEGAL SOURCE. For a legal case, give the name followed by the case number, the name of the court, and the date of the decision.

> Eldred v. Ashcroft. No. 01-618. Supreme Ct. of the US. 15 Jan.
>> 2003. Print.

For an act, give the name followed by the Public Law number of the act, the date it was enacted, and the Statutes at Large cataloging number of the act.

> Museum and Library Services Act of 2003. Pub. L. 108-81. 25
>> Sept. 2003. Stat. 117.991. Print.

48. FILM, VIDEO, OR DVD

> Moore, Michael, dir. *Bowling for Columbine*. United Artists, 2002.
>> *BowlingforColumbine.com*. Web. 30 Sept. 2003.

> *Sideways*. Dir. Alexander Payne. Perf. Paul Giamatti, Virginia
>> Madsen, Thomas Haden Church, and Sandra Oh. 2004.
>> Fox Searchlight, 2005. DVD.

49. TELEVISION OR RADIO PROGRAM

> Komando, Kim. "E-mail Hacking and the Law." *CBS Radio.com*.
>> CBS Radio Inc., 28 Oct. 2003. Web. 11 Nov. 2003.

> "Los Angeles: Silenced Partner." Narr. Paul Winfield.
>> *City Confidential*. Arts and Entertainment Network, 25 Sept.
>> 2003. Television.

50. SOUND RECORDING

> Fountains of Wayne. "Bright Future in Sales." *Welcome Interstate
>> Managers*. S-Curve, 2003. CD.

> Perlman, Itzhak and Pinchas Zukerman, perf. *Bach: Violin
>> Concertos*. By Johann Sebastian Bach. English Chamber Orch.
>> EMI, 2002. CD.

51. MUSICAL COMPOSITION

> Mozart, Wolfgang Amadeus. Symphony no. 41 in C major, K551.

52. LECTURE OR SPEECH

Colbert, Stephen. Speech. White House Correspondents'
Association Dinner. *YouTube*. YouTube, LLC, 29 Apr. 2006.
Web. 20 May 2006.

Eugenides, Jeffrey. Portland Arts and Lectures. Arlene Schnitzer
Concert Hall, Portland, OR. 30 Sept. 2003. Lecture.

53. LIVE PERFORMANCE

Anything Goes. By Cole Porter. Perf. Klea Blackhurst. Shubert
Theater, New Haven. 7 Oct. 2003. Performance.

54. WORK OF ART OR PHOTOGRAPH

Chagall, Marc. *The Poet with the Birds*. 1911. Minneapolis
Inst. of Arts. *artsmia.org*. Web. 6 Oct. 2003.

Kahlo, Frida. *Self-Portrait with Cropped Hair*. 1940. Oil on canvas.
Museum of Mod. Art, New York.

55. MAP OR CHART

Australia. Map. *Perry-Castañeda Library Map Collection*. U of Texas,
1999. Web. 4 Nov. 2003.

California. Map. Chicago: Rand, 2002. Print.

56. ADVERTISEMENT

Microsoft. Advertisement. *Harper's* Oct. 2003: 2-3. Print.

Microsoft. Advertisement. *New York Times*. New York Times,
11 Nov. 2003. Web. 11 Nov. 2003.

57. CARTOON OR COMIC STRIP

Lewis, Eric. "The Unpublished Freud." Cartoon. *New Yorker* 11 Mar.
2002: 80. Print.

Craig 1

David Craig

Professor Turkman

English 219

8 December 2003

Instant Messaging: The Language of Youth Literacy

The English language is under attack. At least, that is what many people would have you believe. From concerned parents to local librarians, everybody seems to have a negative comment on the state of youth literacy today, and many pin the blame on new technology, saying that teachers often must struggle with students who refuse to learn the conventionally correct way to use language.

In the *Chronicle of Higher Education*, Wendy Leibowitz quotes Sven Birkerts of Mount Holyoke College as saying that students "strip-mine what they read" on the Internet. Those casual reading habits, in turn, produce "quickly generated, casual prose" (A67). When asked about the causes of this situation, some point to instant messaging (IM), which coincides with new computer technology.

Instant messaging allows two individuals to engage in real-time, written communication; however, many messagers disregard standard writing conventions. For example, here is part of an IM conversation between two teenage girls:[1]

> Teen One: sorry im talkinto like 10 ppl at a time
>
> Teen Two: u izzyful person
>
> Teen Two: kwel
>
> Teen One: hey i g2g

As this brief conversation shows, participants must use words to communicate via IM, but their words do not have to be in academic or professional English.

Some people feel that instant messaging threatens youth literacy because it creates and compounds undesirable reading and writing

[1]This transcript of an IM conversation was collected on 20 Nov. 2003. The teenagers' names are concealed to protect privacy.

habits and discourages students from learning standard literacy skills. However, the critics' arguments don't hold up. In fact, IM seems to be a beneficial force in the development of youth literacy because it promotes regular contact with words and the use of a written medium for communication.

Regardless of one's views on IM, parents and educators appear to be right about the decline in youth literacy. According to a study from the United States Department of Education's National Center for Education Statistics, the percentage of twelfth graders whose writing ability was "at or above the basic level" of performance dropped from 78 to 74 percent between 1998 and 2002 (Persky, Daane, and Jin 21). And this trend is occurring while IM usage is on the rise. According to the Pew Internet and American Life Project, 54 percent of American youths aged twelve to seventeen have used IM (qtd. in Lenhart and Lewis 20). This figure translates to a pool of some thirteen million young instant messengers. Of this group, Pew reports, half send instant messages every time they go online. American youths apparently spend, at a minimum, nearly three million hours per day on IM. What's more, they seem to be using a new vocabulary.

To establish the existence of an IM language, I analyzed 11,341 lines of text from IM conversations between U.S. residents aged twelve to seventeen. Young messengers voluntarily sent me chat logs. I went through all of the logs, recording the number of times IM language was used in place of conventional English. During the course of my study, I identified four types of IM language: phonetic replacements, acronyms, abbreviations, and inanities. An example of phonetic replacement is using *ur* for *you are*. Another popular type of IM language is the acronym; a common one is *lol*, for *laughing out loud*. Abbreviations are also common in IM, but I discovered that typical abbreviations, such as *etc.*, are not new to the English language. Finally, "inanities" include completely new expressions and nonsensical variations of other words.

In the chat transcripts that I analyzed, the best display of typical IM lingo came from conversations between two thirteen-year-old Texan girls who are avid IM users. Figure 1 graphs how often they used certain phonetic replacements and abbreviations. The *y*-axis plots frequency of replacement, comparing the number of times a word or phrase is used in IM language with the total number of times that it is communicated. The *x*-axis lists specific IM words and phrases.

My research shows that the Texan girls used the first ten phonetic replacements or abbreviations at least 50 percent of the time in their normal IM writing. For example, for every time one of them wrote *see*, there was a parallel time when *c* was used in its place. It appears that the popular IM culture contains at least some elements of its own language. Much of this language seems new: no formal dictionary yet identifies the most common IM words and phrases.

While messaging is widespread and does seem to have its own vocabulary, these two factors alone do not mean it has a damaging influence on youth literacy. However, some people claim that the new technology is a threat to the English language:

> "Abbreviations commonly used in online instant
> messages are creeping into formal essays that
> students write for credit," said [sixth-grade teacher]
> Debbie Frost. . . . "I don't get cohesive thoughts, I
> don't get sentences, they don't capitalize, and they

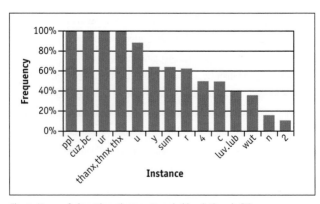

Fig. 1. Usage of phonetic replacements and abbreviations in IM.

have a lot of misspellings and bad grammar," she
said. "With all those glaring mistakes, it's hard to
see the content." ("Young Messagers")

The critics of instant messaging are numerous. Scholars of
metalinguistics, on the other hand, support the claim that IM is not
damaging to those who use it. One of the most prominent components
of IM language is phonetic replacement, in which a word such as
everyone becomes *every1*. This type of wordplay has a special
importance in the development of an advanced literacy. According to
David Crystal, an internationally recognized scholar of linguistics, as
young children learn how words string together to express ideas, they
go through many phases of language play. The rhymes and nonsensical
chants of preschoolers are vital to their learning language, and a
healthy appetite for wordplay leads to a better command of language
later in life (182).

Crystal uses *metalinguistics* to refer to the ability to "step back"
and analyze how language works. "If we are good at stepping back,"
he says, "at thinking in a more abstract way about what we hear and
what we say, then we are more likely to be good at acquiring those
skills which depend on just such a stepping back in order to be
successful--and this means, chiefly, reading and writing. . . . [T]he
greater our ability to play with language, . . . the more advanced will
be our command of language as a whole" (181).

Metalinguistics also involves our ability to write in a variety of
distinct styles and tones. Many critics assume that *either* IM *or*
academic literacy will eventually win out and that the two modes
cannot exist side by side. However, human beings ordinarily develop
a large range of language abilities, from the formal to the relaxed.
Mark Twain, for example, employed local speech when writing
dialogue for *Huckleberry Finn*. Yet few people would argue that
Twain's knowledge of this form of English had a negative impact on
his ability to write in standard English.

Of course, just as Mark Twain used dialects carefully in dialogue,
writers must pay careful attention to the kind of language they use

in any setting. The anonymous owner of the language Web site The Discouraging Word backs up this idea:

> What is necessary, we feel, is that students learn how to shift between different styles of writing--that, in other words, the abbreviations and shortcuts of IM should be used online . . . but that they should not be used in an essay submitted to a teacher. . . . IM might even be considered . . . a different way of reading and writing, one that requires specific and unique skills shared by certain communities.

The analytical ability necessary for writers to choose an appropriate tone and style in their writing is metalinguistic in nature because it involves the comparison of language systems. Thus, young people who possess both IM and traditional skills stand to be better off than their peers who have been trained only in traditional or conventional systems.

Youth literacy does seem to be declining. But the possibility of instant messaging causing the decline seems unlikely when there is evidence of other possible causes. According to the College Board, which collects data from its test takers, enrollment in English composition and grammar classes has decreased in the last decade by 14 percent (Carnahan and Coletti 11). Simply put, schools in the United States are not teaching English as much as they used to. Rather than blaming IM alone for the decline in literacy and test scores, we must look toward our schools' lack of focus on the teaching of conventional English skills.

I found that the use of instant messaging does not threaten the development or maintenance of formal language skills. The current decline in youth literacy is not due to the rise of instant messaging; rather, fewer young students seem to be receiving an adequate education in the use of conventional English. Unfortunately, it may always be fashionable to blame new tools for old problems, but in the case of instant messaging, that blame is not warranted. Although IM may expose literacy problems, it does not create them.

Works Cited

Carnahan, Kristin, and Chiara Coletti. *Ten-Year Trend in SAT Scores Indicates Increased Emphasis on Math Is Yielding Results: Reading and Writing Are Causes for Concern*. New York: College Board, 2002. Print.

Crystal, David. *Language Play*. Chicago: U of Chicago P, 1998. Print.

The Discouraging Word. "Re: Instant Messaging and Literacy." E-mail to the author. 13 Nov. 2003. E-mail.

Leibowitz, Wendy R. "Technology Transforms Writing and the Teaching of Writing." *Chronicle of Higher Education* 26 Nov. 1999: A67-68. Print.

Lenhart, Amanda, and Oliver Lewis. *Teenage Life Online: The Rise of the Instant-Message Generation and the Internet's Impact on Friendships and Family Relationships*. Washington: Pew Internet and Amer. Life Project, 2001. Print.

Persky, Hilary R., Mary C. Daane, and Ying Jin. *The Nation's Report Card: Writing 2002*. NCES 2003-529. Washington: GPO, 2003. Print.

"Young Messagers Ask: Why Spell It Out?" *Columbus Dispatch* 10 Nov. 2002: C1. *LexisNexis Academic*. Web. 14 Nov. 2003.

43 APA Style

Many fields in the social sciences ask students to follow the basic guidelines prescribed by the American Psychological Association (APA) for formatting manuscripts and documenting various kinds of sources. For more information, consult the *Publication Manual of the American Psychological Association,* Sixth Edition, 2010.

43a From assignment to thesis and support

The writing you do in the social sciences may include analyses of the works of others, in position papers or literature reviews (reviews of other studies related to a research topic). Or, you may write about your own research in research reports or case studies. In all cases, developing a strong thesis that states your goal clearly is crucial. Study your assignment carefully, focusing on key terms like *analyze* and *report,* and ask about any aspects that you do not understand, such as how to write a literature review or research report. (For more on beginning a research project, see 38a.) The examples in this section show how one student moved from an assignment to a strong thesis and began crafting an APA-style essay.

Assignment.   Before you begin, make sure you understand the requirements and limits of the assignment. Check whether you are required to include particular elements or sections in your project: an abstract, an introduction, a review of the literature, methods or procedures, results, a discussion, a conclusion, or references.

> Write a brief literature review related to at least one aspect of child development, comparing at least three journal articles addressing the topic and drawing conclusions based on their findings.

Generating ideas about the assignment.   The student had been taking notes on her reading. While going back through the notes to see what aspects of child development she had commented on, she found several notes on interesting and important material on the early detection of child abuse. She decided to try focusing on this aspect.

Working thesis. A working thesis should answer the main question your research poses, given your analysis of current research. The student identified three journal articles that seemed most informative about early detection and then reread them, taking careful notes on the strengths and weaknesses of each study. After detailed comparison of the articles, the student crafted the following working thesis:

> While researchers do not precisely agree on what complex interaction among parent, child, and environment leads to child abuse, they strongly concur on the need for early detection of such abuse.

Evidence. In reviews of literature and reports of research, many disciplines will ask that you summarize key work. You need to understand the evidence used in your sources as well as the evidence you derive in support of your thesis. You will also need to learn to deal with both quantitative and qualitative studies. Quantitative studies emphasize statistical information — from surveys, polls, experiments, and tests — which is often presented in graphs and charts. Qualitative studies are more subjective because they rely on interviews and observations. Here, the instructor asked that students discuss each article in an appropriate section of the review, marking off each section with a heading. These articles then became the evidence for the essay. This student's job as a writer was to analyze each article and to identify specific quotations from it to exemplify the points she was making about it. She needed to understand each article's use of statistics in order to evaluate the data.

Sources. As you prepare your essay, take careful notes on the sources you use (see 39c). Be sure to introduce quotations with a signal phrase (see 40a) and to explain the significance of each quotation. Generally, use only last names when referring to authors. Because APA style emphasizes the timeliness of each source, your text must include the date of every source you cite, either in the signal phrase or in a parenthetical citation (see 43c). Make sure each quotation supports your thesis. Be careful not to plagiarize when

 bedfordstmartins.com/easywriter To access the advice in this chapter online, click on **Documenting Sources.**

you paraphrase and summarize sources (see 40d). APA style generally calls for you to use the **past tense** (*Baker showed*) in literature reviews and the **present tense** only when you discuss the results of an experiment (*the second set of results corroborates*) or for information widely accepted as established (*researchers agree*).

43b APA manuscript format

The following formatting guidelines are adapted from the APA recommendations for preparing manuscripts for publication in journals. However, check with your instructor before preparing your final draft.

Title page.   APA does not provide specific title-page guidelines. Be sure to center the title and include your name, the course name and number, the instructor's name, and the date. In the top right-hand corner, type the words *Running head*, a colon, and a short version of the title (fifty characters or fewer, including spaces using all capital letters). On the same line, flush with the right margin, type the number *1*.

Margins and spacing.   Leave margins of at least one inch at the top and bottom and on both sides of the page. Do not justify the right margin. Double-space the entire text, including headings, set-off quotations (see 23a), content notes, and the list of references. Indent one-half inch, or five spaces, from the left margin for the first line of a paragraph and all lines of a quotation over forty words long.

Short title and page numbers.   Type *Running head* and the short title in the upper left corner of each page. Type the page number in the upper right corner of each page.

Long quotations.   For a long, set-off quotation (one having more than forty words), indent it one-half inch (or five to seven spaces) from the left margin and do not use quotation marks. Place the page reference in parentheses one space after the final punctuation.

Abstract.   If your instructor asks for an abstract with your paper, the abstract should go immediately after the title page, with the word *Abstract* centered about an inch from the top of the page. Double-space the text of the abstract. For most papers, a one-paragraph abstract of about one hundred words will be sufficient to introduce readers to your topic and provide a brief summary of your major thesis and supporting points.

Headings. Headings are used within the text of many APA-style papers. In papers with only one or two levels of headings, center the main headings; italicize the subheadings and position them flush with the left margin. Capitalize all major words; however, do not capitalize **articles**, short **prepositions**, and **coordinating conjunctions** unless they are the first word or follow a colon.

Visuals. Tables should be labeled *Table*, numbered, and captioned. All other visuals (charts, graphs, photographs, and drawings) should be labeled *Figure*, numbered, and captioned with a description and the source information. Remember to refer to each visual in your text, stating how it contributes to the point(s) you are making. Tables and figures should generally appear near the relevant text; check with your instructor for guidelines on placement of visuals.

List of references. Start the list of references on a new page after the text and any footnotes. Identify each page with the short title and the page number, continuing the numbering of the text. Center the title *References* one inch from the top, and double-space between the title and the first entry. Type the first line of each entry flush with the left margin, and indent any subsequent lines one-half inch, or five to seven spaces.

List sources alphabetically by authors' last names. If the author of a source is unknown, alphabetize the source by the first major word of the title.

43c In-text citations

APA style requires parenthetical citations in the text to document quotations, paraphrases, summaries, and other material from a source. These citations include the year of publication and correspond to full bibliographic entries in the list of references.

1. AUTHOR NAMED IN A SIGNAL PHRASE. Generally, use the author's name in a signal phrase to introduce the cited material, and place the date, in parentheses, immediately after the author's name. For a quotation, the page number, preceded by *p.,* appears in parentheses after the quotation.

> Chavez (2003) noted that "six years after slim cigarettes for women were introduced, more than twice as many teenage girls were smoking" (p. 13).

For electronic texts or other works without page numbers, paragraph numbers may be used, preceded by the ¶ symbol or the abbreviation *para.*

> Weinberg (2000) has claimed that "the techniques used in group therapy can be verbal, expressive, or psychodramatic" (¶ 5).

If paragraph numbers are not given, cite the heading and number of the paragraph in that section: (Types of Groups section, para. 1). For a long, set-off quotation (one having more than forty words), place the page reference in parentheses one space after the final punctuation (23a).

2. AUTHOR NAMED IN A PARENTHETICAL REFERENCE. When you do not mention the author in a signal phrase in your text, give the author's name and the date, separated by a comma, in parentheses at the end of the cited material.

One study found that 17% of adopted children in the United States are of a different race than their adoptive parents (Peterson, 2003).

3. TWO AUTHORS. Use both names in all citations. Use *and* in a signal phrase, but use an ampersand (&) in parentheses.

Babcock and Laschever (2003) have suggested that many women do not negotiate their salaries and pay raises as vigorously as their male counterparts do.

A recent study has suggested that many women do not negotiate their salaries and pay raises as vigorously as their male counterparts do (Babcock & Laschever, 2003).

4. THREE TO FIVE AUTHORS. List all the authors' names for the first reference.

Safer, Voccola, Hurd, and Goodwin (2003) reached somewhat different conclusions by designing a study that was less dependent on subjective judgment than were previous studies.

In subsequent references, use just the first author's name plus *et al.*

Based on the results, Safer et al. (2003) determined that the apes took significant steps toward self-expression.

5. SIX OR MORE AUTHORS. Use only the first author's name and *et al.* in every citation.

As Soleim et al. (2002) demonstrated, advertising holds the potential for manipulating "free-willed" consumers.

6. ORGANIZATION AS AUTHOR. If the name of an organization or a corporation is long, spell it out the first time, followed by an abbreviation in brackets. In later references, use the abbreviation only.

FIRST CITATION   (Centers for Disease Control and
                      Prevention [CDC], 2003)

LATER CITATIONS   (CDC, 2003)

7. UNKNOWN AUTHOR. Use the title or its first few words in a signal phrase or in parentheses. Italicize a book or report title; place an article or chapter title in quotation marks.

> The employment profiles for this time period substantiated this trend (*Federal Employment,* 2001).

8. TWO OR MORE AUTHORS WITH THE SAME LAST NAME. If your list of references includes works by different authors with the same last name, include the authors' initials in each citation.

> S. Bartolomeo (2000) conducted the groundbreaking study on teenage childbearing.

9. TWO OR MORE SOURCES IN ONE PARENTHETICAL REFERENCE. List sources by different authors in alphabetical order by authors' last names, separated by semicolons: (Cardone, 1998; Lai, 2002). List works by the same author in chronological order, separated by commas: (Lai, 2000, 2002).

10. SPECIFIC PARTS OF A SOURCE. Use abbreviations (*chap., p., para.,* and so on) in a parenthetical reference to name the part of a work you are citing.

> Mogolov (2003, chap. 9) argued that his research yielded the opposite results.

11. EMAIL AND OTHER PERSONAL COMMUNICATION. Cite any personal letters, email, electronic postings, telephone conversations, or interviews with the person's initial(s) and last name, the identification *personal communication,* and the date. Do not include personal communications in the reference list.

> R. Tobin (personal communication, November 4, 2003) supported his claims about music therapy with new evidence.

12. ELECTRONIC DOCUMENT. Cite a Web or electronic document as you would a print source, using the author's name and date; indicating the chapter or figure, as appropriate; and giving a full citation in your list of references. To cite a quotation, include the page or paragraph numbers, if available.

> Zomkowski argued the importance of "ensuring equitable access to the Internet" (2003, para. 3).

43d Content notes

APA style allows you to use content notes to expand or supplement your text. Indicate such notes in your text by superscript numbers (1). Type the notes themselves on a separate page after the last page of the text, under the heading *Footnotes,* which should be centered at the top of the page. Double-space all entries. Indent the first line of each note one-half inch, or five spaces, but begin subsequent lines at the left margin.

SUPERSCRIPT NUMERAL IN TEXT

The age of the children involved was an important factor in the selection of items for the questionnaire.[1]

FOOTNOTE

[1]Marjorie Youngston Forman and William Cole of the Child Study Team provided great assistance in identifying appropriate items for the questionnaire.

43e List of references

The alphabetical list of the sources cited in your document is called *References.* (If your instructor asks that you list everything you have read — not just the sources you cite — call the list *Bibliography.*) APA style specifies the treatment and placement of four basic elements — author, publication date, title, and other publication information.

- **AUTHOR.** List all authors' last names first, and use only initials for first and middle names. Separate the names of multiple authors with commas, and use an ampersand (&) before the last author's name.

- **PUBLICATION DATE.** Enclose the date in parentheses. Use only the year for books and journals; use the year, a comma, and the month or month and day for magazines; use the year, a comma, and the month and day for newspapers. Do not abbreviate.

- **TITLE.** Italicize titles and subtitles of books and periodicals. Do not enclose titles of articles in quotation marks. For books and articles, capitalize only the first word of the title and subtitle and any proper nouns or proper adjectives. Capitalize all major words in a periodical title.

- **PUBLICATION INFORMATION.** For a book, list the city of publication and the country or postal abbreviation for the

state, a colon, and the publisher's name, dropping *Inc.,*
Co., or *Publishers.* For a periodical, follow the periodical
title with a comma, the volume number (italicized), the
issue number (if appropriate) in parentheses and followed
by a comma, and the inclusive page numbers of the article.
For newspapers and for articles or chapters in books,
include the abbreviation *p.* ("page") or *pp.* ("pages")
before the page numbers.

The following sample entries use hanging indent format, in
which the first line aligns on the left and the subsequent
lines indent one-half inch, or five spaces. This is the cus-
tomary APA format for final copy, including student
papers.

Books. Here is an annotated example of a basic entry for a book:

AUTHOR'S LAST
NAME, THEN   YEAR OF   TITLE (AND SUBTITLE,
INITIAL(S)   PUBLICATION   IF ANY), ITALICIZED

Levick, S. E. (2003). *Clone being: Exploring the psychological and*
   social dimensions. Lanham, MD: Rowman & Littlefield.

INDENT ONE-HALF   PUBLISHER'S CITY, STATE, AND
INCH, OR FIVE SPACES   NAME

DOUBLE-SPACE

1. ONE AUTHOR

Lightman, A. P. (2002). *The diagnosis.* New York, NY: Vintage Books.

2. TWO OR MORE AUTHORS

Walsh, M. E., & Murphy, J. A. (2003). *Children, health, and learning: A guide to the issues.* Westport, CT: Praeger.

3. ORGANIZATION AS AUTHOR

Committee on Abrupt Climate Change, National Research Council.
   (2002). *Abrupt climate change: Inevitable surprises.* Washington, DC: National Academies Press.

Use the word *Author* as the publisher when the organization is both the author and the publisher.

Resources for Rehabilitation. (2003). *A woman's guide to coping
   with disability.* London, England: Author.

4. UNKNOWN AUTHOR

National Geographic atlas of the Middle East. (2003). Washington, DC: National Geographic Society.

5. EDITOR

Dickens, J. (Ed.). (1995). *Family outing: A guide for parents of gays, lesbians, and bisexuals.* London, England: Peter Owen.

6. SELECTION IN A BOOK WITH AN EDITOR

Burke, W. W., & Nourmair, D. A. (2001). The role of personality assessment in organization development. In J. Waclawski & A. H. Church (Eds.), *Organization development: A data-driven approach to organizational change* (pp. 55–77). San Francisco, CA: Jossey-Bass.

7. TRANSLATION

Al-Farabi, A. N. (1998). *On the perfect state* (R. Walzer, Trans.). Chicago, IL: Kazi.

8. EDITION OTHER THAN THE FIRST

Moore, G. S. (2002). *Living with the earth: Concepts in environmental health science* (2nd ed.). New York, NY: Lewis.

9. ONE VOLUME OF A MULTIVOLUME WORK

Barnes, J. (Ed.). (1995). *Complete works of Aristotle* (Vol. 2). Princeton, NJ: Princeton University Press.

10. ARTICLE IN A REFERENCE WORK. If no author is listed, begin with the title.

Dean, C. (1994). Jaws and teeth. In *The Cambridge encyclopedia of human evolution* (pp. 56–59). Cambridge, England: Cambridge University Press.

11. REPUBLICATION

Piaget, J. (1952). *The language and thought of the child.* London, England: Routledge & Kegan Paul. (Original work published 1932)

12. TWO OR MORE WORKS BY THE SAME AUTHOR(S). List two or more works by the same author in chronological order. Repeat the author's name in each entry.

Goodall, J. (1999). *Reason for hope: A spiritual journey.* New York,
   NY: Warner Books.

Goodall, J. (2002). *Performance and evolution in the age of Dar-*
   win: Out of the natural order. New York, NY: Routledge.

Periodicals.   Here is an annotated example of a basic entry
for an article in a journal:

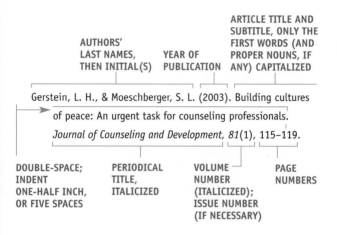

AUTHORS'
LAST NAMES,
THEN INITIAL(S)

YEAR OF
PUBLICATION

ARTICLE TITLE AND
SUBTITLE, ONLY THE
FIRST WORDS (AND
PROPER NOUNS, IF
ANY) CAPITALIZED

Gerstein, L. H., & Moeschberger, S. L. (2003). Building cultures
   of peace: An urgent task for counseling professionals.
   Journal of Counseling and Development, 81(1), 115–119.

DOUBLE-SPACE;
INDENT
ONE-HALF INCH,
OR FIVE SPACES

PERIODICAL
TITLE,
ITALICIZED

VOLUME
NUMBER
(ITALICIZED);
ISSUE NUMBER
(IF NECESSARY)

PAGE
NUMBERS

13. ARTICLE IN A JOURNAL PAGINATED BY VOLUME

O'Connell, D. C., & Kowal, S. (2003). Psycholinguistics: A half
   century of monologism. *The American Journal of Psychology,*
   116, 191–212.

14. ARTICLE IN A JOURNAL PAGINATED BY ISSUE

Hall, R. E. (2000). Marriage as vehicle of racism among women of
   color. *Psychology: A Journal of Human Behavior, 37*(2), 29–40.

15. ARTICLE IN A MAGAZINE

Ricciardi, S. (2003, August 5). Enabling the mobile work force. *PC*
   Magazine, 22, 46.

16. ARTICLE IN A NEWSPAPER

Faler, B. (2003, August 29). Primary colors: Race and fundraising.
   The Washington Post, p. A5.

17. EDITORIAL OR LETTER TO THE EDITOR

Zelneck, B. (2003, July 18). Serving the public at public universities [Letter to the editor]. *The Chronicle Review,* p. B18.

18. UNSIGNED ARTICLE

Annual meeting announcement. (2003, March). *Cognitive
Psychology, 46,* 227.

19. REVIEW

Ringel, S. (2003). [Review of the book *Multiculturalism and the
therapeutic process*]. *Clinical Social Work Journal, 31,* 212–213.

20. PUBLISHED INTERVIEW

Smith, H. (2002, October). [Interview with A. Thompson]. *The
Sun,* pp. 4–7.

21. TWO OR MORE WORKS BY THE SAME AUTHOR IN THE SAME YEAR.
List the works alphabetically by title, and place lowercase
letters (*a, b,* etc.) after the dates.

Shermer, M. (2002a). On estimating the lifetime of civilizations.
Scientific American, 287(2), 33.

Shermer, M. (2002b). Readers who question evolution. *Scientific
American,* 287(1), 37.

Electronic sources.   The *APA Style Guide to Electronic References* (2007) includes guidelines for citing various kinds of
electronic resources. Updated guidelines are maintained at
the APA Web site (www.apa.org).

The basic entry for most sources you access via the
Internet should include the following elements:

- **AUTHOR.** Give the author's name, if available.
- **PUBLICATION DATE.** Include the date of Internet publication or of the most recent update, if available. Use *n.d.*
  ("no date") when the publication date is unavailable.
- **TITLE.** List the title of the document or subject line of the
  message, neither italicized nor in quotation marks.
- **PUBLICATION INFORMATION.** For articles from online
  journals, newspapers, or reference databases, give the
  publication title and other publishing information as you
  would for a print periodical.
- **RETRIEVAL INFORMATION.** For a work from a database,
  do the following: If the article has a DOI (digital object identi-

fier), include that number after publication information. If there is no DOI, write *Retrieved from* followed by the URL for the journal's home page (not the database home page). For a work found on a Web site, write *Retrieved from* and include the URL. If the URL will not fit on one line, break it before a punctuation mark, but do not add a hyphen.

22. ARTICLE IN AN ONLINE PERIODICAL. Give the information as you would for a print document. Include both volume and issue numbers for all journal articles. If the article has a DOI, include it. If not, include the URL for the article or for the home page (if the URL is long). For newspaper articles accessible from a searchable Web site, give the site URL only.

> Barringer, F. (2008, February 7). In many communities, it's not
> easy going green. *The New York Times*. Retrieved from
> http://www.nytimes.com

> Hacker, J. S. (2006). The privatization of risk and the growing
> economic insecurity of Americans. *Items and Issues, 5*(4),
> 16–23. Retrieved from http://publications.ssrc.org/items
> /items5.4/Hacker.pdf

23. ARTICLE FROM A DATABASE. Give the information as you would for a print document. Include both volume and issue numbers for all journal articles. If the article has a DOI, include it, and omit the name of the database. If there is no DOI, include the name of the database and any document number.

> Hazleden, R. (2003, December). Love yourself: The relationship
> of the self with itself in popular self-help texts. *Journal of
> Sociology, 39*(4), 413–428. Retrieved from http://jos
> .sagepub.com

> Morley, N.J., Ball, L.J., & Ormerod, T.C. (2006). How the detection
> of insurance fraud succeeds and fails. *Psychology, Crime, &
> Law, 12*(2), 163–180. doi: 10.1080/10683160512331316325

24. DOCUMENT FROM A WEB SITE. Include all of the following information that is available: the author's name, the publication date (or *n.d.* if no date is given), the title, *Retrieved from*, and the URL. Provide your date of access only if no publication date is available.

Behnke, P.C. (2006, February 22). The homeless are everyone's problem. *Authors' Den*. Retrieved from http://www .authorsden.com/visit/viewArticle.asp?id=21017

What parents should know about treatment of behavioral and emotional disorders in preschool children. (2006). *APA Online*. Retrieved from http://www.apa.org/releases /kidsmed.html

25. CHAPTER OR SECTION OF A WEB DOCUMENT. After the chapter or section title, type *In* and give the document title, with identifying information, if any, in parentheses.

Salamon, Andrew. (n.d.). War in Europe. In *Childhood in Times of War* (chap. 2). Retrieved April 11, 2005, from http:// remember.org/jean

26. EMAIL MESSAGE OR REAL-TIME COMMUNICATION. Do not include entries for email messages or real-time communications (such as IMs) in the list of references; instead, cite these sources in your text as forms of personal communication.

27. ONLINE POSTING. For a listserv message, provide both the name of the list and the URL of the archived message. For a newsgroup posting, end with the name of the news-group.

Troike, R. C. (2001, June 21). Buttercups and primroses [Msg 8]. Message posted to the American Dialect Society's electronic mailing list, archived at http://listserv.linguistlist.org /archives/ads-l.html

Wittenberg, E. (2001, July 11). Gender and the Internet [Msg 4]. Message posted to news://comp.edu.composition

28. SOFTWARE OR COMPUTER PROGRAM

PsychMate [Software]. (2003). Available from Psychology Software Tools: http://pstnet.com/products/psychmate

Other sources

29. GOVERNMENT DOCUMENT

Office of the Federal Register. (2003). *The United States government manual 2003/2004*. Washington, DC: U.S. Government Printing Office.

U.S. Public Health Service. (1999). *The surgeon general's call to action to prevent suicide*. Retrieved from http://www.mentalhealth.org /suicideprevention/calltoaction.asp

30. DISSERTATION. If you retrieve a dissertation from a Web site, give the type of dissertation, the institution, and year after the title, and provide a retrieval statement.

Meeks, M. G. (2006). *Between abolition and reform: First-year writing programs, e-literacies, and institutional change* (Doctoral dissertation, University of North Carolina, 2006). Retrieved from http://dc.lib.unc.edu/cgi-bin/showfile.exe?CISOROOT= /etd&CISOPTR=212

31. TECHNICAL OR RESEARCH REPORT

McCool, R., Fikes, R., & McGuinness, D. (2003). *Semantic web tools for enhanced authoring* (Report No. KSL-03-07). Stanford, CA: Knowledge Systems Laboratory.

32. CONFERENCE PROCEEDINGS

Mama, A. (2001). Challenging subjects: Gender and power in African contexts. In *Proceedings of Nordic African Institute Conference: Rethinking power in Africa*. Uppsala, Sweden, 9–18.

33. FILM, VIDEO, OR DVD

Moore, M. (Director). (2003). *Bowling for Columbine* [Motion picture]. United States: MGM.

34. TELEVISION PROGRAM, SINGLE EPISODE

Imperioli, M. (Writer), & Buscemi, S. (Director). (2002). Everybody hurts [Television series episode]. In D. Chase (Executive Producer), *The Sopranos*. New York, NY: Home Box Office.

35. PODCAST. For a podcast, include as much of the following information as you can find: the writer or producer; the date produced or posted; the title of the podcast; the title of the series, if any; an identifying number, if any, in brackets; and the retrieval information.

O'Brien, K. (Writer). (2008, January 31). Developing countries. *KUSP's Life in the fast lane* [Audio podcast]. Retrieved from http://www.kusp.org/shows/fast.html

SAMPLE APA TITLE PAGE

Running head: LEADERSHIP ROLES   1

Leadership Roles in a Small-Group Project

Merlla McLaughlin
Professor Bushnell
Communications 102
February 22, 2004

SAMPLE APA ABSTRACT

Running head: LEADERSHIP ROLES   2

Abstract

Using the interpersonal communications research of J. K. Brilhart and G. J. Galanes as well as that of W. Wilmot and J. Hocker, along with T. Hartman's Personality Assessment, I observed and analyzed the leadership roles and group dynamics of my project collaborators in a communications course. Based on results of the Hartman Personality Assessment, I predicted that a single leader would emerge. However, complementary individual strengths and gender differences encouraged a distributed leadership style, in which the group experienced little confrontation. Conflict, because it was handled positively, was crucial to the group's progress.

SAMPLE APA FIRST TEXT PAGE

Leadership Roles in a Small-Group Project

Although classroom lectures provide students with volumes of information, many experiences can be understood only by living them. So it is with the workings of a small, task-focused group. What observations can I make after working with a group of peers on a class project? And what have I learned as a result?

Leadership Expectations and Emergence

The six members of this group were selected by the instructor; half were male and half were female. By performing the Hartman Personality Assessment (Hartman, 1998) in class, we learned that Hartman has associated key personality traits with the colors red, blue, white, and yellow (see Table 1). The assessment identified most of us as "Blues," concerned with intimacy and caring. Because of the bold qualities associated with "Reds," I expected that Nate, our only "Red" member, might become our leader. (Kaari, the only "White," seemed poised to become the peacemaker.) However, after Nate missed the first two meetings, it seemed that Pat, who contributed often during our first three meetings, might emerge as leader. Pat has strong communications skills and a commanding presence and displays sensitivity to others.

Table 1

Hartman's Key Personality Traits

Trait category	Color			
	Red	Blue	White	Yellow
Motive	Power	Intimacy	Peace	Fun
Strengths	Loyal to tasks	Loyal to people	Tolerant	Positive
Limitations	Arrogant	Self-righteous	Timid	Uncommitted

Note. Table is adapted from information found at *The Hartman Personality Profile,* by N. Hayden. Retrieved February 24, 2004, from http://students.cs.byu.edu/~nhayden/Code/index.php

SAMPLE APA LIST OF REFERENCES

Running head: LEADERSHIP ROLES   7

                              References

Brilhart, J. K., & Galanes, G. J. (1998). *Effective group discussion*
        (9th ed.). Boston, MA: McGraw-Hill.

Hartman, T. (1998). *The color code: A new way to see yourself, your
        relationships, and your life*. New York, NY: Scribner.

Hayden, N. (n.d.). *The Hartman Personality Profile*. Retrieved February
        15, 2004, from http://students.cs.byu.edu/~nhayden/Code
        /index.php

Wilmot, W., & Hocker, J. (1998). *Interpersonal conflict* (5th ed.).
        Boston, MA: McGraw-Hill.

44 *Chicago* Style

The style guide of the University of Chicago Press has long been used in history and some other fields in the humanities. The fifteenth edition of *The Chicago Manual of Style,* published in 2003, provides a complete guide to *Chicago* style, including two systems for citing sources. This chapter presents the notes and bibliography system.

44a From assignment to thesis and support

Developing a strong thesis that states your goal clearly is crucial to writing an effective essay. Study your assignment carefully, focusing on key terms like *explore, discuss,* or *argue,* and ask for clarification if any part of the assignment is unclear. (For more on beginning a research project, see 38a.) The examples in this section show how one student moved from an assignment to a strong thesis and began crafting a *Chicago*-style essay.

Assignment. Before you begin, make sure you understand the requirements and limits of the assignment. What is the scope of the assignment: How many and what kinds of sources should you use? How long is your project supposed to be? When is it due?

One student in a course focusing on the history of education received the following assignment:

> Write an essay in which you explore some aspect of the history of American women's entry into higher education. Develop an argument about which forces were most instrumental in helping women gain access to higher education.

Generating ideas about the assignment. Ask questions about the topic of your project. As you focus your questions by brainstorming, reading and rereading sources, and talking with others, you develop a starting point for your research. For this history-of-education project, the student decided to begin by interviewing a local historian of education. From the interview, the student learned that women were first admitted to college in the United States at about the same time that African Americans were first admitted.

He then jotted down a series of questions about why women and African Americans had not been allowed to enroll in college and how they had finally gained access. With this list in mind, he decided to focus on the admission of African American women to higher education in the United States.

Working thesis. A working thesis should answer the main question your research poses (see 1c). After a session with a reference librarian, the student identified well-respected books and credible Web sites that provided bibliographies and links to other information about African Americans in higher education. He decided to focus on one school, Oberlin College, which many sources reported as the first college to admit women and African Americans. As he began to build on his research, he crafted the following working thesis:

> Although we may never know definitively why Oberlin College opened its doors to women and African Americans, a study of archival materials and contemporary news accounts as well as of important secondary texts suggests that the school's philosophy, its faculty, and its major supporters were key factors in bringing about this change.

Evidence. Most of your evidence will likely come from historical sources (see 38b). Finding those sources and evaluating them takes on major importance, and your instructor and a reference librarian can help you get started most efficiently. You may be able to find good primary sources on the Web, but don't accept these sources at face value without making sure they are credible (see 39a). You might begin with a list of questions, and then make sure you identify sufficient sources to find answers. You might even use these questions as headings in your essay and as a guide for organizing your material.

Sources. Be sure to take careful notes on the sources you use (see 39c). Introduce quotations with a signal phrase (see 40a) and explain the significance of the quotation. When you

 bedfordstmartins.com/easywriter To access the advice in this chapter online, click on **Documenting Sources.**

first mention a source, use that person's full name (*A. J. Meier argues*); thereafter, use the last name only (*Meier suggests one possibility*). Check that all your quotations are accurate and that they support your thesis. Be careful not to plagiarize when you paraphrase and summarize sources (40d). Finally, note that *Chicago* style requires you to use the **present tense** in signal phrases that introduce quotations or other source material (*citing Bebout's studies, Meier <u>points</u> out*).

44b *Chicago* manuscript format

Title page.   About halfway down the title page, center the full title of your paper and your name. Unless otherwise instructed, at the bottom of the page also list the course name, the instructor's name, and the date submitted. Do not type a number on this page, but do count it; consequently, number the first page of text page 2.

Margins and spacing.   Leave one-inch margins at the top, bottom, and sides of your pages. Double-space the entire text, including block quotations. Single-space entries in notes and the bibliography, but double-space between the entries.

Page numbers.   Number all pages (except the title page) in the upper right-hand corner. Also use a short title or your name before page numbers.

Long quotations.   For a long quotation, indent one-half inch (or five spaces) from the left margin and do not use quotation marks. In general, *Chicago* defines a long quotation as one hundred words or eight lines, though you may decide to set off shorter quotes for emphasis (see 23a).

Headings.   *Chicago* style allows, but does not require, headings. Many students and instructors find them helpful. (See 5c for guidelines on using headings and subheadings.)

Visuals.   Visuals (photographs, drawings, charts, graphs, and tables) should be placed as near as possible to the relevant text. (See 5d for guidelines on incorporating visuals into your text.) Tables should be labeled *Table*, numbered, and captioned. All other visuals should be labeled *Figure* (abbreviated *Fig.*), numbered, and captioned. Remember to refer to each visual in your text, pointing out how it contributes to the point(s) you are making.

Notes.   Notes can be footnotes (each appearing at the bottom of the page on which its citation appears in the text) or endnotes (all appearing on a separate page at the end of the text under the heading *Notes*). Be sure to check your instructor's preference. The first line of each note is indented one-half inch, or five spaces, and begins with a number followed by a period and one space before the first word. All remaining lines of the entry are flush with the left margin. Single-space footnotes with a double space between each note; double-space endnotes.

Bibliography.   Begin the list of sources on a separate page after the main text and any endnotes. Continue numbering the pages consecutively. Center the title *Bibliography* (without underlining, italics, or quotation marks) one inch below the top of the page. Double-space, and begin each entry at the left margin. Indent the second and subsequent lines of each entry one-half inch, or five spaces. Single-space within entries, and double-space between entries.

List sources alphabetically by authors' last names or by the first major word in the title if the author is unknown. See page 266 for an example of a *Chicago*-style bibliography.

44c In-text citations, notes, and bibliography

In *Chicago* style, use superscript numbers (1) to mark citations in the text. Number citations sequentially throughout the text; each should correspond to a note that contains either publication information about the source cited or explanatory or supplemental material not included in the main text. Place the superscript number for each note near the cited material—at the end of the relevant quotation, sentence, clause, or phrase. Type the number after any punctuation mark except the dash; do not leave space between the superscript and the preceding letter or punctuation mark.

IN THE TEXT

Sweig argues that Castro and Che Guevara were not the only key players in the Cuban Revolution of the late 1950s.[19]

IN THE FIRST NOTE

19. Julia Sweig, *Inside the Cuban Revolution* (Cambridge, MA: Harvard University Press, 2002), 9.

IN SUBSEQUENT NOTES. After giving complete information the first time you cite a work, shorten any additional references to that work: list only the author's name followed by a comma, a shortened version of the title followed by a comma, and the page number. If the reference is to the same source cited in the previous note, you can use the Latin abbreviation *Ibid.* (for "in the same place") instead of the name and title.

19. Julia Sweig, *Inside the Cuban Revolution* (Cambridge, MA: Harvard University Press, 2002), 9.

20. Ibid., 13.

21. Ferguson, "Comfort of Being Sad," 63.

22. Sweig, *Cuban Revolution*, 21.

The alphabetical list of the sources in the paper is usually titled *Bibliography*. If *Sources Consulted, Works Cited,* or *Selected Bibliography* better describes your list, however, any of these titles are acceptable.

In the bibliographic entry for a source, include the same information as in the first note for that source, but omit the specific page reference. However, give the *first* author's name last name first, followed by a comma and the first name; separate the main elements of the entry with periods rather than commas; type the first line flush with the left margin and indent subsequent lines of each entry; and do not enclose the publication information for books in parentheses. List bibliographic entries alphabetically by authors' last names or, if an author is unknown, by the first major word in the title.

IN THE BIBLIOGRAPHY

Sweig, Julia. *Inside the Cuban Revolution*. Cambridge, MA: Harvard University Press, 2002.

DIRECTORY TO *CHICAGO*-STYLE NOTES AND BIBLIOGRAPHIC ENTRIES

The following examples demonstrate how to format both notes and bibliographic entries according to *Chicago* style. The note, which is numbered, appears first; the bibliographic entry, which is not numbered, appears below the note.

Books

1. ONE AUTHOR

1. James S. Hirsch, *Riot and Remembrance: The Tulsa Race War and Its Legacy* (Boston: Houghton Mifflin, 2002), 119.

Hirsch, James S. *Riot and Remembrance: The Tulsa Race War and Its Legacy.* Boston: Houghton Mifflin, 2002.

2. MULTIPLE AUTHORS

2. Margaret Macmillan and Richard Holbrooke, *Paris 1919: Six Months That Changed the World* (New York: Random House, 2003), 384.

Macmillan, Margaret, and Richard Holbrooke. *Paris 1919: Six Months That Changed the World.* New York: Random House, 2003.

When there are more than three authors, you may give the first-listed author followed by *et al.* or *and others* in the note. In the bibliography, however, list all the authors' names.

2. Stephen J. Blank and others, *Conflict, Culture, and History: Regional Dimensions* (Miami: University Press of the Pacific, 2002), 276.

Blank, Stephen J., Lawrence E. Grinter, Karl P. Magyar, Lewis B. Ware, and Bynum E. Weathers. *Conflict, Culture, and History: Regional Dimensions.* Miami: University Press of the Pacific, 2002.

3. UNKNOWN AUTHOR

3. *Broad Stripes and Bright Stars* (Kansas City, MO: Andrews McMeel Publishing, 2002), 10.

Broad Stripes and Bright Stars. Kansas City, MO: Andrews McMeel Publishing, 2002.

4. EDITOR

4. James H. Fetzer, ed., *The Great Zapruder Film Hoax: Deceit and Deception in the Death of JFK* (Chicago: Open Court Publishing, 2003), 56.

Fetzer, James H., ed. *The Great Zapruder Film Hoax: Deceit and Deception in the Death of JFK.* Chicago: Open Court Publishing, 2003.

5. SELECTION IN AN ANTHOLOGY OR CHAPTER IN A BOOK, WITH AN EDITOR

5. Denise Little, "Born in Blood," in *Alternate Gettysburgs*, ed. Brian Thomsen and Martin H. Greenberg (New York: Berkley Publishing Group, 2002), 245.

Little, Denise. "Born in Blood." In *Alternate Gettysburgs*, edited
   by Brian Thomsen and Martin H. Greenberg, 242–55. New
   York: Berkley Publishing Group, 2002.

6. TRANSLATION

   6. Suetonius, *The Twelve Caesars*, trans. Robert Graves (London:
Penguin Classics, 1989), 202.

Suetonius. *The Twelve Caesars*. Translated by Robert Graves. London: Penguin Classics, 1989.

7. EDITION OTHER THAN THE FIRST

   7. Charles G. Beaudette, *Excess Heat: Why Cold Fusion Research Pre-
vailed*, 2nd ed. (South Bristol, ME: Oak Grove Press, 2002), 313.

Beaudette, Charles G. *Excess Heat: Why Cold Fusion Research Pre-
   vailed*. 2nd ed. South Bristol, ME: Oak Grove Press, 2002.

8. MULTIVOLUME WORK

   8. John Watson, *Annals of Philadelphia and Pennsylvania in the
Olden Time*, vol. 2 (Washington, DC: Ross & Perry, 2003), 514.

Watson, John. *Annals of Philadelphia and Pennsylvania in the
   Olden Time*. Vol. 2. Washington, DC: Ross & Perry, 2003.

9. REFERENCE WORK. Use *s.v.*, for the Latin *sub verbo* ("under
the word"), to help your reader find the entry.

   9. *Encarta World Dictionary*, s.v. "carpetbagger."

Do not list reference works in your bibliography.

Periodicals

10. ARTICLE IN A JOURNAL

   10. Karin Lützen, "The Female World: Viewed from Denmark,"
Journal of Women's History 12, no. 3 (2000): 36.

Lützen, Karin. "The Female World: Viewed from Denmark." *Journal
   of Women's History* 12, no. 3 (2000): 34–38.

11. ARTICLE IN A MAGAZINE

   11. Douglas Brinkley and Anne Brinkley, "Lawyers and Lizard-
Heads," *Atlantic Monthly*, May 2002, 56.

Brinkley, Douglas, and Anne Brinkley. "Lawyers and
    Lizard-Heads." *Atlantic Monthly,* May 2002, 55–61.

12. ARTICLE IN A NEWSPAPER

    12. Caroline E. Mayer, "Wireless Industry to Adopt Voluntary
Standards," *Washington Post,* September 9, 2003, sec. E.

Mayer, Caroline E. "Wireless Industry to Adopt Voluntary
    Standards." *Washington Post,* September 9, 2003, sec. E.

Electronic sources

13. NONPERIODICAL WEB SITE

    13. Rutgers University, "Picture Gallery," *The Rutgers Oral History
Archives of World War II,* http://fas-history .rutgers.edu/oralhistory/
orlhom.htm (accessed November 7, 2003).

Rutgers University. "Picture Gallery." *The Rutgers Oral History
    Archives of World War II.* http://fas-history .rutgers.edu/
    oralhistory/orlhom.htm (accessed November 7, 2003).

14. ONLINE BOOK

    14. Janja Bec, *The Shattering of the Soul* (Los Angeles: The Simon
Wiesenthal Center, 1997), http://motlc.wiesenthal.com/resources/
books/shatteringsoul/index.html (accessed November 6, 2003).

Bec, Janja. *The Shattering of the Soul.* Los Angeles: The Simon
    Wiesenthal Center, 1997. http://motlc.wiesenthal.com/
    resources/books/shatteringsoul/index.html (accessed
    November 6, 2003).

15. ARTICLE IN AN ELECTRONIC JOURNAL

    15. Damian Bracken, "Rationalism and the Bible in Seventh-
Century Ireland," *Chronicon* 2 (1998), http://www.ucc.ie/chronicon/
bracfra.htm (accessed November 1, 2003).

Bracken, Damian. "Rationalism and the Bible in Seventh-Century
    Ireland." *Chronicon* 2 (1998). http://www.ucc.ie/chronicon/
    bracfra.htm (accessed November 1, 2003).

16. ARTICLE IN AN ONLINE MAGAZINE

    16. Kim Iskyan, "Putin's Next Power Play," *Slate,* November 4,
2003, http://slate.msn.com/id/2090745 (accessed November 7, 2003).

Iskyan, Kim. "Putin's Next Power Play." *Slate,* November 4, 2003.

    http://slate.msn.com/id/2090745 (accessed November 7, 2003).

17. ARTICLE FROM A DATABASE

    17. Peter DeMarco, "Holocaust Survivors Lend Voice to History," *Boston Globe*, November 2, 2003, http://www.lexisnexis.com (accessed November 19, 2003).

    DeMarco, Peter. "Holocaust Survivors Lend Voice to History."

        Boston Globe, November 2, 2003. http://www.lexisnexis.com

        (accessed November 19, 2003).

18. EMAIL AND OTHER PERSONAL COMMUNICATIONS. Cite email messages and other personal communications, such as letters and telephone calls, in the text or in a note only, not in the bibliography. (*Chicago* style recommends hyphenating *email*.)

    18. Kareem Adas, e-mail message to author, February 11, 2004.

Other sources

19. PUBLISHED OR BROADCAST INTERVIEW

    19. Condoleezza Rice, interview by Charlie Rose, *The Charlie Rose Show,* PBS, October 30, 2003.

    Rice, Condoleezza. Interview by Charlie Rose. *The Charlie Rose*

        Show. PBS, October 30, 2003.

Interviews you conduct are considered personal communications.

20. VIDEO OR DVD

    20. Edward Norton and Edward Furlong, *American History X*, DVD, directed by Tony Kaye (1998; Los Angeles: New Line Studios, 2002).

    Norton, Edward, and Edward Furlong. *American History X*. DVD.

        Directed by Tony Kaye 1998. Los Angeles: New Line Studios,

        2002.

21. CD-ROM

    21. *The Civil War*, CD-ROM (Fogware Publishing, 2000).

    The Civil War. CD-ROM. Fogware Publishing, 2000.

22. PAMPHLET, REPORT, OR BROCHURE. Information about the author or publisher may not be readily available, but give enough information to identify your source.

22. Jamie McCarthy, *Who Is David Irving?* (San Antonio, TX: The Holocaust History Project, 1998).

McCarthy, Jamie. *Who Is David Irving?* San Antonio, TX: The Holocaust History Project, 1998.

23. GOVERNMENT DOCUMENT

23. U.S. House Committee on Ways and Means, *Report on Trade Mission to Sub-Saharan Africa,* 108th Cong., 1st sess. (Washington, DC: U.S. Government Printing Office, 2003), 28.

U.S. House Committee on Ways and Means. *Report on Trade Mission to Sub-Saharan Africa*. 108th Cong., 1st sess. Washington, DC: U.S. Government Printing Office, 2003.

SAMPLE *CHICAGO* TITLE PAGE

Marbury v. Madison and the
Origins of Judicial Review
Kelly Darr

History 214
Professor Bishop
March 4, 2004

Darr 2

Marbury v. Madison and the

Origins of Judicial Review

The Supreme Court of the United States is a very prestigious and powerful branch of American government today. Perhaps the most notable demonstration of the Court's power was its decision concerning the presidential election of 2000, a decision that resulted in George W. Bush becoming president.[1] The Court has not always held this position, however. When the government system was developed in the late eighteenth century, the powers of the judicial branch were fairly undefined. In 1803, Chief Justice John Marshall, with his decision in *Marbury v. Madison,* began to define the duties of the Court by claiming for the Supreme Court the power of judicial review. Judicial review has been upheld ever since, and many people take the practice for granted. There is controversy around Marshall's decision, however, with some claiming that judicial review was not the intent of the nation's founders. Two questions must be asked: Did Marshall overstep his bounds when he declared judicial review for the Court? If so, why has his decision been upheld for two hundred years? An examination of the actual case, *Marbury v. Madison,* and of Marshall's reasons for his decision is the first step to answering these questions.

This case was complicated by personal and political opposition. It was brought to Court by William Marbury, whose commission as justice of the peace by John Adams was withheld by Thomas Jefferson when he became president. Jefferson's act was prompted by Adams's attempt to fill the national judiciary with Federalist judges on the eve before Jefferson took office. Due to a mistake by John Marshall himself (at the time the secretary of state under Adams), however, the commissions were not delivered. Jefferson, who did not appreciate the last-minute attempt to fill the offices with Federalists, refused to deliver the commissions after he took office. Marbury and a few other men sued James Madison, secretary of state under

SAMPLE *CHICAGO* ENDNOTES

Notes

1. *Bush v. Gore,* 531 U.S. 1998 (2000), http://supct.law.cornell
.edu/supct/html/00-949.ZPC.html (accessed February 8, 2004).

2. John A. Garraty, *Quarrels That Have Shaped the Constitution* (New York: Harper and Row, 1987), 7–14.

3. Ibid., 19.

4. William C. Louthan, *The United States Supreme Court: Lawmaking in the Third Branch of Government* (Englewood Cliffs, NJ: Prentice-Hall, 1991), 51.

5. Thomas J. Higgins, *Judicial Review Unmasked* (West Hanover, MA: Christopher Publishing House, 1981), 40–41.

6. *Marbury v. Madison,* 5 U.S. 137 (1803).

7. Louthan, *Supreme Court,* 51.

8. Ibid.

9. Ibid., 50-51.

10. Higgins, *Judicial Review,* 40–41.

11. Ibid., 32.

12. Ibid., 34.

SAMPLE *CHICAGO* BIBLIOGRAPHY

Darr 7

Bibliography

Bush v. Gore. 531 U.S. 1998 (2000). http://supct.law.cornell.edu/supct/html/00-949.ZPC.html (accessed February 8, 2004).

Garraty, John A. *Quarrels That Have Shaped the Constitution.* New York: Harper and Row, 1987.

Higgins, Thomas J. *Judicial Review Unmasked.* West Hanover, MA: Christopher Publishing House, 1981.

Louthan, William C. *The United States Supreme Court: Lawmaking in the Third Branch of Government.* Englewood Cliffs, NJ: Prentice-Hall, 1991.

Marbury v. Madison, 5 U.S. 137 (1803).

45 CSE Style

Writers in the physical sciences, the life sciences, and mathematics often use the documentation style set forth by the Council of Science Editors (CSE). Guidelines for citing print sources can be found in *Scientific Style and Format: The CSE Manual for Authors, Editors, and Publishers*, Seventh Edition, 2006.

45a From assignment to thesis and support

Developing a clear thesis is crucial to writing a successful paper. Focus on important terms in the assignment and ask for clarification of anything you do not understand. (For more on beginning a research project, see 38a.) The examples in this section show how one student moved from an assignment to a thesis and began crafting a CSE-style essay.

Assignment. Before you begin, make sure you understand the requirements and limits of the assignment. What is the scope of the assignment: How many and what kinds of sources should you use? How long is your project supposed to be? When is it due? Understand the kinds of writing you may be asked to do — for example, a literature review, a lab notebook, or a research report. Also be sure you know what structural elements your project needs. You may be required to include an abstract, an introduction, a statement of purpose, a literature review, a list of materials, a time line, an explanation of methods, results, a discussion, a conclusion, or a list of references.

One student in a biology course received the following assignment:

> Choose a current subject of research in which you are interested and, based on at least ten reputable and current sources, write a report that synthesizes the research findings.

Generating ideas about the assignment. Ask questions that will lead you toward a topic for your project. As you

---

bedfordstmartins.com/easywriter To access the advice in this chapter online, click on **Documenting Sources.**

focus the questions by brainstorming, reading and rereading sources, talking with others, and considering other information you know, you develop a starting point for your research. This student brainstormed with two of her classmates about biology topics in the news. As they discussed nutrition information, outbreaks of disease, and miracle cures, they began to talk about what they had heard about stem-cell research.

Working thesis.   A working thesis should answer the main question your research poses (see 1c). The student used her university library's databases to find abstracts and full texts of articles in recent publications on stem-cell research. These led her to reports on the Web site of the National Institutes of Health and other relevant sites. From these reports, she learned about the hypotheses underlying embryonic stem-cell research. She created the following working thesis:

> Although still in its early stages, embryonic stem-cell research has the potential to further the scientific understanding of human cell development and may someday offer new hope for patients with diseases now seen as incurable.

Evidence.   Research reviews call for understanding and summarizing key sources (see 38b). The student had to be sure she understood the research described and the presentation of data in each of the required ten reliable sources that made up her evidence. Her job as a writer was to analyze the research and findings from each source, objectively present the information she had gathered, and select effective quotations or passages for paraphrase or summary in support of her conclusion.

Sources.   Take careful notes on the sources you use (see 39c). Be sure to introduce quotations with a signal phrase (see 40a) and to explain the significance of any quotation. Generally, use only last names when referring to authors. Make sure each quotation, paraphrase, or summary provides evidence for your thesis, and be careful not to plagiarize when you paraphrase and summarize sources (see 40d).

45b CSE manuscript format

Title page.   Center the title of your paper. Beneath it, center your name. Include other relevant information, such as the course name and number, the instructor's name, and the date submitted.

Margins and spacing.   Leave standard margins at the top and bottom and on both sides of each page. Double-space the text and the references list.

Page numbers.   Type a short version of the paper's title and the page number in the upper right-hand corner of each page.

Abstract.   CSE style often calls for a one-paragraph abstract (about one hundred words). The abstract should be on a separate page, right after the title page, with the title *Abstract* centered one inch from the top of the page.

Headings.   CSE style does not require headings, but it notes that they can help readers quickly find the contents of a section of the paper.

Tables and figures.   Tables and figures must be labeled *Table* or *Figure* and numbered separately, one sequence for tables and one for figures. Give each table and figure a short, informative title. Be sure to introduce each table and figure in your text and comment on its significance.

List of references.   Start the list of references on a new page at the end of the essay, and continue to number the pages consecutively. Center the title *References* one inch from the top of the page, and double-space before beginning the first entry.

45c In-text citations

In CSE style, citations within an essay follow one of three formats.

- The *citation-sequence format* calls for a superscript number ([1]) or a number in parentheses after any mention of a source. The sources are numbered in the order they appear in the text.

- The *citation-name format* also calls for a superscript number ([2]) or a number in parentheses after any mention of a source. The sources are numbered in the order of the alphabetized list of references.

- The *name-year format* calls for the last name of the author and the year of publication in parentheses after any mention of a source. If the last name appears in a signal phrase, the name-year format allows for giving only the year of publication in parentheses.

Before deciding which system to use, check a current journal in the field, or ask an instructor about the preferred style in a particular course or discipline.

1. IN-TEXT CITATION USING CITATION-SEQUENCE OR CITATION-NAME FORMAT

VonBergen[1] provides the most complete discussion of this phenomenon.

For the citation-sequence and citation-name formats, you would use the same superscript *1* ([1]) for each subsequent citation of this work by VonBergen.

2. IN-TEXT CITATION USING NAME-YEAR FORMAT

VonBergen provides the most complete discussion of this phenomenon (2003).

Hussar's two earlier studies of juvenile obesity (1995, 1999) examined only children with diabetes.

The classic examples of such investigations (Morrow 1968; Bridger and others 1971; Franklin and Wayson 1972) still shape the assumptions of current studies.

45d List of references

The citations in the text of an essay correspond to items on a list called *References*.

- If you use the citation-sequence format, number and list the references in the order in which the references are *first* cited in the text.

- If you use the citation-name format, list and number the references in alphabetical order.
- If you use the name-year format, list the references, unnumbered, in alphabetical order.

In the following examples, you will see that the citation-sequence and citation-name formats call for listing the date after the publisher's name in references for books and after the periodical name in references for articles. The name-year format calls for listing the date immediately after the author's name in any kind of reference.

CSE style also specifies the treatment and placement of the following basic elements:

- **AUTHOR.** List all authors last name first, and use only initials for first and middle names. Do not place a comma after the author's last name, and do not place periods after or spaces between the initials. Use a period after the last initial of the last author listed.
- **TITLE.** Do not italicize or underline titles and subtitles of books and periodicals. Do not enclose titles of articles in quotation marks. For books and articles, capitalize only the first word of the title and any proper nouns or proper adjectives. Abbreviate and capitalize all major words in a periodical title.

As you refer to the following sample entries, pay attention to how publication information (publishers for books, details about periodicals for articles) and other specific elements are punctuated.

Books

1. ONE AUTHOR
Citation-sequence and citation-name

> 1. Buchanan M. Nexus: small worlds and the groundbreaking theory of networks. New York: Norton; 2003.

Name-year

> Buchanan M. 2003. Nexus: small worlds and the groundbreaking theory of networks. New York: Norton.

2. TWO OR MORE AUTHORS
Citation-sequence and citation-name

> 2. Wojciechowski BW, Rice NM. Experimental methods in kinetic studies. 2nd ed. St. Louis (MO): Elsevier Science; 2003.

Name-year

> Wojciechowski BW, Rice NM. 2003. Experimental methods in kinetic studies. 2nd ed. St. Louis (MO): Elsevier Science.

3. ORGANIZATION AS AUTHOR
Citation-sequence and citation-name

> 3. World Health Organization. The world health report 2002: reducing risks, promoting healthy life. Geneva (Switzerland): The Organization; 2002.

Place the organization's abbreviation at the beginning of the name-year entry and use it in the corresponding in-text citation. Alphabetize the entry by the full name, not by the abbreviation.

Name-year

> [WHO] World Health Organization. 2002. The world health report 2002: reducing risks, promoting healthy life. Geneva (Switzerland): The Organization.

4. BOOK PREPARED BY EDITOR(S)

Citation-sequence and citation-name

> 4. Torrence ME, Isaacson RE, editors. Microbial food safety in animal agriculture: current topics. Ames: Iowa State University Press; 2003.

Name-year

> Torrence ME, Isaacson RE, editors. 2003. Microbial safety in animal agriculture: current topics. Ames: Iowa State University Press.

5. SECTION OF A BOOK WITH AN EDITOR

Citation-sequence and citation-name

> 5. Kawamura A. Plankton. In: Perrin MF, Wursig B, Thewissen JGM, editors. Encyclopedia of marine mammals. San Diego (CA): Academic Press; 2002. p. 939–942.

Name-year

> Kawamura A. 2002. Plankton. In: Perrin MF, Wursig B, Thewissen JGM, editors. Encyclopedia of marine mammals. San Diego (CA): Academic Press. p. 939–942.

6. CHAPTER OF A BOOK

Citation-sequence and citation-name

> 6. Honigsbaum M. The fever trail: in search of the cure for malaria. New York: Picador; 2003. Chapter 2, The cure; p. 19–38.

Name-year

> Honigsbaum M. 2003. The fever trail: in search of the cure for malaria. New York: Picador. Chapter 2, The cure; p. 19–38.

7. PAPER OR ABSTRACT IN CONFERENCE PROCEEDINGS

Citation-sequence and citation-name

7. Gutierrez AP. Integrating biological and environmental factors in crop system models. Integrated Biological Systems Conference; 2003 Apr 14–16; San Antonio, TX. Beaumont (TX): Agroeconomics Research Group; 2003. 77 p. 14–15.

Name-year

Gutierrez AP, editor. 2003. Integrating biological and environmental factors in crop system models. Integrated Biological Systems Conference; 2003 Apr 14–16; San Antonio, TX. Beaumont (TX): Agroeconomics Research Group. 77 p. 14–15.

Periodicals. For rules on abbreviating journal titles, consult the CSE manual, or ask an instructor or a librarian to refer you to other examples.

8. ARTICLE IN A JOURNAL

Citation-sequence and citation-name

8. Mahmud K, Vance ML. Human growth hormone and aging. New Engl J Med. 2003;348(2):2256–2257.

Name-year

Mahmud K, Vance ML. 2003. Human growth hormone and aging. New Engl J Med. 348(2):2256–2257.

9. ARTICLE IN A WEEKLY JOURNAL

Citation-sequence and citation-name

9. Holden C. Future brightening for depression treatments. Science. 2003 Oct 31:810–813.

Name-year

Holden C. 2003. Future brightening for depression treatments. Science. Oct 31:810–813.

10. ARTICLE IN A MAGAZINE

Citation-sequence and citation-name

10. Livio M. Moving right along: the accelerating universe holds secrets to dark energy, the Big Bang, and the ultimate beauty of nature. Astronomy. 2002 Jul:34–39.

Name-year

> Livio M. 2002 Jul. Moving right along: the accelerating universe holds secrets to dark energy, the Big Bang, and the ultimate beauty of nature. Astronomy. 34–39.

11. ARTICLE IN A NEWSPAPER

Citation-sequence and citation-name

> 11. Kolata G. Bone diagnosis gives new data but no answers. New York Times (National Ed.). 2003 Sep 28;Sect 1:1(col 1).

Name-year

> Kolata G. 2003 Sep 28. Bone diagnosis gives new data but no answers. New York Times. Sect 1:1(col 1).

Electronic sources. These examples use the citation-sequence or citation-name system. To adapt them to the name-year system, delete the superscripts and reorder the information in the entries, placing the date immediately after the author's name.

The basic entry for most sources you access electronically should include the following elements:

- **AUTHOR.** Give the author's name, if available, last name first, followed by the initial(s) and a period.
- **TITLE.** For book, journal, and article titles, follow the style for print materials. For all other types of electronic material, reproduce the wording that appears on the screen.
- **MEDIUM.** Indicate, in brackets, that the source is not in print format by using designations such as [Internet] or [database on the Internet].
- **PLACE OF PUBLICATION.** After the city, use the two-letter abbreviation for the state, in parentheses. Very well-known cities and publishers whose names include the state may be listed without a state designation. If the city is inferred, put the city and state in brackets, followed by a colon. If the city cannot be inferred, use the words *place unknown* in brackets, followed by a colon.
- **PUBLISHER.** Include the individual or organization that produces or sponsors the site. You may include a designation for the country, in parentheses, after the publisher's name. If no publisher can be determined, use the words *publisher unknown* in brackets.
- **DATES.** Cite three dates if possible: the date the publication appeared on the Internet or the copyright date; the

latest date of any update or revision; and the date of access. Use the format "year month day" and precede the date of copyright with a *c*, as in *c2000*. (In the following examples, dates are grouped together after the publisher's name. Check with your instructor to see if this style is acceptable.)

- **PAGE, DOCUMENT, VOLUME, AND ISSUE NUMBERS.** When citing a portion of a larger work or site, list the inclusive page numbers or document numbers of the specific item being cited. For journals or journal articles, include volume and issue numbers.

- **ADDRESS.** Include the URL or other electronic address; use the phrase *Available from:* to introduce the address. Only URLs that end with a slash are followed by a period.

12. ARTICLE IN AN ONLINE JOURNAL

12. Perez P, Calonge TM. Yeast protein kinase C. J Biochem [Internet]. 2002 Oct [cited 2003 Nov 3];132(4): 513–517. Available from: http://edpex104.bcasj.or.jp/jb-pdf/132-4/jb132-4-513.pdf

13. ARTICLE IN AN ONLINE NEWSPAPER

13. Brody JE. Reasons, and remedies, for morning sickness. New York Times Online [Internet]. 2004 Apr 27 [cited 2004 Apr 30]:[about 24 paragraphs]. Available from: http://www.nytimes.com/2004/04/27/health/27BROD.html

14. ONLINE BOOK

14. Patrick TS, Allison JR, Krakow GA. Protected plants of Georgia [Internet]. Social Circle (GA): Georgia Dept of Natural Resources; c1995 [cited 2003 Dec 3]. Available from: http://www.georgiawildlife.com/content/displaycontent.asp?txtDocument=89&txtPage=9

15. WEB SITE

15. Geology and public policy [Internet]. Boulder (CO): Geological Society of America; c2003 [updated 2003 Apr 8; cited 2003 Apr 13]. Available from: http://www.geosociety.org/science/govpolicy.htm

16. GOVERNMENT WEB SITE. Include a designation for the country, in parentheses, after the name of the site sponsor or publisher.

16. Health disparities: minority cancer awareness [Internet].

Atlanta (GA): Centers for Disease Control and Prevention (US);

[updated 2004 Apr 27; cited 2005 May 1]. Available from:

http://www.cdc.gov/cancer/minorityawareness.htm

17. MATERIAL FROM AN ONLINE DATABASE. Because CSE does not provide guidelines for citing an article from an online database, this model has been adapted from CSE guidelines for citing an online periodical article.

17. Shilts E. Water wanderers. Can Geographic.

2002;122(3):72–77. Expanded Academic ASAP [database on the

Internet]. Farmington Hills (MI): Thomson Gale. 2002 [cited 2004

Jan 27]. Available from: http://web4.infotrac.galegroup.com/

itw/; Document No.: A86207443.

SAMPLE CSE TITLE PAGE

Field Measurements of Photosynthesis
and Transpiration Rates in Dwarf Snapdragon
(*Chaenorrhinum minus* Lange):
An Investigation of Water Stress Adaptations

Tara Gupta

Proposal for a Summer Research Fellowship
Colgate University
February 25, 2004

SAMPLE CSE TEXT PAGE

Water Stress Adaptations 2

Introduction

Dwarf snapdragon (*Chaenorrhinum minus*) is a weedy pioneer
plant found growing in central New York during spring and summer.
Interestingly, the distribution of this species has been limited almost
exclusively to the cinder ballast of railroad tracks[1] and to sterile
strips of land along highways.[2] In these harsh environments, charac-
terized by intense sunlight and poor soil water retention, one would
expect *C. minus* to exhibit anatomical features similar to those of
xeromorphic plants (species adapted to arid habitats). However, this
is not the case. T. Gupta and R. Arnold (unpublished) have found
that the leaves and stems of *C. minus* are not covered by a thick,
waxy cuticle but rather with a thin cuticle that is less effective in
inhibiting water loss through diffusion. The root system is not long
and thick, capable of reaching deeper, moister soils; instead, it is
thin and diffuse, permeating only the topmost (and driest) soil hori-
zon. Moreover, in contrast to many xeromorphic plants, the stomata
(pores regulating gas exchange) are not found in sunken crypts or
cavities in the epidermis that retard water loss from transpiration.

Despite a lack of these morphological adaptations to water
stress, *C. minus* continues to grow and reproduce when morning dew
has been its only source of water for up to five weeks (R. Arnold,
personal communication). Such growth involves fixation of carbon by
photosynthesis and requires that the stomata be open to admit sufficient carbon dioxide. Given the dry, sunny environment, the time
required for adequate carbon fixation must also mean a significant
loss of water through transpiration as open stomata exchange carbon
dioxide with water. How does *C. minus* balance the need for carbon
with the need to conserve water?

Purposes of the Proposed Study

The above observations have led me to an exploration of the
extent to which *C. minus* is able to photosynthesize under conditions

SAMPLE CSE LIST OF REFERENCES

Water Stress Adaptations 6

References

1. Wildrlechner MP. Historical and phenological observations of the spread of *Chaenorrhinum minus* across North America. Can J Bot. 1983;61(1):179-187.

2. Dwarf Snapdragon [Internet]. Olympia (WA): Washington State Noxious Weed Control Board [updated 2001 July 7; cited 2004 Jan 25]. Available from: http://www.wa.gov/agr/weedboard/ weed_info/dwarfsnapdragon.html

3. Boyer JS. Plant productivity and environment. Science. 1982 Nov 6: 443–448.

4. Manhas JG, Sukumaran NP. Diurnal changes in net photosynthetic rate in potato in two environments. Potato Res. 1988; 31:375–378.

5. Doley DG, Unwin GL, Yates DJ. Spatial and temporal distribution of photosynthesis and transpiration by single leaves in a rainforest tree, *Argyrodendron peralatum*. Aust J Plant Physiol. 1988; 15(3):317–326.

6. Kallarackal J, Milburn JA, Baker DA. Water relations of the banana. III. Effects of controlled water stress on water potential, transpiration, photosynthesis and leaf growth. Aust J Plant Physiol. 1990;17(1):79–90.

7. Idso SB, Allen SG, Kimball BA, Choudhury BJ. Problems with porometry: measuring net photosynthesis by leaf chamber techniques. Agron. 1989;81(4):475–479.

absolute phrase See *phrase.*

active voice The form of a verb when the subject performs the action: *Lata <u>sang</u> the chorus again.* See also *voice.*

adjective A word that modifies, quantifies, identifies, or describes a noun or a word or words acting as a noun. Most adjectives precede the noun or other word(s) they modify (*a <u>good</u> book*), but a **predicate adjective** follows the noun or pronoun it modifies (*the book is <u>good</u>*).

adjective clause See *clause.*

adjective forms Changes in an adjective from the **positive** degree (*tall, good*) to the **comparative** (comparing two — *taller, better*) or the **superlative** (comparing more than two — *tallest, best*). Short regular adjectives (*tall*) add *-er* and *-est*, but most adjectives of two syllables or more form the comparative by adding *more* (*more beautiful*) and the superlative by adding *most* (*most beautiful*). A few adjectives have irregular forms (*good, better, best*), and some (*only, forty*) do not change form.

adverb A word that qualifies, modifies, limits, or defines a verb, an adjective, another adverb, or a clause, frequently answering the questions *where? when? how? why? to what extent?* or *under what conditions?* Adverbs derived from adjectives and nouns commonly end in the suffix *-ly. She will <u>soon</u> travel <u>south</u> and will <u>probably</u> visit her <u>very</u> favorite sister.* See also *conjunction.*

adverb clause See *clause.*

adverb forms Changes in an adverb from the **positive** degree (*eagerly*) to the **comparative** (comparing two — *more eagerly*) or the **superlative** (comparing more than two — *most eagerly*). Most adverbs add *more* to form the comparative and *most* to form the superlative, but a few add *-er* and *-est* or have irregular forms (*fast, faster, fastest; little, less, least*).

adverbial particle A preposition combined with a verb to create a phrasal verb.

agreement The correspondence of a pronoun with the word it refers to (its antecedent) in person, number, and gender or of a verb with its subject in person and number. See also *antecedent, gender, number, person.*

antecedent The specific noun that a pronoun replaces and to which it refers. A pronoun and its antecedent must agree in person, number, and gender. *<u>Ginger Rogers</u> moved <u>her</u> feet as no one else has.*

appositive A noun or noun phrase that identifies or adds identifying information to a preceding noun phrase. *Zimbardo,* *an innovative researcher*, designed the Stanford Prison Experiment. *My sister Janet has twin boys.*

appositive phrase See *appositive.*

argument A text that makes and supports a **claim**. See also *evidence, warrant.*

article *A, an,* or *the,* the most common adjectives. *A* and *an* are **indefinite**; they do not specifically identify the nouns they modify. *I bought an apple and a peach. The* is **definite**, or specific. *The peach was not ripe.*

auxiliary verb A verb that combines with the base form or with the present or past participle of a main verb to form a verb phrase. The primary auxiliaries are forms of *do, have,* and *be. Did he arrive? We have eaten. She is writing.* **Modal** auxiliaries such as *can, may, shall, will, could, might, should, would,* and *ought* [*to*] have only one form and show possibility, necessity, obligation, and so on.

base form The form of a verb that is listed in dictionaries, such as *go* or *listen.* For all verbs except *be,* it is the same as the first-person singular form in the present tense.

Boolean operator A word like *and* or *or* that allows for computer database searches using multiple words. Example: *Kahlo, Frida and American literature.*

case The form of a noun or pronoun that reflects its grammatical role in a sentence. Nouns and indefinite pronouns can be **subjective, possessive,** or **objective,** but they change form only in the possessive case. *The dog* (subjective) *barked. The dog's* (possessive) *tail wagged. The mail carrier called the dog* (objective). The personal pronouns *I, he, she, we,* and *they,* as well as the relative or interrogative pronoun *who,* have different forms for all three cases. *We* (subjective) *took the train to Chicago. Our* (possessive) *trip lasted a week. Maria met us* (objective) *at the station.* See also *person, pronoun.*

claim An arguable statement.

clause A group of words containing a subject and a predicate. An **independent clause** can stand alone as a sentence. *The car hit the tree.* A **dependent clause,** as the name suggests, is grammatically subordinate to an independent clause, linked to it by a subordinating conjunction or a relative pronoun. A dependent clause can function as an adjective, an adverb, or a noun. *The car hit the tree that stood at the edge of the road* (**adjective clause**). *The car hit the tree when it went out of control* (**adverb clause**). *The car hit what grew at the side of the road* (**noun clause**). See also *nonrestrictive element, restrictive element.*

collective noun A noun that refers to a group or collection (*herd, mob*).

comma splice An error resulting from joining two independent clauses with only a comma.

common noun See *noun*.

comparative or **comparative degree** The form of an adjective or adverb used to compare two things (*happier, more quickly*). See also *adjective forms, adverb forms*.

complement A word or group of words completing the predicate in a sentence. A **subject complement** follows a linking verb and renames or describes the subject. It can be a **predicate noun** (*Anorexia is an <u>illness</u>*) or a **predicate adjective** (*Karen Carpenter was <u>anorexic</u>*). An **object complement** renames or describes a direct object (*We considered her a <u>prodigy</u> and her behavior <u>extraordinary</u>*).

complete predicate See *predicate*.

complete subject See *subject*.

complex sentence See *sentence*.

compound adjective A combination of words that functions as a single adjective (<u>*blue-green*</u> *sea,* <u>*ten-story*</u> *building,* <u>*get-tough*</u> *policy,* <u>*high school*</u> *outing,* <u>*north-by-northwest*</u> *journey*). Most, but not all, compound adjectives need hyphens to separate their individual elements.

compound noun A combination of words that functions as a single noun (*go-getter, in-law, Johnny-on-the-spot, oil well, southeast*).

compound predicate See *predicate*.

compound sentence See *sentence*.

compound subject See *subject*.

conjunction A word or words that join words, phrases, clauses, or sentences. **Coordinating conjunctions** (*and, but, for, nor, or, so,* or *yet*) join grammatically equivalent elements (*Marx <u>and</u> Engels* [two nouns]; *Marx wrote one essay, <u>but</u> Engels wrote the other* [two independent clauses]). **Correlative conjunctions** (such as *both . . . and; either . . . or;* or *not only . . . but also*) are used in pairs to connect grammatically equivalent elements (*<u>neither</u> Marx <u>nor</u> Engels; Marx <u>not only</u> studied the world <u>but also</u> changed it*). A **subordinating conjunction** (such as *although, because, if, that,* or *when*) introduces a dependent clause and connects it to an independent clause. *Marx moved to London, <u>where</u> he did most of his work. Marx argued <u>that</u> religion was an "opiate."* A **conjunctive adverb** (such as *consequently, moreover,* or *nevertheless*) modifies an independent clause following another independent clause. A conjunctive adverb generally follows a semicolon and is followed by a comma. *Thoreau lived simply at Walden; <u>however</u>, he regularly joined his aunt for tea in Concord.*

conjunctive adverb. See *conjunction*.

coordinating conjunction See *conjunction*.

correlative conjunction See *conjunction*.

count noun See *noun*.

dangling modifier A word, phrase, or clause that does not logically modify any element in the sentence to which it is attached. *Studying Freud, the meaning of my dreams became clear* is incorrect because *the meaning* could not have been studying Freud. *Studying Freud, I began to understand the meaning of my dreams* is correct because now *I* was doing the studying.

definite article The word *the*. See also *article*.

degree See *adjective forms, adverb forms*.

dependent clause A word group containing a subject and a predicate, but unable to stand alone as a sentence; usually begins with a subordinating conjunction (*because, although*) or a relative pronoun (*that, which*). See also *clause*.

direct address Construction that uses a noun or pronoun to name the person or thing being spoken to. *Hey, Jack. You, get moving.*

direct discourse A quotation that reproduces a speaker's exact words, marked with quotation marks.

direct object A noun or pronoun receiving the action of a transitive verb. *McKellan recited Shakespearean soliloquies*. See also *indirect object*.

evidence Support for an argument's claim.

expletive A construction that introduces a sentence with *there* or *it*, usually followed by a form of *be*. *There are four candidates for this job. It was a dark and stormy night.*

first person See *person*.

fragment A group of words that is not a grammatically complete sentence but is punctuated as one. See also *sentence fragment*.

fused sentence A sentence in which two independent clauses are run together without a conjunction or punctuation between them. Also known as a **run-on sentence**.

future tense See *simple tense*.

gender The classification of a noun or pronoun as masculine (*god, he*) feminine (*goddess, she*), or neuter (*godliness, it*).

gerund A verbal form ending in *-ing* and functioning as a noun. *Sleeping is a bore.*

helping verb See *auxiliary verb*.

imperative mood The form of a verb used to express a command or a request. An imperative uses the base form of the verb and may or may not have a stated subject. *Leave*. *You be quiet*. *Let's go*. See also *mood*.

indefinite article The words *a* and *an*. See also *article*.

indefinite pronoun A word such as *each*, *everyone*, or *nobody* that does not refer to a specific person or thing. See also *pronoun*.

independent clause A word group containing a subject and a predicate that can stand alone as a sentence. See also *clause*.

indicative mood The form of a verb used to state a fact or an opinion or to ask a question. *Washington crossed the Delaware*. *Did he defeat the Hessians?* See also *mood*.

indirect discourse A paraphrased quotation that does not repeat another's exact words and hence is not enclosed in quotation marks. *Coolidge said that if nominated he would not run.*

indirect object A noun or pronoun identifying to whom or to what or for whom or for what a transitive verb's action is performed. The indirect object almost always precedes the direct object. *I handed the dean my application and told her that I needed financial aid.* See also *direct object*.

indirect question A sentence pattern in which a question is the basis of a subordinate clause. An indirect question should end with a period, not a question mark. *Everyone wonders why young people continue to start smoking*. (The question, phrased directly, is "Why do young people continue to start smoking?")

indirect quotation See *indirect discourse*.

infinitive The base form of a verb, preceded by *to* (*to go*, *to run*, *to hit*). An infinitive can serve as a noun, an adverb, or an adjective. *To go would be unthinkable* (noun). *We stopped to rest* (adverb). *The company needs space to grow* (adjective). An infinitive can be in either the active (*to hit*) or passive (*to be hit*) voice and in either the present (*to* [*be*] *hit*) or perfect (*to have* [*been*] *hit*) tense. An **infinitive phrase** consists of an infinitive together with its modifiers, objects, or complements. See *phrase*.

intensifier A modifier that increases the emphasis of the word or words it modifies. *I would very much like to go. I'm so happy.* Despite their name, intensifiers are stylistically weak; they are best avoided in academic and professional writing.

interjection A grammatically independent word or group of words that is usually an exclamation of surprise, shock, dismay, or the like. *Ouch! For heaven's sake, what do you think you're doing?*

intransitive verb A verb that does not need a direct object to complete its meaning. *The children laughed.*

irregular verb A verb whose past tense and past participle are not formed by adding *-ed* or *-d* to the base form, such as *see, saw, seen.*

keyword A word or phrase used to search a computer database. In a World Wide Web or Internet search, it is typed into the search engine's dialog box.

linking verb A verb that joins a subject with a subject complement or complements. Common linking verbs are *appear, be, become, feel,* and *seem. The argument <u>appeared</u> sound. It <u>was</u> actually a trick.* See also *verb.*

main clause An independent clause. See *clause.*

main verb The verb that carries the central meaning in a verb phrase, such as *given* in the phrase *could be given.*

misplaced modifier A word, phrase, or clause positioned so that it appears to modify a word other than the one the writer intended. *<u>With a credit card</u>, the traveler paid for the motel room and opened the door.* Unless the writer intended to indicate that the traveler used the credit card to open the door, *with a credit card* should follow *paid* or *room.*

modal See *auxiliary verb.*

modifier A word, phrase, or clause that acts as an adjective or an adverb and qualifies the meaning of another word, phrase, or clause. See also *adjective, adverb, clause, phrase.*

mood The form of a verb that indicates the writer's or speaker's attitude toward the idea expressed by the verb. Different moods are used to state a fact or an opinion or to ask a question (indicative); to give a command or request (imperative); and to express a wish, a suggestion, a request or requirement, or a condition that does not exist (subjunctive). *The sea <u>is</u> turbulent* (indicative). *<u>Stay</u> out of the water* (imperative). *I wish the water <u>were</u> calm enough for swimming* (subjunctive). See also *imperative mood, indicative mood, subjunctive mood.*

noncount noun See *noun.*

nonrestrictive element A word, phrase, or clause that modifies but does not change the essential meaning of a sentence element. A nonrestrictive element is set off from the rest of the sentence with commas, dashes, or parentheses. *Quantum physics, <u>which is a difficult subject</u>, is fascinating.* See also *restrictive element.*

noun A word that names a person, place, object, concept, action, or the like. Nouns serve as subjects, objects, complements, and appositives. Most nouns form the plural with the addition of *-s* or *-es* and the possessive with the addition of *'s* (see *number, case*). **Common nouns** (*president, state, month*) name classes or general groups. **Proper nouns** (*Bill Clinton, Florida, July*) name particular persons or things and are capitalized.

Collective nouns (*family, committee, jury*) refer to a group of related elements. **Count nouns** (*women, trees*) refer to things that can be directly counted. **Noncount nouns** (*sand, rain, violence*) refer to collections of things or to ideas that cannot be directly counted.

noun clause See *clause.*

noun phrase See *phrase.*

number The form of a noun or pronoun that indicates whether it is singular (*book, I, he, her, it*) or plural (*books, we, they, them, their*).

object A word or words, usually a noun or pronoun, influenced by a transitive verb, a verbal, or a preposition. See also *direct object, indirect object, object of a preposition.*

object complement See *complement.*

objective case See *case.*

object of a preposition A noun or pronoun connected to a sentence by a preposition. The preposition, the object, and any modifiers make up a **prepositional phrase**. *I went to the party without her.*

participial phrase A phrase consisting of a participle and any modifiers, objects, and complements and acting as an adjective. See also *participle, phrase.*

participle A verbal with properties of both an adjective and a verb. Like an adjective, a participle can modify a noun or pronoun; like a verb, it has present and past forms and can take an object. The **present participle** of a verb always ends in *-ing* (*going, being*). The **past participle** usually ends in *-ed* (*ruined, injured*), but many verbs have irregular forms (*gone, been, brought*). Present participles are used with the auxiliary verb *be* to form the **progressive tenses** (*I am making, I will be making, I have been making*). Past participles are used with the auxiliary verb *have* to form the **perfect tenses** (*I have made, I had made, I will have made*) and with *be* to form the passive voice (*I am seen, I was seen*). These combinations of auxiliary verbs and participles are known as **verb phrases**. See also *adjective, phrase, tense, verbal, voice.*

parts of speech The eight grammatical categories into which words can be grouped depending on how they function in a sentence. Many words act as different parts of speech in different sentences. The parts of speech are *adjectives, adverbs, conjunctions, interjections, nouns, prepositions, pronouns,* and *verbs.*

passive voice The form of a verb when the subject is being acted on rather than performing the action. *The batter was hit by a pitch.* See also *voice.*

past participle See *participle.*

past perfect or **past perfect tense** The form a verb takes to show that an action or a condition was completed before another event in the past (*The virus <u>had killed</u> six people before investigators learned of its existence*). See also *tense*.

past subjunctive See *subjunctive mood*.

past tense See *simple tense*.

perfect progressive or **perfect progressive tense** The form a verb takes to show an action or a condition that continues up to some point in the past, present, or future (*The workers <u>had been striking</u> for a month before they signed the contract; She <u>has been complaining</u> for days; The experiment <u>will have been continuing</u> for a year next May*). See also *tense*.

perfect tense The form a verb takes to show a completed action in the past, present, or future (*They <u>had hoped</u> to see the parade but ended up stuck in traffic; I <u>have</u> never <u>understood</u> this equation; By tomorrow, the governor <u>will have vetoed</u> the bill*). See also *tense*.

person The relation between a subject and its verb, indicating whether the subject is speaking about itself (**first person** — *I* or *we*), being spoken to (**second person** — *you*), or being spoken about (**third person** — *he, she, it*, or *they*). *Be* has several forms depending on the person (*am, is*, and *are* in the present tense and *was* and *were* in the past tense). Other verbs change form only in the present tense with a third-person singular subject (*I fall, you fall, she falls, we fall, they fall*).

personal pronoun See *pronoun*.

phrasal verb A verb that combines with a preposition. *The plane <u>took off</u>*.

phrase A group of words that functions as a single unit but lacks a subject, verb, or both. An **absolute phrase** modifies an entire sentence. It usually includes a noun or pronoun followed by a participle (sometimes implied) or participial phrase. *<u>The party having ended</u>, everyone left*. A **gerund phrase** includes a gerund and its objects, complements, and modifiers. It functions as a noun, acting as a subject, a complement, or an object. *<u>Exercising regularly and sensibly</u> is a key to good health* (subject). An **infinitive phrase** includes an infinitive and its objects, complements, and modifiers. It functions as an adjective, an adverb, or a noun. *The Pacific Coast is the place <u>to be</u>* (adjective). *She went <u>to pay her taxes</u>* (adverb). *<u>To be young again</u> is all I want* (noun). A **noun phrase** includes a noun and its modifiers. *<u>A long, rough road</u> crossed <u>the barren desert</u>*. A **participial phrase** includes a present or past participle and its objects, complements, and modifiers. It functions as an adjective. *<u>Absentmindedly climbing the stairs</u>, he stumbled. They bought a house <u>built in 1895</u>*. A **prepositional phrase** is introduced by a preposition and ends with a noun or pronoun, called the object of the preposition. It functions as an adjective, an adverb, or a noun. *The gas <u>in the laboratory</u> was leaking* (adjective). *The firefighters went <u>to the lab</u> to check* (adverb). *The smell came from inside a wall* (noun). A **verb phrase** is composed of a main verb and one or more auxiliaries, acting as a single verb in the sentence predicate. *I should have come to the review session.*

plural The form of a noun, pronoun, or adjective that refers to more than one person or thing, such as *books, we,* or *those.*

positive or **positive degree** The basic form of an adjective or adverb (*cold, quick*). See also *adjective forms, adverb forms.*

possessive or **possessive case** The form of a noun or pronoun that shows possession. Nouns and indefinite pronouns in the possessive case use apostrophes (*Harold's, the children's, everyone's, your parents'*), while personal pronouns in the possessive case do not (*my, mine, its, yours, hers*). See also *case.*

possessive pronoun A word used in place of a noun that shows possession. See also *possessive, pronoun.*

predicate The verb and related words in a clause or sentence. The predicate expresses what the subject does, experiences, or is. The **simple predicate** is the verb or verb phrase. *For years the YMHA has been a cultural center in New York City.* The **complete predicate** includes the simple predicate and any modifiers, objects, or complements. *John gave Sarah an engagement ring.* A **compound predicate** has more than one simple predicate. *The athletes swam in a relay and ran in a marathon.*

predicate adjective See *complement.*

predicate noun See *complement.*

prefix An addition to the beginning of a word that alters its meaning (*anti-French, undress*).

preposition A word or group of words that indicates the relationship of a noun or pronoun, called the *object of the preposition,* to another part of the sentence. *He was at the top of the ladder before the others had climbed to the fourth rung.* See also *phrase.*

prepositional phrase A group of words beginning with a preposition and ending with its object. A prepositional phrase can function as an adjective, an adverb, or a noun. See also *phrase.*

present participle See *participle.*

present perfect or **present perfect tense** The form a verb takes to show that an action or a condition has been completed before the present (*The team has worked together well*). See also *tense.*

present progressive The form a verb takes to show an action or a condition that is ongoing in the present (*He is planning a sales presentation*). See also *tense.*

present tense See *simple tense.*

primary source A research source that offers firsthand knowledge of its subject.

progressive tense The form a verb takes to show an action or a condition that is continuing in the past, present, or future (*He was singing too loudly to hear the telephone; The economy is surging; Business schools will be competing for this student*). See also *tense*.

pronoun A word used in place of a noun, usually called the antecedent of the pronoun. **Indefinite pronouns** do not refer to specific nouns and include *any, each, everybody, some,* and similar words. *Many are called, but few are chosen.* **Personal pronouns** (*I, you, he, she, it, we, you,* and *they*) refer to particular people or things. They have different forms (*I, me, my, mine*) depending on their case. (See also *case*.) **Possessive pronouns** (*my, mine, our, his/her, your, their*) denote possession. **Relative pronouns** (*who, whom, whose, which, that, what, whoever, whomever, whichever,* and *whatever*) connect a dependent clause to a sentence. *I wonder who will win the prize.*

proper noun See *noun*.

regular verb A verb whose past tense and past participle are formed by adding *-d* or *-ed* to the base form (*care, cared, cared; look, looked, looked*). See also *irregular verb*.

relative pronoun See *pronoun*.

restrictive element A word, phrase, or clause that limits the essential meaning of the sentence element it modifies or provides necessary identifying information about it. A restrictive element is not set off from the rest of the sentence with commas, dashes, or parentheses. *The tree that I hit was an oak.* See also *nonrestrictive element*.

run-on sentence See *fused sentence*.

secondary source A research source that reports information from research done by others. See also *primary source*.

second person See *person*.

sentence A group of words containing a subject and a predicate and expressing a complete thought. In writing, a sentence begins with a capital letter and ends with a period, a question mark, or an exclamation point. A **compound sentence** contains two or more independent clauses linked with a coordinating conjunction, a correlative conjunction, or a semicolon. *I did not wish to go, but she did.* See also *clause*.

sentence fragment A group of words that is not a grammatically complete sentence but is punctuated as one. Usually a fragment lacks a subject, a verb, or both or is a dependent clause that is not attached to an independent clause. In academic and professional writing, fragments should be revised to be complete sentences.

simple past tense See *tense*.

simple predicate See *predicate*.

simple subject See *subject*.

simple tense Past (*It _happened_*), present (*Things _fall_ apart*), or future (*You _will succeed_*) forms of verbs. See also *tense*.

singular The form of a noun, a pronoun, or an adjective that refers to one person or thing, such as *book*, *it*, or *this*.

split infinitive The often awkward intrusion of an adverb between *to* and the base form of the verb in an infinitive (*to better serve* rather than *to serve better*).

squinting modifier A misplaced word, phrase, or clause that could refer equally, but with different meanings, to words either preceding or following it. For example, in *Playing poker _often_ is dangerous*, the position of *often* fails to indicate whether the writer meant that frequent poker playing is dangerous or that poker playing is often dangerous.

subject The noun or pronoun and related words that indicate who or what a sentence is about. The **simple subject** is the noun or pronoun. The **complete subject** is the simple subject and its modifiers. In *_The timid gray mouse_ fled from the owl*, *mouse* is the simple subject; *The timid gray mouse* is the complete subject. A **compound subject** includes two or more simple subjects. *_The mouse and the owl_ heard the fox.*

subject complement See *complement*.

subjective case See *case*.

subjunctive mood The form of a verb used to express a wish, a suggestion, a request or requirement, or a condition that does not exist. The present subjunctive uses the base form of the verb. *I asked that he _be_ present. Long _live_ the Queen!* The past subjunctive uses the same verb form as the past tense except for the verb *be*, which uses *were* for all subjects. *If I _were_ president, I would change things.* See also *mood*.

subordinate clause A dependent clause. See *clause*.

subordinating conjunction A word or phrase such as *although*, *because*, or *even though* that introduces a dependent clause and joins it to an independent clause. See also *conjunction*.

suffix An addition to the end of a word that alters the word's meaning or part of speech, as in *migrate* (verb) and *migra_tion_* (noun) or *late* (adjective or adverb) and *late_ness_* (noun).

superlative The form of an adjective or adverb used in a comparison of three or more items (*happiest*, *most gladly*). See also *adjective forms*, *adverb forms*.

syntax The arrangement of words in a sentence in order to reveal the relation of each to the whole sentence and to one another.

tense The form of a verb that indicates the time at which an action takes place or a condition exists. The times expressed by tense are basically **present, past,** and **future.** Each tense has **simple** (*I enjoy*), **perfect** (*I have enjoyed*), **progressive** (*I am enjoying*), and **perfect progressive** (*I have been enjoying*) forms.

third person See *person.*

transition A word or phrase that signals a progression from one sentence or part of a sentence to another.

transitive verb A verb that takes a direct object, which receives the action expressed by the verb. A transitive verb may be in the active or passive voice. *The artist <u>drew</u> the sketch. The sketch <u>was drawn</u> by the arist.* See also *verb.*

verb A word or group of words, essential to a sentence, that expresses what action a subject takes or receives or what the subject's state of being is. *Edison <u>invented</u> the incandescent bulb. Gas lighting <u>was becoming</u> obsolete.* Verbs change form to show tense, number, voice, and mood. See also *auxiliary verb, intransitive verb, irregular verb, linking verb, mood, person, regular verb, tense, transitive verb, verbal, voice.*

verbal A verb form that functions as a noun, an adjective, or an adverb. The three kinds of verbals are gerunds, infinitives, and participles. See also *gerund, infinitive, participle.*

verbal phrase A phrase using a gerund, a participle, or an infinitive. See *phrase.*

verb phrase See *phrase.*

verb tense See *tense.*

voice The form of a verb that indicates whether the subject is acting or being acted on. When a verb is in the **active voice**, the subject performs the action. *Parker <u>played</u> the saxophone fantastically.* When a verb is in the **passive voice**, the subject receives the action. *The saxophone <u>was played</u> by Parker.* The passive voice is formed with the appropriate tense of the verb *be* and the past participle of the transitive verb. See also *verb.*

warrant Assumptions, sometimes unstated, that connect an argument's claims to the reasons for making the claims.

Glossary of Usage

Conventions of usage might be called the "good manners" of discourse. And just as our notions of good manners vary from culture to culture and time to time, so do conventions of usage. The word *ain't*, for instance, now considered inappropriate in academic and professional discourse, was once widely used by the most proper British speakers and is still commonly used in some spoken U.S. dialects. In short, matters of usage, like other language choices you must make, depend on what your purpose is and on what is appropriate for a particular audience at a particular time. This glossary provides usage guidelines for some commonly confused or otherwise problematic words and phrases.

a, an Use *a* with a word that begins with a consonant (*a* book), a consonant sound such as "y" or "w" (*a* euphoric moment, *a* one-sided match), or a sounded *h* (*a* hemisphere). Use *an* with a word that begins with a vowel (*an* umbrella), a vowel sound (*an* X-ray), or a silent *h* (*an* honor).

accept, except The verb *accept* means "receive" or "agree to." *Except* is usually a preposition that means "aside from" or "excluding." *All the plaintiffs* except *Mr. Kim decided to* accept *the settlement.*

advice, advise The noun *advice* means "opinion" or "suggestion"; the verb *advise* means "offer advice." *Charlotte's mother* advised *her to dress warmly, but Charlotte ignored the* advice.

affect, effect As a verb, *affect* means "influence" or "move the emotions of"; as a noun, it means "emotions" or "feelings." *Effect* is a noun meaning "result"; less commonly, it is a verb meaning "bring about." *The storm* affected *a large area. Its* effects *included widespread power failures. The drug* effected *a major change in the patient's* affect.

aggravate The formal meaning is "make worse." *Having another mouth to feed* aggravated *their poverty.* In academic and professional writing, avoid using *aggravate* to mean "irritate" or "annoy."

all ready, already *All ready* means "fully prepared." *Already* means "previously." *We were* all ready *for Lucy's party when we learned that she had* already *left.*

all right, alright Avoid the spelling *alright.*

all together, altogether *All together* means "all in a group" or "gathered in one place." *Altogether* means "completely" or "everything considered." *When the board members were* <u>*all*</u> <u>*together*</u>*, their mutual distrust was* <u>*altogether*</u> *obvious.*

allude, elude *Allude* means "refer indirectly." *Elude* means "avoid" or "escape from." *The candidate did not even* <u>*allude*</u> *to her opponent. The suspect* <u>*eluded*</u> *the police for several days.*

allusion, illusion An *allusion* is an indirect reference. An *illusion* is a false or misleading appearance. *The speaker's* <u>*allusion*</u> *to the Bible created an* <u>*illusion*</u> *of piety.*

already See *all ready, already.*

alright See *all right, alright.*

altogether See *all together, altogether.*

among, between In referring to two things or people, use *between.* In referring to three or more, use *among. The relationship* <u>*between*</u> *the twins is different from that* <u>*among*</u> *the other three children.*

amount, number Use *amount* with quantities you cannot count; use *number* for quantities you can count. *A small* <u>*number*</u> *of volunteers cleared a large* <u>*amount*</u> *of brush.*

an See *a, an.*

and/or Avoid this term except in business or legal writing. Instead of *fat and/or protein,* write *fat, protein, or both.*

any body, anybody, any one, anyone *Anybody* and *anyone* are pronouns meaning "any person." <u>*Anyone*</u> [or <u>*anybody*</u>] *would enjoy this film. Any body* is an adjective modifying a noun. <u>*Any*</u> <u>*body*</u> *of water has its own ecology. Any one* is two adjectives or a pronoun modified by an adjective. *Customers could buy only two sale items at* <u>*any one*</u> *time. The winner could choose* <u>*any one*</u> *of the prizes.*

anyplace In academic and professional discourse, use *anywhere* instead.

anyway, anyways In writing, use *anyway,* not *anyways.*

apt, liable, likely *Likely to* means "probably will," and *apt to* means "inclines or tends to." In many instances, they are interchangeable. *Liable* often carries a more negative sense and is also a legal term meaning "obligated" or "responsible."

as Avoid sentences in which it is not clear if *as* means "when" or "because." For example, does *Carl left town* <u>*as*</u> *his father was arriving* mean "at the same time as his father was arriving" or "because his father was arriving"?

as, as if, like In academic and professional writing, use *as* or *as if* instead of *like* to introduce a clause. *The dog howled* <u>*as if*</u> [not <u>*like*</u>] *it were in pain. She did* <u>*as*</u> [not <u>*like*</u>] *I suggested.*

assure, ensure, insure *Assure* means "convince" or "promise"; its direct object is usually a person or persons. *She* <u>*assured*</u> *voters she would not raise taxes. Ensure* and *insure* both mean "make certain," but *insure* usually refers specifically to protection against financial loss. *When the city rationed water to <u>ensure</u> that the supply would last, the Browns could no longer afford to <u>insure</u> their car-wash business.*

as to Do not use *as to* as a substitute for *about*. *Karen was unsure <u>about</u>* [not *<u>as to</u>*] *Bruce's intentions.*

at, where See *where*.

awful, awfully *Awful* and *awfully* mean "awe-inspiring" and "in an awe-inspiring way." In academic and professional writing, avoid using *awful* to mean "bad" (*I had an <u>awful</u> day*) and *awfully* to mean "very" (*It was <u>awfully</u> cold*).

awhile, a while Always use *a while* after a preposition such as *for, in,* or *after*. *We drove <u>awhile</u> and then stopped for <u>a while</u>.*

bad, badly Use *bad* after a linking verb such as *be, feel,* or *seem*. Use *badly* to modify an action verb, an adjective, or another verb. *The hostess felt <u>bad</u> because the dinner was <u>badly</u> prepared.*

because of, due to Use *due to* when the effect, stated as a noun, appears before the verb *be*. *His illness was <u>due to</u> malnutrition.* (*Illness*, a noun, is the effect.) Use *because of* when the effect is stated as a clause. *He was sick <u>because of</u> malnutrition.* (*He was sick*, a clause, is the effect.)

being as, being that In academic or professional writing, use *because* or *since* instead of these expressions. *<u>Because</u>* [not *<u>being as</u>*] *Romeo killed Tybalt, he was banished to Padua.*

beside, besides *Beside* is a preposition meaning "next to." *Besides* can be a preposition meaning "other than" or an adverb meaning "in addition." *No one <u>besides</u> Francesca would sit <u>beside</u> him.*

between See *among, between*.

breath, breathe *Breath* is a noun; *breathe*, a verb. *"<u>Breathe</u>," said the nurse, so June took a deep <u>breath</u>.*

bring, take Use *bring* when an object is moved from a farther to a nearer place; use *take* when the opposite is true. *<u>Take</u> the box to the post office; <u>bring</u> back my mail.*

but, yet Do not use these words together. *He is strong <u>but</u>* [not *<u>but yet</u>*] *gentle.*

but that, but what Avoid using these as substitutes for *that* in expressions of doubt. *Hercule Poirot never doubted <u>that</u>* [not *<u>but that</u>*] *he would solve the case.*

can, may *Can* refers to ability and *may* to possibility or permission. *Since I <u>can</u> ski the slalom well, I <u>may</u> win the race.*

can't hardly *Hardly* has a negative meaning; therefore, *can't hardly* is a double negative. This expression is commonly used in some varieties of English but is not used in academic English. *Tim <u>can</u>* [not *<u>can't</u>*] *hardly wait.*

can't help but This expression is redundant. Use the more formal *I cannot but go* or less formal *I can't help going* rather than *I can't help but go.*

censor, censure *Censor* means "remove that which is considered offensive." *Censure* means "formally reprimand." *The newspaper censored stories that offended advertisers. The legislature censured the official for misconduct.*

complement, compliment *Complement* means "go well with." *Compliment* means "praise." *Guests complimented her on how her earrings complemented her gown.*

comprise, compose *Comprise* means "contain." *Compose* means "make up." *The class comprises twenty students. Twenty students compose the class.*

conscience, conscious *Conscience* means "a sense of right and wrong." *Conscious* means "awake" or "aware." *After lying, Lisa was conscious of a guilty conscience.*

consensus of opinion Use *consensus* instead of this redundant phrase. *The family consensus was to sell the old house.*

consequently, subsequently *Consequently* means "as a result"; *subsequently* means "then." *He quit, and subsequently his wife lost her job; consequently, they had to sell their house.*

continual, continuous *Continual* means "repeated at regular or frequent intervals." *Continuous* means "continuing or connected without a break." *The damage done by continuous erosion was increased by the continual storms.*

could of *Have,* not *of,* should follow *could, would, should,* or *might. We could have* [not *of*] *invited them.*

criteria, criterion *Criterion* means "standard of judgment" or "necessary qualification." *Criteria* is the plural form. *Image is the wrong criterion for choosing a president.*

data *Data* is the plural form of the Latin word *datum,* meaning "fact." Although *data* is used informally as either singular or plural, in academic or professional writing, treat *data* as plural. *These data indicate that fewer people are smoking.*

different from, different than *Different from* is generally preferred in academic and professional writing, although both phrases are widely used. *Her lab results were no different from* [not *than*] *his.*

discreet, discrete *Discreet* means "tactful" or "prudent." *Discrete* means "separate" or "distinct." *The leader's discreet efforts kept all the discrete factions unified.*

disinterested, uninterested *Disinterested* means "unbiased." *Uninterested* means "indifferent." *Finding disinterested jurors was difficult. She was uninterested in the verdict.*

distinct, distinctive *Distinct* means "separate" or "well defined." *Distinctive* means "characteristic." *Germany includes many <u>distinct</u> regions, each with a <u>distinctive</u> accent.*

doesn't, don't *Doesn't* is the contraction for *does not.* Use it with *he, she, it,* and singular nouns. *Don't* stands for *do not;* use it with *I, you, we, they,* and plural nouns.

due to See *because of, due to.*

each other, one another Use *each other* in sentences involving two subjects and *one another* in sentences involving more than two.

effect See *affect, effect.*

elicit, illicit The verb *elicit* means "draw out." The adjective *illicit* means "illegal." *The police <u>elicited</u> from the criminal the names of others involved in <u>illicit</u> activities.*

elude See *allude, elude.*

emigrate from, immigrate to *Emigrate from* means "move away from one's country." *Immigrate to* means "move to another country." *We <u>emigrated</u> from Norway in 1999. We <u>immigrated</u> to the United States.*

ensure See *assure, ensure, insure.*

enthused, enthusiastic Use *enthusiastic* rather than *enthused* in academic and professional writing.

equally as good Replace this redundant phrase with *equally good* or *as good.*

every day, everyday *Everyday* is an adjective meaning "ordinary." *Every day* is an adjective and a noun, meaning "each day." *I wore <u>everyday</u> clothes almost <u>every day</u>.*

every one, everyone *Everyone* is a pronoun. *Every one* is an adjective and a pronoun, referring to each member of a group. *Because he began after <u>everyone</u> else, David could not finish <u>every one</u> of the problems.*

except See *accept, except.*

explicit, implicit *Explicit* means "directly or openly expressed." *Implicit* means "indirectly expressed or implied." *The <u>explicit</u> message of the ad urged consumers to buy the product, while the <u>implicit</u> message promised popularity if they did so.*

farther, further *Farther* refers to physical distance. *How much <u>farther</u> is it to Munich? Further* refers to time or degree. *I want to avoid <u>further</u> delays.*

fewer, less Use *fewer* with nouns that can be counted. Use *less* with general amounts that you cannot count. *The world will be safer with <u>fewer</u> bombs and <u>less</u> hostility.*

finalize *Finalize* is a pretentious way of saying "end" or "make final." *We <u>closed</u> [not <u>finalized</u>] the deal.*

firstly, secondly, etc. *First, second,* etc., are more common in U.S. English.

flaunt, flout *Flaunt* means to "show off." *Flout* means to "mock" or "scorn." *The drug dealers <u>flouted</u> authority by <u>flaunting</u> their wealth.*

former, latter *Former* refers to the first and *latter* to the second of two things previously mentioned. *Kathy and Anna are athletes; the <u>former</u> plays tennis, and the <u>latter</u> runs.*

further See *farther, further.*

good, well *Good* is an adjective and should not be used as a substitute for the adverb *well*. *Gabriel is a <u>good</u> host who cooks <u>well</u>.*

good and *Good and* is colloquial for "very"; avoid it in academic and professional writing.

hanged, hung *Hanged* refers to executions; *hung* is used for all other meanings.

hardly See *can't hardly.*

herself, himself, myself, yourself Do not use these reflexive pronouns as subjects or as objects unless they are necessary. *Jane and I* [not *<u>myself</u>*] *agree. They invited John and me* [not *<u>myself</u>*].

he/she, his/her Better solutions for avoiding sexist language are to write out *he or she*, to eliminate pronouns entirely, or to make the subject plural. Instead of writing *Everyone should carry <u>his/her</u> driver's license*, try *<u>Drivers</u> should carry <u>their</u> licenses* or *<u>People</u> should carry <u>their</u> driver's licenses.*

himself See *herself, himself, myself, yourself.*

hisself Use *himself* instead in academic or professional writing.

hopefully *Hopefully* is often misused to mean "it is hoped," but its correct meaning is "with hope." *Sam watched the roulette wheel <u>hopefully</u>* [not *<u>Hopefully</u>, Sam will win*].

hung See *hanged, hung.*

illicit See *elicit, illicit.*

illusion See *allusion, illusion.*

immigrate to See *emigrate from, immigrate to.*

impact Avoid the colloquial use of *impact* or *impact on* as a verb meaning "affect." *Population control may <u>reduce</u>* [not *<u>impact</u>*] *world hunger.*

implicit See *explicit, implicit.*

imply, infer To *imply* is to suggest indirectly. To *infer* is to guess or conclude on the basis of an indirect suggestion. *The note <u>implied</u> they were planning a small wedding; we <u>inferred</u> we would not be invited.*

inside of, outside of Use *inside* and *outside* instead. *The class regularly met <u>outside</u>* [not *<u>outside of</u>*] *the building.*

insure See *assure, ensure, insure.*

interact, interface *Interact* is a vague word meaning "do something that somehow involves another person." *Interface* is computer jargon; when used as a verb, it means "discuss" or "communicate." Avoid both verbs in academic and professional writing.

irregardless, regardless *Irregardless* is a double negative. Use *regardless.*

is when, is where These vague expressions are often incorrectly used in definitions. *Schizophrenia is a psychotic condition in which* [not *is when* or *is where*] *a person withdraws from reality.*

its, it's *Its* is the possessive form of *it. It's* is a contraction for *it is* or *it has. It's important to observe the rat before it eats its meal.*

kind, sort, type These singular nouns should be modified with *this* or *that,* not *these* or *those,* and followed by other singular nouns, not plural nouns. *Wear this kind of dress* [not *those kind of dresses*].

kind of, sort of Avoid these colloquialisms. *Amy was somewhat* [not *kind of*] *tired.*

later, latter *Later* means "after some time." *Latter* refers to the second of two items named. *Juan and Chad won all their early matches, but the latter was injured later in the season.*

latter See *former, latter* and *later, latter.*

lay, lie *Lay* means "place" or "put." Its main forms are *lay, laid, laid.* It generally has a direct object, specifying what has been placed. *She laid her books on the desk. Lie* means "recline" or "be positioned" and does not take a direct object. Its main forms are *lie, lay, lain. She lay awake until two.*

leave, let *Leave* means "go away." *Let* means "allow." *Leave alone* and *let alone* are interchangeable. *Let me leave now, and leave* [or *let*] *me alone from now on!*

lend, loan In academic and professional writing, do not use *loan* as a verb; use *lend* instead. *Please lend me your pen so that I may fill out this application for a loan.*

less See *fewer, less.*

let See *leave, let.*

liable See *apt, liable, likely.*

lie See *lay, lie.*

like See *as, as if, like.*

likely See *apt, liable, likely.*

literally *Literally* means "actually" or "exactly as stated." Use it to stress the truth of a statement that might otherwise be understood as figurative. Do not use *literally* as an intensifier in a figurative statement. *Mirna was literally at the edge of her seat* may be accurate, but *Mirna is so hungry that she could <u>literally</u> eat a horse* is not.

loan See *lend, loan*.

loose, lose *Lose* is a verb meaning "misplace." *Loose* is an adjective that means "not securely attached." *Sew on that <u>loose</u> button before you <u>lose</u> it.*

lots, lots of Avoid these informal expressions meaning "much" or "many" in academic or professional discourse.

man, mankind Replace these terms with *people, humans, humankind, men and women,* or similar wording.

may See *can, may*.

may be, maybe *May be* is a verb phrase. *Maybe* is an adverb that means "perhaps." *He <u>may be</u> the head of the organization, but <u>maybe</u> someone else would handle a crisis better.*

media *Media* is the plural form of the noun *medium* and takes a plural verb. *The <u>media are</u> [not <u>is</u>] obsessed with scandals.*

might of See *could of*.

moral, morale A *moral* is a succinct lesson. *The <u>moral</u> of the story is that generosity is rewarded.* *Morale* means "spirit" or "mood." *Office <u>morale</u> was low.*

myself See *herself, himself, myself, yourself*.

nor, or Use *either* with *or* and *neither* with *nor*.

number See *amount, number*.

off of Use *off* without *of*. *The spaghetti slipped <u>off</u> [not <u>off of</u>] the plate.*

OK, O.K., okay All are acceptable spellings, but avoid the term in academic and professional discourse.

on account of Use this substitute for *because of* sparingly or not at all.

one another See *each other, one another*.

or See *nor, or*.

outside of See *inside of, outside of*.

owing to the fact that Avoid this and other wordy expressions for *because*.

per Use the Latin *per* only in standard technical phrases such as *miles per hour.* Otherwise, find English equivalents. *As mentioned in* [not *As per*] *the latest report, the country's average food consumption each day* [not *per day*] *is only 2,000 calories.*

percent, percentage Use *percent* with a specific number; use *percentage* with an adjective such as *large* or *small. Last year, 80 <u>percent</u> of the members were female. A large <u>percentage</u> of the members are women.*

plenty *Plenty* means "enough" or "a great abundance." *They told us America was a land of <u>plenty</u>.* Colloquially, it is used to mean "very," a usage you should avoid in academic and professional writing. *He was very [not plenty] tired.*

plus *Plus* means "in addition to." *Your salary plus mine will cover our expenses.* Do not use *plus* to mean "besides" or "moreover." *That dress does not fit me. Besides [not Plus], it is the wrong color.*

precede, proceed *Precede* means "come before"; *proceed* means "go forward." *Despite the storm that preceded the ceremony, it proceeded on schedule.*

pretty Avoid using *pretty* as a substitute for "rather," "somewhat," or "quite." *Bill was quite [not pretty] disagreeable.*

principal, principle When used as a noun, *principal* refers to a head official or an amount of money; when used as an adjective, it means "most significant." *Principle* means "fundamental law or belief." *Albert went to the principal and defended himself with the principle of free speech.*

proceed See *precede, proceed.*

quotation, quote *Quote* is a verb, and *quotation* is a noun. *He quoted the president, and the quotation [not quote] was preserved in history books.*

raise, rise *Raise* means "lift" or "move upward." (Referring to children, it means "bring up.") It takes a direct object; someone raises something. *The guests raised their glasses to toast.* *Rise* means "go upward." It does not take a direct object; something rises by itself. *She saw the steam rise from the pan.*

rarely ever Use *rarely* by itself, or use *hardly ever.* *When we were poor, we rarely went to the movies.*

real, really *Real* is an adjective, and *really* is an adverb. Do not substitute *real* for *really.* In academic and professional writing, do not use *real* or *really* to mean "very." *The old man walked very [not real or really] slowly.*

reason is because Use either *the reason is that* or *because* — not both. *The reason the copier stopped is that [not is because] the paper jammed.*

reason why This expression is redundant. *The reason [not reason why] this book is short is market demand.*

regardless See *irregardless, regardless.*

respectfully, respectively *Respectfully* means "with respect." *Respectively* means "in the order given." *Karen and David are, respectively, a juggler and an acrobat. The children treated their grandparents respectfully.*

rise See *raise, rise.*

set, sit *Set* usually means "put" or "place" and takes a direct object. *Sit* refers to taking a seat and does not take an object. *Set your cup on the table, and sit down.*

should of See *could of.*

since Be careful not to use *since* ambiguously. In <u>*Since*</u> *I broke my leg, I've stayed home, since* might be understood to mean either "because" or "ever since."

sit. See *set, sit.*

so In academic and professional writing, avoid using *so* alone to mean "very." Instead, follow *so* with *that* to show how the intensified condition leads to a result. *Aaron was* <u>*so*</u> *tired* <u>*that*</u> *he fell asleep at the wheel.*

someplace Use *somewhere* instead in academic and professional writing.

some time, sometime, sometimes *Some time* refers to a length of time. *Please leave me* <u>*some time*</u> *to dress. Sometime* means "at some indefinite later time." <u>*Sometime*</u> *I will take you to London. Sometimes* means "occasionally." <u>*Sometimes*</u> *I eat sushi.*

sort See *kind, sort, type.*

sort of See *kind of, sort of.*

stationary, stationery *Stationary* means "standing still"; *stationery* means "writing paper." *When the bus was* <u>*stationary*</u>, *Pat took out* <u>*stationery*</u> *and wrote a note.*

subsequently See *consequently, subsequently.*

supposed to, used to Be careful to include the final -*d* in these expressions. *He is* <u>*supposed to*</u> *attend.*

sure, surely Avoid using *sure* as an intensifier. Instead, use *surely* (or *certainly* or *without a doubt*). *I was* <u>*surely*</u> *glad to see you.*

take See *bring, take.*

than, then Use *than* in comparative statements. *The cat was bigger* <u>*than*</u> *the dog.* Use *then* when referring to a sequence of events. *I won, and* <u>*then*</u> *I cried.*

that, which A clause beginning with *that* singles out the item being described. *The book* <u>*that*</u> *is on the table is a good one* specifies the book on the table as opposed to some other book. A clause beginning with *which* may or may not single out the item, although some writers use *which* clauses only to add more information about an item being described. *The book,* <u>*which*</u> *is on the table, is a good one* contains a *which* clause between the commas. The clause simply adds extra, nonessential information about the book; it does not specify which book.

theirselves Use *themselves* instead in academic and professional writing.

then See *than, then.*

to, too, two *To* generally shows direction. *Too* means "also." *Two* is the number. *We,* <u>*too*</u>, *are going* <u>*to*</u> *the meeting in* <u>*two*</u> *hours.* Avoid using *to* after *where.* *Where are you flying* [not *flying* <u>*to*</u>]?

two See *to, too, two.*

type See *kind, sort, type*.

uninterested See *disinterested, uninterested*.

unique *Unique* means "the one and only." Do not use it with adverbs that suggest degree, such as *very* or *most*. *Adora's paintings are <u>unique</u>* [not *<u>very unique</u>*].

used to See *supposed to, used to*.

very Avoid using *very* to intensify a weak adjective or adverb; instead, replace the adjective or adverb with a stronger, more precise, or more colorful word. Instead of *very nice*, for example, use *kind, warm, sensitive, endearing*, or *friendly*.

way, ways When referring to distance, use *way*. *Graduation was a long <u>way</u>* [not *<u>ways</u>*] *off*.

well See *good, well*.

where Use *where* alone, not with words such as *at* and *to*. *<u>Where</u> are you going* [not *going <u>to</u>*]?

which See *that, which*.

who's, whose *Who's* is the contraction of *who* and *is* or *has*. *<u>Who's</u> on the patio? Whose* is a possessive form. *<u>Whose</u> sculpture is in the garden? <u>Whose</u> is on the patio?*

would of See *could of*.

yet See *but, yet*.

your, you're *Your* shows possession. *Bring <u>your</u> sleeping bag along. You're* is the contraction of *you* and *are*. *<u>You're</u> in the wrong sleeping bag.*

yourself See *herself, himself, myself, yourself*.

Acknowledgments

Photo credits: **p. 25 (top)**, Reprinted with permission of the National Endowment for the Humanities; **p. 25 (bottom)**, *Business Week*, The McGraw-Hill Company, NY; **p. 26**, Photo by Lee Celano of Joseph C. Phillips. *Newsweek;* **p. 36**, Reprinted with permission from Microsoft Corporation; **p. 45 (top)**, © 1996–2005 National Geographic Society. All rights reserved. Reproduced by permission; **p. 45 (bottom)**, United States Department of Health and Human Services, Center for Disease Control and Prevention; **p. 46 (top)**, © 2005 Bartleby.com. www.bartleby.com. Reproduced by permission; **p. 46 (bottom)**, United States Postal Service; **p. 51**, "Democracy" cartoon: Ares. www.caglecartoons.com; **p. 51**, photo: Brand X Pictures/fotosearch; **p. 171 (left)**, Reprinted with permission. *Michigan Quarterly Review*, 40:3, Summer 2001; **p. 171 (right)**, © *Sports Illustrated*, Time, Inc.; **p. 179**, excerpt from pp. 909–34 in *Human Rights Quarterly* 25 (2003). © 2003 by The Johns Hopkins University Press. Reprinted by permission; **p. 181**, © 2004 "State of the Birds" by Greg Butcher, first published in *Audubon* magazine, September–October 2004, reprinted by permission; **p. 209**, © 2002 James B. Twitchell. By permission of Columbia University Press. Reprinted with the permission of the publisher; **p. 213**, Anita Hamilton. Excerpt from "All the Right Questions." From *Time*, April 5, 2004, pp. 65–6. © 2004 TIME, Inc. Reprinted by permission; **p. 215**, "Outsourcing War," by Singer, P. W. *Foreign Affairs*, 00157120, Mar/Apr 2005, vol. 84, issue 2; **p. 219**, Published with permission from the Nobel Foundation. © The Nobel Foundation 2005.

Index

For Multilingual Writers

Throughout *EasyWriter,* boxed tips offer help on the following topics for writers whose first language is not English.

CONTENTS